To the long-suffering Russian people
in the hope of a new, and better, future.

Putin's Russia

Putin's Russia

Past Imperfect, Future Uncertain

Edited by
Dale R. Herspring

ROWMAN & LITTLEFIELD PUBLISHERS, INC.
Lanham • Boulder • New York • Oxford

ROWMAN & LITTLEFIELD PUBLISHERS, INC.

Published in the United States of America
by Rowman & Littlefield Publishers, Inc.
A Member of the Rowman & Littlefield Publishing Group
4501 Forbes Boulevard, Suite 200, Lanham, Maryland 20706
www.rowmanlittlefield.com

PO Box 317, Oxford, OX2 9RU, United Kingdom

British Library Cataloguing in Publication Information Available

Library of Congress Cataloging-in-Publication Data

Putin's Russia : past imperfect, future uncertain / [edited by] Dale R. Herspring.
    p. cm.
    Includes bibliographical references and index.
    ISBN 0-7425-1967-8 (cloth : alk. paper) — ISBN 0-7425-1968-6 (pbk. : alk. paper)
    1. Russia (Federation)—Politics and government—1991– 2. Putin, Vladimir Vladimirovich, 1952– I. Herspring, Dale R. (Dale Roy)
DK510.763 .P88 2002   2002011140

Printed in the United States of America

I would like to suggest that at this point the country does not need a leader of strategic proportions, but an effective manager.

—P. Vayl

Contents

Foreword

Ambassador James J. Collins

One unexpected outcome of the terrorist attacks on New York and Washington was Russia's return to centrality in America's foreign policy and security calculus. President Putin's embrace of the U.S.-led antiterrorist coalition and the outpouring of sympathy from Russia's people captured the imagination of Americans and rekindled interest in this complex, rich, but elusive country whose fate has been inextricably tied to our own over the past two-and-a-half centuries. This volume provides an excellent introduction to the multihued tapestry of today's Russia and to the personality, vision, and politics of its young president. The authors discuss the individuals, issues, and circumstances central to Russia today, and they help us understand the environment that is defining Russia's transition from its Soviet imperial past. The book is especially valuable for its portrayal, when taken as a whole, of the ambiguities and inconsistencies that characterize a Russia still deeply in search of itself as a society, its place in the international system, and its future direction.

For most readers, Russia's direction and future is directly linked to the personality and vision of Vladimir Putin, its enigmatic, often controversial, and, until recently, largely unknown young president. When Boris Yeltsin sprang his own Y2K surprise on the eve of the new millennium by announcing early retirement and selecting Putin to succeed him, this last confounding stroke by Russia's master of the political surprise was greeted by most of his compatriots with a mixture of hope that the aimless drift of the late Yeltsin era had ended, and deep uncertainty about the man to whom their country had been entrusted. The uncertainty was understandable. Emerging from Russia's faceless bureaucracy, Putin at that time was all but unknown. He had neither known political affiliation nor political experience anyone could point to. In St. Petersburg he had worked in the shadow of the city's reformist mayor, Anatoly Sobchak, and his earlier activities as an intelligence officer had for obvious reason been hidden from public view. Nor had his short tenure in office at the national level—as Kremlin staffer, director of the Federal Security Service (FSB), and national security adviser—given Russia's political class familiarity with his views. Indeed, it was only in his few months as prime minister that this unexpected president-to-be had come before the public, and that tenure, dominated by the renewal of warfare in Chechnya, raised as many questions as it resolved. So it was scarcely surprising that on the mind of nearly every Russian, foreign official, journalist, and political figure on New Year's Day 2000 was the question, "Who is Vladimir Putin and what does he represent?"

Nevertheless, Putin was not unfamiliar to everyone. As ambassador I had come to know the new acting president in different capacities. I had encountered him occasionally as a Kremlin insider working in the presidential administration. I had met with him more often during his service as FSB director, national security adviser, and prime minister. In those encounters Putin came across to me as an intelligent, exceptionally well-informed interlocutor. He addressed issues pragmatically and logically, without emotion. He was precise in presenting his positions and views. He impressed me as a man who internalized issues and spoke to them from a base of solid understanding and mastery of detail. Putin also had a personable side, although he was often difficult to read as an individual. With visitors he was a gracious host, employing a sense of humor effectively to put guests at ease at the outset of meetings devoted even to the most difficult issues. And in conversation he was a careful listener who responded to his partners' points and made clear where he agreed or disagreed, or deliberately chose to leave an issue open. But with all this, Putin revealed little of himself or his personal thinking, and he remained a political mystery to the nation he would lead.

Two years of the Putin presidency have now changed that. The contours of the Putin vision have begun to emerge more clearly as he and his team address Russia's pressing economic and social issues and define their nation's future international role. The chapters that follow discuss how the new administration has shaped the Putin presidency to date by confronting the critical issues of Russia's revival and recovery. They offer a good beginning for those who seek to understand not just who Mr. Putin is and how he seeks to define and direct his nation, but also to comprehend the environment within which this Russian president must make the critical decisions for his country.

As the authors of the subsequent chapters discuss, Putin first developed as a presidential candidate many of the ideas that would later define his presidency. Certain political themes served to differentiate him from his predecessor while establishing his credentials to deal in new ways with Russia's pressing problems. Thus, he emphasized restoring the strength and authority of the Russian state and promoted his image as a decisive, active, and engaged leader. Sensing the emotional appeal of patriotic themes, he stressed from the very first moment that as president he would insure that Russia set its own domestic and international course and define its own interests. And, taking account of the fatigue from political stalemate between the pro- and anti-Yeltsin camps, he conveyed readiness to make room for all who shared his goal of restoring Russia to greatness, specifically including those who felt alienated by Yeltsin's determined struggle with the communists. This was, it seemed at the time, very much the leader of a new generation who understood and accepted the dynamics of Russia's post-communist and post–Cold War international circumstances, the necessity to find accommodation with the forces at work in Russia's fledgling and imperfect market democracy, and the need to create and maintain the support of a centrist majority if he were to become an effective political leader of the Russia of the twenty-first century.

That Russia, it is important to recall, was already far removed from its Soviet past. A decade of the Yeltsin revolution had dismantled the Soviet empire, uprooted the communist political structure, and planted the roots of a market-based economic system. Russia also had taken giant steps to end the Soviet era's self-imposed isolation and to normalize relations with its neighbors and the broader international community. Nevertheless, Yeltsin, as he observed poignantly in his farewell to the Russian people, had failed to achieve a recovery from economic collapse. Moreover, after several years of weakened and increasingly ineffective leadership by an ailing president, Russia's fragile political system had become dysfunctional. Reform efforts had stalled; immature democratic institutions provided weak and unresponsive governance; and Russia's citizens suffered from lawlessness, corruption, and arbitrary bureaucratic rapacity that seemed to drag the country down with each passing crisis of leadership.

It was this Russia that Yeltsin entrusted to his successor, and these issues that Putin began to address as he took up his duties at the stroke of midnight, January 1, 2000. He began to set in motion a program of radical change no less ambitious than that begun by his predecessor a decade earlier. That program, developed by a close group of young advisors whom Putin assembled around him in his earliest days, and implemented subsequently by a newly formed Putin-structured coalition, has not only begun to define the Putin presidency but has already been instrumental in setting Russia on a new course. At home, the components of this program have already done much to jump-start a second phase in the modernization of Russia's society, political system, and economy. Several chapters of this book examine key elements of this program as they document some of the Putin team's greatest achievements. Among these are market reforms that have carried Russia farther than was possible in much of the previous decade and have fostered a remarkable economic recovery, the passage of a major legislative package that is transforming fundamental elements of Russia's socioeconomic and legal culture, and an ambitious program to redefine the relationships between central and regional authority in a way that will answer the eternal challenge of governing Russia's vast territory effectively. At the same time the authors raise many of the persistent questions that Putin's agenda has posed for the future health of Russian democracy and economic recovery. The implications for human rights and democracy of the debilitating and dehumanizing war in Chechnya remain a scar on the Putin record for which neither he nor any in his team have answers; and the handling of press and media issues in ways that suggest discomfort with truly pluralistic freedom of expression leave serious questions about the Putin leadership's capacity to subject government to open public scrutiny.

The final chapters of this volume are devoted to issues that in recent years have been at the heart of Russians' efforts to define themselves and their place in the post–Cold War world. Much attention has been paid to President Putin's moves in response to the attacks on New York and Washington on September 11. But, as the chapters on Russia's defense and foreign policy suggest, Putin's realism and sense for realpolitik have guided his vision for Russia's future place as a great power from his earliest days in office. Central in this regard, Putin has been almost brutally frank with his own people about Russian weaknesses—military, economic, and diplomatic—and the limits thus imposed on his nation's options and choices for national defense and international leadership. The authors of these chapters rightly point to Putin's repeated return to the need to restore and modernize Russia's economic, military, and political structures to revive its international fortunes. And they note that Putin has consistently urged his people to take a realistic view of their international circumstances. He has, thus, crafted pragmatic responses to actions by the West that have reshaped the structures of European security and transformed the strategic framework of relations with the United States, preserving his options and avoiding confrontations that Russia would not win.

For many, the declaration of his intent to take Russia into the coalition against terrorism came as a surprise, one not without serious controversy internally. But Putin's conviction that his country's destiny lay with Europe and the West was evident almost from the outset of his presidency and appeared to represent a core element of his vision for Russia's future. In his first meetings with Western leaders, including Secretary of State Madeleine Albright for example, Putin set forth certain principles he maintained would guide his approach to Russia's international position. Most significantly, I recall, he categorically insisted almost from the first moment that in his worldview Russia was a part of the West and would develop only in that context. He made clear, of course, that Russia would actively pursue normal and productive relations with all its neighbors. But, his early comments were a not-very-subtle rejection of competing strategies that emphasized a multipolar world in which Russia stood as a counterweight to American dominance or a Eurasian school of thinking that sought to set Russia apart from its European roots. That he later would seize on the opportunity afforded by September 11 to push his country dramatically westward was fully in keeping with these early inclinations.

Readers of this volume may well ask themselves at the end many of the same questions they had at the outset. They will look in vain for a unidimensional answer to the question, "Who is Putin?" Nor are there uniform or consistent answers to critical questions about the future of Russia's fragile democracy and developing market economy. Rather, what emerges is a complex and uneven tapestry whose design and weaving are far from complete. For Americans, with an abiding and deep interest in how Russia will evolve, it is perhaps of greatest significance that President Putin remains steadfast in his conviction that Russia's future lies with the Euro-Atlantic world. The challenge will be to recognize the opportunity that conviction represents and to approach the accomplishments and failures of this Russian president with patient realism about the difficult and complex transition through which he must guide his nation.

Acknowledgments

Anyone who teaches Russian politics today bemoans the lack of material available on Putin, the Putin administration, what he and his government have accomplished (and not accomplished) in the first years of his presidency, and where he is leading the country. We have only his autobiography, in the form of a set of interviews, and several sketchy biographies.[1] In addition, a number of studies of the Yeltsin period provide an excellent basis for understanding his handpicked successor.[2] But it soon became clear to me and my close friend and colleague Jake Kipp that there is very little analysis of this very different Russian leader and the policies he is following. Some see him as a reincarnated KGB officer taking the country backward into a world of authoritarian repression, while others consider him a major reformer leading Russia to greater democracy and political stability.

This led us to write an article on Putin, which was favorably received.[3] Yet it was evident from the beginning that we needed to go beyond that essay to provide students and other interested readers with a broader, more in-depth study of the man and his regime in the context of Russia's current condition. Recognizing the complexity of the problems facing Putin and the different approaches he has taken to deal with the country's many problems, I asked a group of experts to join me in trying to understand Russia since January 1, 2000, when Putin became first acting president and later was elected president. We do not all agree on what Putin has done or where he is taking the country. After all, he has been in power for only a short time, but his regime has already had a tremendous impact on Russia. This book represents an effort to shed some light on this unusual Russian leader and the policies he has advocated and implemented.

This volume never would have been possible, however, had the contributors not accepted my somewhat harsh, even Prussian-like discipline. In spite of my constant e-mails and questions, they all put up with me graciously and came through with excellent chapters on subjects as varied as corruption and foreign policy to democratization and the war in Chechnya. I am grateful for their forbearance and patience. I would like to stress, however, that I alone bear responsibility for the content of the introduction and conclusion.

I would also be remiss if I did not express my appreciation to ITAR-TASS to include the many photos in this book. My hope is that they will help readers attach faces to the many confusing (to American students) names of important individuals discussed in this book.

I also want to express my thanks and appreciation to Susan McEachern for her help in editing and organizing this book. This is the third book I have put together under her editorship, and as usual, whatever value this work has is due, in large part, to her help. Michael McFaul's encouragement to me to take on this project is also deeply appreciated and played a major role in my decision to attempt to put a book on Putin together at this point in time.

Speaking personally, I would also like to thank Dr. Jon Wefald, president of Kansas State University, for his help and support at some critical junctures in my academic career. His backing has been invaluable on more than one occasion, and it has been deeply appreciated.

Finally, I want to thank my wife for putting up with my frequent absences while I worked in my study putting this volume together.

NOTES

1. Vladimir Putin, *First Person* (New York: Public Affairs, 2000). For biographies, see Yuri Bortsov, *Vladimir Putin* (Moscow: Feniks, 2001) and Alexander Rahr, *Wladimir Putin, Der Deutsche im Kreml* (Munich: Universitas Verlag, 2000). Among the better articles on Putin, see Peter Rutland, "Putin's Path to Power," *Post-Soviet Affairs* 16, no. 4 (December 2000): 313–54.

2. Two of the best are Lilia Shevtsova, *Yeltsin's Russia: Myths and Reality* (Washington, D.C.: Carnegie Institution, 2001) and Michael McFaul, *Russia's Unfinished Revolution: Political Change from Gorbachev to Putin* (Ithaca, N.Y.: Cornell University Press, 2001).

3. Dale R. Herspring and Jacob Kipp, "Searching for the Elusive Mr. Putin," *Problems of Post-Communism* (September 2001).

Chapter One

Introduction

Dale R. Herspring

When Vladimir Putin became interim president of Russia on January 1, 2000, he was confronted with a staggering array of daunting problems. As he put it, "Russia is in the midst of one of the most difficult periods in its history. For the first time in the past 200–300 years, it is facing a real threat of sliding into the second, and possibly even third echelon of world states."[1] The country's economy was in shambles, its political system was in chaos, and its social and moral structure was in an advanced state of decay. To make matters worse, Putin was virtually unknown, both in Russia and abroad. A former KGB officer, he had returned to his native Leningrad from a KGB assignment in East Germany only ten years previously to become an assistant to Anatoly Sobchak, his former professor, at Leningrad State University. And now the obscure Putin was the country's president!

Putin's reign has been short in the context of Russian history, but these few years have been critical in Russia's development and allow us to begin to make some tentative judgments about his and his regime's performance to date. With this in mind, we will focus on two key questions in this book. First, to what degree has he and his regime been successful (or unsuccessful) in dealing with Russia's problems? Second, and perhaps even more important, where does he seem to be leading the country? What are his goals for Russia, or does he even know where he is taking this beleaguered nation? Before we attempt to shed light on these questions, however, let us take a closer look at this man, an individual who is attempting to rebuild Russia internally, while at the same time regain the international prestige it lost under Yeltsin.

PUTIN, THE MAN

The published facts about Putin's career are sketchy, but the following discussion will at least permit the reader to understand the major events that influenced his life.[2]

1

Putin was born in 1952 in what was then Leningrad (now again St. Petersburg). While in school, he trained in judo and in 1974 became the Leningrad city champion. In his autobiography he credits judo as the turning point in his life. "If I hadn't gotten involved in sports, I'm not sure how my life would have turned out. It was sports that dragged me off the streets."[3] His lifelong dream was to become a member of the KGB. Indeed, he recalls going to the local KGB office while still in high school and telling a somewhat startled officer, "I want to get a job with you."[4] He was advised instead to attend the university and study law.

After graduating from Leningrad State University in 1975 with a degree in law, Putin applied again to the KGB, this time successfully. He was sent to Moscow for initial training and was then assigned to foreign intelligence in Leningrad, where he spent the majority of his time spying on foreigners and Russians who had contacts with them. He studied German and was eventually posted to Dresden in the German Democratic Republic, where he and his wife spent five years and their two daughters were born. This was also where he perfected his German. Putin was no "natural" in the world of espionage, but he learned the craft quickly and effectively, according to one German agent he controlled.[5]

In 1989, Putin returned to Russia and became head of the Foreign Section (Inotdel) at Leningrad State University. In that capacity he served as an assistant for international affairs to his former law professor, Anatoly Sobchak, who was the university's rector. A year later, Sobchak, becoming a major force in Leningrad politics, asked Putin to move to city hall as his advisor on international affairs. In 1991, Sobchak became Leningrad's mayor and appointed Putin chairman of the city's foreign relations committee. It was not long before Sobchak gave him responsibility for a number of reform programs, including foreign investments, where Putin impressed those who dealt with him as a man who could get things done.[6] Indeed, it was during his time in St. Petersburg that he made his reputation as an outstanding administrator.[7]

In 1996 Sobchak failed in his bid for re-election amid charges of corruption, and it appeared that Putin's post-KGB career was at an end. Having heard of Putin's reputation as a "doer," however, Anatoly Chubais, a well-connected advisor to Yeltsin, got him a job working with Pavel Borodin, who was head of a staff closely associated with Yeltsin. Yeltsin took notice of Putin, and in the tumultuous administrative upheavals of the Russian executive in 1998, he was appointed first deputy head of the presidential administration in charge of relations with the regions, and later that year head of the Federal Security Service (the successor to the KGB), a move he claimed made him unhappy because of the secretive life it would entail. "It put you in a constant state of tension. All the papers are secret. This isn't allowed, that isn't allowed."[8] Shortly thereafter, he was put in control of the body that coordinated all of Russia's security and intelligence ministries. Not bad for a former KGB lieutenant colonel.

On August 9, 1999, the ailing Yeltsin surprised the world by appointing Putin as his prime minister and designated successor. On December 31, Yeltsin again astonished everyone by resigning his post and making Putin Russia's acting president. Yeltsin knew his time was limited and wanted to ensure his protégé had the best possible chance to win the forthcoming presidential elections. On March 26, 2000, Putin stood for election and won over 52 percent of the vote in the first round—enough to avoid a runoff. He became Russia's only second elected president.

PUTIN'S APPROACH TO POLITICS

Perhaps because of his KGB background, Putin gives the impression that he believes that even the most difficult problem can be resolved, provided the decisionmaker will follow through and take personal responsibility for the outcome. In short, his past experience made him into a dedicated problem solver. Anatoly Sobchak called him a "determined, even stubborn young man."[9] Once he made up his mind—whether it was to be a judo champion, a KGB officer, or a presidential aide—his bosses could rely on him to see a problem through. Graham Humes, who dealt with Putin while Humes was director general of CARESBAC, an international humanitarian organization in St. Petersburg, talks of the important role Putin played in the city. He overcame one bureaucratic obstacle after another to ensure that humanitarian aid from abroad was delivered in a timely and fair manner.[10] Putin faced a different challenge during his tenure in charge of regional affairs in dealing with the country's regional governors while working for Yeltsin. The latter, who had given the governors considerable autonomy in return for their support, was concerned about their tendency to side with former Russian Prime Minister Yevgeny Primakov and the mayor of Moscow, Yuri Luzhkov, in the battle for political power. Yeltsin asked Putin to break up this budding alliance, which Putin took on. In a short time, the governors had become more neutral when it came to power struggles in Moscow.[11]

In contrast to his predecessors, Putin claims to be nonideological. As he put it in his millennium speech shortly after he took over from Yeltsin, "I am against the restoration of an official state ideology in Russia in any form."[12] Putin appears less interested in an ideological system, than in using any strategy that will work to attack a problem. The ultimate pragmatist, he has been known to try the solutions of left as well as right.

Putin also gives the impression that he tries to be highly rational in his approach to dealing with issues. As a former KGB colleague put it, "He's always in control of his emotions, keeping his cards close to his chest. He must have a weakness, but I don't know what it is."[13] In the policymaking arena, he seems both thoughtful and methodical. To quote two Russian writers, "We have to say this for Putin: he is not in a hurry to make a choice with regards to the reforms and the methods of their implementation. He is taking his time, waiting for his team to be formed to the end."[14]

Putin's style is also administrative, in that he expects the bureaucracy to implement his mandates, and his decisions tend to be of the gradual, incremental type that one would expect from someone who spent his life in an organization like the KGB. As Bortsov put it in comparing Putin with Aleksandr Kerensky (the ill-fated head of the short-lived noncommunist government in the immediate aftermath of the czar's fall in 1917), "Aleksandr Fedorovich Kerensky was an irresponsible romantic, but Vladimir Putin is pragmatic, and it is for that reason in his policies from the beginning he has taken the tactical approach of 'the possible.' Putin is a statesman—Kerensky was not, Putin is for stability, Kerensky was for a revolution, Putin is a man of action, Kerensky was an outstanding orator."[15] In this sense, Putin also stands in contrast to Yeltsin, who was a revolutionary in the sense that he destroyed the old system, especially the control of the Communist Party, and attempted to introduce a new one. In short, Putin is a leader who appears to believe in structured, stable decisionmaking.

Despite his early reputation as a "laid back" KGB agent,[16] during his civilian period he quickly developed a more active image. Putin delegates, but he is also deeply involved in dealing with the problem of the moment. Bortsov put it best when he commented on the difference between Boris Yeltsin and Vladimir Putin: "The principal difference was that the text was written for Boris Nikolaevich, while Vladimir Vladimirovich writes the theses."[17] This hands-on approach is also evident in Putin's dealings with the various departments and agencies in the Russian government. Take Chechnya, for example. As he noted in his autobiography, his initial response to the conflict was centralization and improved coordination. "I met with the top officials of the Ministry of Defense, the General Staff and the Interior Ministry. We met almost every day—sometimes twice a day, morning and evening. And with a lot of fine-tuning, the ministries were consolidated. The first thing I had to do was overcome the disarray among the ministries."[18] In the same vein, Putin believes in personal responsibility—a trait that has again been evident in Chechnya, where Moscow's military operations have been anything but successful.[19]

Pragmatic solutions to immediate tasks, however, depend on the definition of the problem. And Putin's worldview appears to play a role. He spent his career in the state apparatus, within an agency tasked with being the sword and shield of the regime. He comes to problem solving with a bias toward governmental actions and a notion of society as subservient to the interests of the state. He belongs to a long tradition of Russian statesmen who have sought change through autocratic action from above to mold society.[20]

If Putin's character contains an "ism," it would be a statism that, like nationalism, embraces a deep-seated desire to restore Russia to the greatness of its Soviet years, especially through the exercise of state power. His words are instructive: "Patriotism is a source of courage, staunchness and strength of our people. If we lose patriotism and national pride and dignity, which are connected with it, we will lose ourselves as a nation capable of great achievements."[21] Revealingly, Putin's personal hero is Peter the Great, the leader most associated with opening Russia to the West.[22] Indeed, if Putin has a bias in the foreign policy realm, it is toward the West in general, and the United States and Germany in particular. German was one of his best subjects in school and he served there long enough to become quite comfortable in the language—fluent enough to address the Bundestag in German when he visited in 2001. Indeed, his affinity for Germany was strong enough that one of his biographers called him the "German in the Kremlin."[23] Those who worked with him, however, considered him primarily a Europeanist,[24] and his actions in the aftermath of the attack on the Pentagon and the World Trade Towers show that he also favors strong ties with the United States.

Despite Putin's desire to restore Russia to its great-power status, there is no evidence that he is allied with the jingoistic right. He is clearly what Bortsov called a "healthy conservative."[25] Putin's major concern is to rebuild Russia so that it plays the kind of role in the world it did twenty or thirty years ago, and he is not bashful about saying so.

This brings us to the question, how well does the short biographical sketch match up against Putin's first years in office? To what degree did he act in accordance with the personality characteristics described earlier? To try and shed some light on Putin, the man, we asked Ambassador James Collins, newly returned from four years as U.S. ambassador in Moscow, to comment on Putin and his regime. Ambassador Collins observed Putin's rise at close range, and met with him on numerous occasions. Ambassador Collins not only sat in on many private meetings with Putin, including many of the U.S.–Russian summits, he also met and talked with almost all of the individuals mentioned in this book. His perspective on the issues covered in this book is unique.

RUSSIA IN CONTEXT

As a number of analyses of the Yeltsin period have shown, Yeltsin's primary concern was to maintain his own power. Toward that end, he did nothing to create the kind of political infrastructure that would establish a functioning democracy in the Western sense of the term. As Lilia Shevtsova put it, "His

worst mistake both for Russia and himself, has been his failure to establish
strong political institutions and stable rules of the game. He has displayed
little respect for the law. More often than not, he has obeyed only his sense
of political expedience, apparently placing the highest priority on his own
political ambitions."[26] Indeed, for a while one of the best sports for Moscow
watchers was to bet on (a) how long Yeltsin's current prime minister would
last, and (b) who would replace him as Yeltsin proceeded to play musical
chairs with his top officials. The minute anyone appeared to grow too powerful or became a political liability, Yeltsin removed him. Yeltsin believed that
Russia could only survive if it had a strong president.

One could argue that in the aftermath of his 1993 war with the Duma,
Yeltsin had no choice but to create a constitution that enshrined the idea of
a super-presidency. With recalcitrant legislators, communists, and hundreds
if not thousands of other opponents, he had no alternative. However, as
Shevtsova noted, "Many people, even in Russia, at first hoped that the
'super-presidency' that Yeltsin established was only temporary. But this structure, designed to overcome deadlocks and to serve as a major reform force,
has now become the main source of political disarray."[27]

A temporary super-presidency might have worked if Yeltsin had been a different leader. However, his ill health, his alcoholism, his acceptance of cronyism and corruption, and his fear of competitors undermined his effectiveness.
Furthermore, as time wore on, instead of developing political institutions
such as the Duma, he fought one battle after another with it until he generally ignored it in favor of presidential decrees. His actions were often contradictory and his leadership weak at best.

This meant that when Putin came to power Russia had a constitution that
put almost all power in the hands of the country's president. In the meantime, nothing had been done to create a "rule of law," a system that would
not only enable justice to be dispensed in a fair and impartial manner, but
would allow the millions of daily interactions between individuals and firms
and the government to be regulated. Similarly, political parties—with the
exception of the Communist Party—were nonexistent. By Soviet standards,
the press was free, as was the media in general. However, as a result of Yeltsin's need of their support during his 1996 election campaign, the majority
of the country was owned by the oligarchs, a small group of powerful and
wealthy individuals. In the meantime, many of the country's eighty-nine
regions paid little attention to Moscow. They passed whatever local laws they
preferred, even if they ran counter to the Russian constitution. The country's
economy was in shambles after the August 1998 crash of the ruble. Finally,
the military was mired in what appeared to be an unwinnable war in Chechnya, and the Kremlin's standing on the world stage was at an all-time low.

Putin and his followers have attempted to deal with these problems. It
would be wrong, however, to look upon Putin either as Russia's savior or as

its Satan. I personally am agnostic. I believe it is too early to say where Putin is taking Russia. As citizens of a Western democracy, we may disagree with many of his and his colleagues' actions. Yet the most important issue, at least in my opinion, is how effective has he been in creating a politically stable and economically viable polity. Here, the jury is out; and indeed the reader will find disagreement among this book's contributors on this question.

Some will argue that he has done very little; that his actions are half-measures at best, while others will maintain that he has taken some (admittedly small and preliminary) steps toward moving the country in the direction of political and economic stability. Some will also note that this "progress" has come at a cost. They will maintain that democracy (as that term is understood in the West) has been weakened, while others will suggest that the creation of viable economic and political institutions may have to take priority at this stage, considering Russia's disastrous state.

One of the key prerequisites of any democracy is the existence of attitudes that support it—the presence of beliefs in support of concepts such as compromise, secret ballots, respect for the law, a belief that power comes from the people (i.e., the presence of an active as opposed to a passive citizenry), the existence of groups of individuals who are not controlled by a single party or state, etc.

Timothy Colton and Michael McFaul struggle with this vitally important issue by looking at grassroots attitudes in Russia, especially toward democracy and political practices. Contrary to popular wisdom, they conclude that despite Russia's illiberal tendencies, most citizens support democratic values and ideas. Just as important, however, is the problem of institutionalizing democracy. Toward this end, Thomas Remington focuses on the oft-overlooked Duma, Russia's parliament, and the issue of creating viable political parties. Yeltsin fought with parliament, while Putin is trying to work with it, even if not as democratically as many in the West would prefer. The key point is that unless democratization is institutionalized in the form of genuinely functional political parties, many argue that the outlook for democracy in Russia is mixed at best.

When it comes to the question of democracy, there are no more important issues than press freedom and corruption. In the first instance, Masha Lipman, herself a journalist, and Michael McFaul take a critical look at how the relatively free media that existed under Yeltsin has fared under Putin. The trends are disturbing—at least if one supports the kind of free press we have in the West. Similarly, Virginie Coulloudon analyzes what Putin has done (or not) to deal with the ever-present problems of corruption and judicial reform. Unless meaningful steps are undertaken, the outlook for everything from protecting human rights to attracting foreign investment will be bleak at best.

Indeed, almost all observers are united on one point: unless Russia is able to create a stable, healthy economy, there is little chance that it will evolve in the direction of the kind of democratic polity that most Russians seek. Indeed, Putin has focused repeatedly on this problem, and noted just how critical it is in his millennium speech when he observed, "It will take us approximately fifteen years and an annual growth of our Gross Domestic Product by 8 percent a year to reach the per capita GDP level of present-day Portugal or Spain, which are not among the world's industrialized leaders."[28] Toward this end, James Millar takes a careful and critical look at the evolution of the Russian economy under Yeltsin and then Putin in an effort to shed light on the prospects for success in this area. Furthermore, it is clear to anyone who has followed events in Russia that if there is one group that has had the most profound impact on the country's economic and political structure, it is the oligarchs. Peter Rutland considers their role and his chapter on the oligarchs looks at how Putin has approached these highly influential individuals.

Too often books such as this one tend to ignore security and military questions. It reminds me of a book published in the 1930s that I read long ago that said it would not discuss the military "because it is an occupation that we hope will not be used again." However, in the case of Russia, it is impossible to overlook the issue of security. It plays a vital role in Russia's future whether we like it or not. Thus, Dale Herspring considers whether Putin has been successful in reforming that beleaguered institution. At the same time, no analysis of the military would be complete without an in-depth discussion of the never-ending wars in Chechnya, which Jake Kipp provides. As a historian, Jake Kipp knows only too well the key role that historical animosities play in this part of the world.

Chechnya is far from Putin's only regional worry. Nikolai Petrov and Darrell Slider explore Putin's efforts to reassert Moscow's authority, first over the rest of the country, and second in the world at large. One of the strategies Yeltsin used to gain the support of local politicians was to give them as much autonomy as they could seize. While that may have helped Yeltsin in his battle with the communists, it left Putin with a highly decentralized political system—one in which the Kremlin exerted only limited authority over its far-flung territory, as Nikolai Petrov and Darrell Slider note. Putin appears to have regained some of the control that Yeltsin lost, but at a cost to local autonomy.

Dale Herspring and Peter Rutland consider Moscow's attempt to influence the world beyond the near abroad, the realm of foreign policy, where Russia has fallen from the cosmic heights of a superpower to what some observers have referred to dismissively as "a third world country with nuclear weapons." Putin both wants to see Russia reestablish its position in the world for nationalistic reasons and because he understands that Russia's economic recovery is to a large degree dependent in particular on its ties with the United States and Western Europe.

This leaves us with our first question noted earlier: Where is Putin taking Russia? Dale Herspring explores this issue in his conclusion. What can we (and the Russian people) expect from Putin in the future? Political prognoses are an inexact science at best, and none of us would claim to know the future. Yet the more we understand the present and the past, the better are our chances to prepare for what may come.

NOTES

1. Vladimir Putin, "Russia at the Turn of the Millennium," *Pravitel'stvo Rossiyskoy Federatsii*, January 17, 2000, at www.government.gov.ru/english/statVP_engl_1.html.

2. Much of the following biographical information is taken from Herspring and Kipp, "Searching for the Elusive Mr. Putin," *Problems of Post Communism* (September/October 2001).

3. Vladimir Putin, *First Person* (New York: Public Affairs, 2000), 19.

4. Putin, *First Person*, 23.

5. Mark Franchetti, "Spy Tells How Putin Blew It as KGB Rookie," *New York Times*, March 11, 2001.

6. See Graham Hume's discussion of Putin's role and effectiveness at this time. "Vladimir Vladimirovich Putin in 1994: A Personal Reflection," E-Notes, Foreign Policy Research Institute, January 14, 2001.

7. Yuri Bortsov, *Vladimir Putin* (Moscow: Feniks, 2001), 132.

8. Putin, *First Person*, 131.

9. Ann-Marie O'Neill, Julian Varoli, John Garelik, and Glen Mikelbank, "Vladimir Putin, Russia's Martial-Arts-Loving President in Waiting Remains an Enigma," *People's Weekly*, February 28, 2000.

10. Hume, "Vladimir Vladimorovich Putin in 1994."

11. Masha Gessen, "Putin Himself First," *New Republic*, January 17, 2000, 23.

12. Putin, "Russia at the Turn of the Millennium," 5.

13. Franchetti, "Spy Tells How Putin Blew It as a KGB Rookie."

14. "Putin in 2001: A Burden of Choice," *Ponedelnik*, no. 6 (February 2001) in *Johnson's List*, February 13, 2001.

15. Bortsov, *Vladimir Putin*, 215.

16. Rahr, Alexander, *Wladimir Putin, der "Deutsche" im kreml* (Munich: Universitas, 2000), 64.

17. Bortsov, *Vladimir Putin*, 175.

18. Putin, *First Person*, 140–41.

19. Bortsov, *Vladimir Putin*, 199.

20. Ariel Cohen, "From Yeltsin to Putin," *Policy Review*, no. 100 (April/May 2000): 35–49.

21. Putin, "Russia at the Turn of the Millennium," 6.

22. See Bortsov, *Vladimir Putin*, 111.

23. Rahr, *Wladimir Putin*.

24. Bortsov, *Vladimir Putin*, 122.

Dale R. Herspring

25. Bortsov, *Vladimir Putin*, 277.

26. Lilia Shevtsova, *Yeltsin's Russia, Myths and Reality* (Washington, D.C.: Carnegie Endowment for International Peace, 1993).

27. Shevtsova, *Yeltsin's Russia, Myths and Reality*, 3.

28. Putin, "Russia at the Turn of the Millennium," 5.

Part One

POLITICS

Chapter Two

Putin and Democratization
Timothy J. Colton and Michael McFaul

A new narrative about post-Soviet Russia has been taking hold in policy, media, and academic circles and shows signs of entrenching as a new conventional wisdom. By this reading, Russia's experiment with democracy has failed. So misconceived and mismanaged were the political and economic reforms of the 1990s that they have fueled mass disenchantment with democratic norms and brought authoritarianism back into repute. Russians, in short, are said to be giving up on democracy.

Westerners who subscribe to this point of view can readily support it with evidence from Russian sources. A national poll of adult Russians conducted by the Center for the Study of Public Opinion (VTsIOM) in Moscow, in January 2000, found that 75 percent were in accord with a statement that order is more important than democracy and should be pursued even if it entails violations of democratic procedures and abridgements of personal freedom.[1] Commenting on Vladimir Putin's election as president in March 2000, the esteemed head of VTsIOM, Professor Yuri Levada, concluded, "Putin can do what he wants. . . . Russians value might more than principles now."[2] In repeated instances of democratic backsliding during the Putin era, including the emasculation of the Federation Council and the closure of NTV and TV-6, the people seem indifferent.[3] Other surveys seem to confirm that "Russian support for civil liberties is weak, especially when they are asked concrete questions rather than abstract ones."[4]

Some observers go a step further, anchoring present-day antidemocratic sentiment in an unbroken continuum of Russian values and traditions. Russians, they say, are culturally predisposed—by Orthodox Christianity, by the paternalistic mores of village life, by centuries of tsarist rule, and most recently by Marxism-Leninism and cradle-to-grave socialism—to desire an overweening state and a dominant leader. Nikolai Biryukov and Victor Serge-

yev write that the problems of the past decade are but the latest in a long line
of mishaps:

> So far there have been six failures [of democracy] during the last ninety years.
> These take into account the First, Second, and Fourth State Duma in 1906,
> 1907, and 1917; the Constituent Assembly in 1918; the Congress of Peoples'
> Deputies and the Supreme Soviet of the USSR and the Russian Federation in
> 1991 and 1993. Given this, it is more than appropriate to ask why all attempts
> to institute representative authority in Russia seem to come to an apparently
> inevitable dramatic, not to say tragic, end? Since these events occurred under
> different historic circumstances and different regimes, it is also appropriate—in
> our inquiry concerning factors that prevent development of representative
> democracy in Russia—to turn to those features in Russian society that undergo
> slow changes and remain relatively invariable under all political regimes. Political
> culture is, presumably, the first to be considered.[5]

Biryukov and Sergeyev are in select company. Distinguished scholars of
comparative politics—Seymour Martin Lipset, Samuel Huntington, and Russell Bova, among them—hold that societal acceptance of Western democratic
values is an indispensable prop of democratic institutions.[6] In the Russian
case, the exact influences identified as having molded the popular mindset
vary from account to account, but the gloomy conclusion about Russians'
ingrained and immutable hostility to democracy is a common thread.[7] As a
result, Russia's difficulties in consolidating democracy in the past decade do
not come as a shock: they essentially betray continuity with Russia's communist *and* pre-communist legacies, and a lack of receptivity to values imported
artificially from the remote West. In a sense, this emphasis on Russian culture
and values casts the people as "co-conspirators" in bringing about democratic failure.[8] Some make an analogous argument about Russian attitudes
toward private property and markets, as in Stephen Cohen's statement that
"a fully capitalist system is in conflict with Russia's tradition."[9]

Putin's rise to power and stellar approval ratings seem at first blush to confirm this take on Russian culture and history. After a decade of chaos, Russians, it may be reasoned, yearned for a Kremlin strongman who would
deliver order and stability. Putin's ruthless use of force against the Chechens
made him a national hero and the easy winner of the 2000 presidential election, and he followed up his electoral victory with curbs on press freedoms
and other democratic rights. In the cultural mirror, the neo-authoritarian
drift may be exactly what the Russians want and deserve. This argument is
not inconvenient for President Putin, and is propagated subtly by analysts
and politicians in his camp.

This chapter challenges key elements of the emerging master narrative of
Russian politics. Without questioning the many illiberal features of Russia's
current political system, we use data on Russian public opinion to offer a

more nuanced and complex picture of grassroots attitudes. We build on a substantial body of empirical work on public attitudes in Russia and the other post-Soviet states. Although surveys of the mass of the population have furnished many insights into popular attitudes toward democracy, these insights have tended to be offered in highly summarized and compressed form. Attitudes toward democracy as such have not, by and large, been the exclusive or even the principal focus in the published research. Instead, measures of these attitudes have been utilized for other scholarly purposes—in particular, for understanding voting behavior, the links between political values and economic perceptions, and continuity and change in popular beliefs over time.

Our objective here is to take the time to profile Russian attitudes toward democracy and political practices in more depth and detail than other studies have provided. The data we quarry are a byproduct of a research project directed primarily, like so many others, at a different objective—in this case, to investigation of the Russian electoral cycle of 1999–2000. We agree with the conventional view that Russian democratic institutions are performing miserably and that leaders, especially since Putin's ascent to power, have done much to compromise and erode democratic practices.[10] The political system in Russia today is at best an illiberal democracy. However, we maintain that its many and obvious limitations are not caused by, or for that matter consistently reinforced by, popular attitudes toward democracy. Although Russian citizens in many ways share our negative assessment of the way their national institutions work, it would be wrong to jump to the conclusion that they single-mindedly spurn democratic values and ideas *per se*. Even Putin's own electorate is more pro-democratic than the talk of Russia's authoritarian trend would have it.

This chapter explores this ground in seven parts. The first maps voter attitudes about the way Russian "democracy" works. It documents that people in Russia are anything but satisfied with their government. The second part reviews popular attitudes toward the general idea or concept of democracy as a system, showing, contrary to some assertions, that democracy is not a dirty word among Russian voters. In the third part, we turn to attitudes toward specific components of a democratic system, revealing that support for these concrete aspects of democracy is likely stronger than for the concept of democracy in the abstract. The fourth part takes up the thorny issue of trade-offs between order and democracy. Our results offer a somewhat different picture than previous analyses and imply that Russians are not as eager to give up their individual liberties as has long since been suspected. Next we briefly profile the supporters of democracy in sociodemographic terms. Then we look specifically at Putin's supporters in the 2000 presidential election, revealing that they are not markedly less attached to democratic practices than the country as a whole. We conclude by placing Russia in a comparative context and teasing out some recommendations for Western policy.

POPULAR ASSESSMENTS OF
DEMOCRATIC PRACTICE IN RUSSIA

For the last decade, Russia's leaders, now chosen in contested elections, have assured the citizenry over and over again that their country's new system of government is a democracy. Putin frequently echoes this refrain. Our polling data testify categorically that Russians on the whole do *not* believe what they have repeatedly been told. When asked in 1999 whether their political system could be considered a democracy at all (see the second column of table 2.1), slightly more than half of survey respondents told interviewers that it could not; only about 20 percent agreed that Russia is a democratic country. To make matters worse, the proportion of the population that considers Russia to be democratically governed has been on the *decrease* in recent years, not on the increase. When Boris Yeltsin was elected to a second term in 1996, about 35 percent of Russian voters thought their homeland was a democracy and about 30 percent thought it was not, or not nearly as many naysayers as there were to be in 1999 (see the first column of table 2.1).

Responses to a question about "how democracy is developing" manifest a

Table 2.1.   Agreement with Statement: "The political system that exists in Russia today is a democracy," 1996 and 1999

Position	1996[a] (percentage)	1999[b] (percentage)
Fully agree	3	4
Agree	27	15
Indifferent	18	19
Disagree	20	39
Completely disagree	5	13
Don't know	17	11

Note: Percentages may not add to 100 due to rounding.
[a] Interviews after 1996 presidential election (N = 2,472 weighted cases).
[b] Interviews before 1999 parliamentary election (N = 1,919 weighted cases).

Table 2.2.   Satisfaction with How Democracy Is Developing in Russia, 1996 and 1999

Position	1996[a] (percentage)	1999[b] (percentage)
Fully satisfied	1	1
Satisfied	25	11
Dissatisfied	42	56
Completely dissatisfied	15	24
Don't know	17	9

Note: Percentages may not add to 100 due to rounding.
[a] Interviews after 1996 presidential election (N = 2,472 weighted cases).
[b] Interviews before 1999 parliamentary election (N = 1,919 weighted cases).

similarly bleak trend (see table 2.2). About one-quarter of Russians felt satisfaction in 1996 with the course of democratization, or nearly as many as were dissatisfied. In 1999 the proportion of satisfied individuals had shrunk to barely 10 percent and 80 percent proclaimed themselves dissatisfied with the political trend.

By any gauge, frustration with the operations of contemporary Russian government is rampant. The vast majority of citizens believe that their governmental authorities do their job inadequately, as the top panel of table 2.3 shows conclusively. On a five-point scale for ranking government performance, almost two-thirds of Russians take one of the two pronouncedly negative positions; a mere 5 percent adopts one of the two positive positions. When individuals are asked about governmental responsiveness and accountability, the picture they paint is no more flattering. Twenty-five percent of

Table 2.3.   Satisfaction with the Russian Political System, 1999–2000

Question/Answer	Percentage
Rate the Russian political scale on a 5 point scale, "where 1 means that things are working very poorly and 5 means things are working very well."	
1 (very poorly)	37
2	27
3	27
4	3
5 (very well)	2
Don't know	4
Position on statement, "It seems to me government officials do not especially care what people like me think."	
Fully agree	25
Agree	59
Indifferent	9
Disagree	6
Completely disagree	0
Don't know	2
Position on statement, "People like me have no say in what the government does."	
Fully agree	14
Agree	42
Indifferent	11
Disagree	25
Completely disagree	4
Don't know	4

Note: Interviews after 1999 parliamentary election (N = 1,846 weighted cases). Percentages may not add to 100 due to rounding.

our respondents in 1999–2000 fully agreed and 60 percent agreed with the assertion that government officials "do not especially care what people like me think," with only 6 percent dissenting. In reaction to the statement, "people like me have no say in what the government does," 14 percent fully agreed and 42 percent agreed, with 29 percent disagreeing.

Given the magnitude of the discontent with the current order, it is perhaps to be expected that many in Russia will be nostalgic for the alternative most familiar to them from life experience—the Soviet one-party system. The vast majority of Russians at the present time are convinced that the dismantling of the Soviet Union was a mistake (see table 2.4). Fewer than 15 percent of our polling respondents in 1999 disagreed in whole or in part with the statement that the USSR "should never under any circumstances have been dissolved." Those who agreed with the statement outnumbered them about six-to-one. A cornerstone of Russia's vaunted democratic revolution is looked upon with almost universal disdain one decade after it came about.

The sources of warm memories of the Soviet period are many, and no doubt include feelings of a private and nonpolitical nature. In the political realm, many Russians would be only too pleased to resurrect the Soviet Union's authoritarian regime, as the figures in table 2.5 show. Presented with a four-way choice between an unreformed Soviet system, a reformed Soviet system, the current political system, and "democracy of the Western type," a clear preponderance of our respondents in 1999 fancied some version of the Soviet model, and only about one in five preferred the current political order or a Western democracy. Notice, however, that the most widely desired outcome is a *democratized* version of the Soviet system, not the dictatorship that Mikhail Gorbachev inherited in 1985 and subsequently demolished. Notice also the intriguing discrepancy between table 2.5 and table 2.4. About three-quarters of Russians in 1999 beheld the passing of the Soviet Union with regret; but only about one-quarter wished for a return to the unmodified Soviet political system. Even among respondents who strongly believed the dissolution of the USSR to have been a mistake, fewer than 40 percent favored reinstatement of an unreformed Soviet-type polity.

Table 2.4. Agreement with Statement: "The Soviet Union should never under any circumstances have been dissolved," 1999

Position	Percentage
Fully agree	38
Agree	35
Indifferent	11
Disagree	12
Completely disagree	1
Don't know	3

Note: Interviews before 1999 parliamentary election (N = 1,919 weighted cases).

Table 2.5.   Preferred Political System for Russia, 1999–2000

Preference	Percentage
The Soviet system we had in our country before *perestroyka*	25
The Soviet system, but in a different, more democratic form	41
The political system that exists today	12
Democracy of the Western type	9
Other response or Don't know	12

Note: Interviews after 1999 parliamentary election (N = 1,846 weighted cases). Percentages may not add to 100 due to rounding.

POPULAR ATTITUDES TOWARD
THE IDEA OF DEMOCRACY

In all democracies, especially new ones, dissatisfaction with the practice of democracy has the potential to erode the normative preference for democracy.[11] This is most certainly the case in the Russian Federation. For example, mass support for democracy writ large dropped in the aftermath of the confrontation between the parliament and President Yeltsin in September–October 1993.[12] Ordinary people did not like the practice of politics they were witnessing. Since it was called democracy, their support for democracy and the "democrats" declined. Today, though, many Russian citizens seem to recognize the difference between the democracy practiced in Russia and the ideal or norm of democracy that Russia has failed to achieve. As already noted, voters expressed anger at the condition of their political system in our 1999–2000 polls. And yet, when they were interrogated about the idea of democracy, the gestalt was very different.

Answers to the most straightforward of the questions we posed—"Do you in general support the idea of democracy?"—are contained in the top section of table 2.6. About two out of three respondents endorsed the concept of democracy, while fewer than one in five opposed it. As a general proposition, then, Russians overwhelmingly embrace democracy. Contrary to many journalistic reports, "democracy" has not degenerated into a dirty word for most Russian voters.

In response to a crude binary choice—democracy or not—an affirmative answer to this question may not tell us much about either understanding of or deep commitment to the concept. We thus inserted several variations on the same overall theme into our survey questionnaire. For one thing, we had our interviewers ask if democracy is an appropriate way for Russia to be governed. Russian voters, after all, may suppose that democracy is fine in theory or an appropriate way for governing in rich Western countries, but still unsuitable for their homeland. Domestic commentators do often dismiss democracy as a luxury Russia cannot afford right now. However, the typical

Table 2.6.   Attitudes toward the Idea of Democracy, 1999–2000

Question/Answer	Percentage
"Do you in general support the idea of democracy or do you come out against the idea of democracy?"[a]	

Support it	64
Against it	18
Don't know	18

"How good would democracy be for governing Russia?"[b]	

Very good way	8
Fairly good way	52
Fairly bad way	18
Very bad way	6
Don't know	16

Agreement with statement, "Democracy may have many problems, but it is better than any other form of government."[b]	

Fully agree	6
Agree	41
Indifferent	20
Disagree	15
Completely disagree	2
Don't know	17

Agreement with statement, "In a democracy, citizens have more control over their leaders than in nondemocratic systems."[b]	

Fully agree	9
Agree	43
Indifferent	16
Disagree	13
Completely disagree	2
Don't know	17

Note: Percentages may not add to 100 due to rounding.
[a] Interviews before 1999 parliamentary election (N = 1,919 weighted cases).
[b] Interviews after 1999 parliamentary election (N = 1,846 weighted cases).

Russian voter, as the second panel of table 2.6 indicates, is of a different opinion. Sixty percent of our respondents felt in 1999–2000 that democracy was a very good or a fairly good model for Russia, with far fewer, 24 percent, portraying it as fairly bad or very bad.

Equally noteworthy, Russians also seem to realize that no political system is perfect. In reply to the Churchillian question about democracy in relation to the alternatives, a plurality of voters goes along with democracy as the best form of government when compared to other systems (see table 2.6). When asked about government accountability, most Russian citizens, we reported above, do not think that their own government is responsive to their needs. In principle, however, they believe that democracies in general give citizens more control over their leaders than dictatorships do. The answers to this item are revealing, since most Russians of voting age, except for the very youngest, have direct personal experience with dictatorial rule.

It is tempting to speculate that the general notion of democracy is for Russians a proxy for the affluent way of life associated with the Western nations. Our data do not allow us to sound out this possibility in depth, but we do find evidence that envy of the West is *not* the all-consuming force it once might have been and that not all Russians perceive democracy as a monopoly of the Western community.

The best clue comes from a polling question about the extent of emulation of Western experience. We asked survey respondents to choose among three formulations of Russia's optimal strategy. Almost none of our informants selected the option that connotes slavish imitation of the West. Opinion divided nearly evenly between those looking to the West as a partial if not exclusive model and those wanting Russia to shun the West and hew to its own exclusive path. Table 2.7 juxtaposes those responses with the distribution of opinion on our questions concerning the idea of democracy and the best political system for Russia. Among those who took a position on Westernization, support for the ideal of democracy was highest among persons who favored at least some learning from the West. But even among defenders of a separate national path for Russia, a majority (52 percent) said they favored democracy in principle, whereas a minority (28 percent) came out against it. The pattern is similar for political system preference. An unreformed Soviet political system comes out slightly ahead of the most widely preferred option, a reformed Soviet system, only among the respondents who do not voice a position on Westernization. Proponents of a separate national path are considerably more likely than individuals who favor wholesale or selective borrowing from the West to prefer an unreformed Soviet system, but even in that category a slight plurality prefers a reformed Soviet system.

It is clear, in other words, that a significant portion of the Russian population acquiesces in the abstract idea of democracy without necessarily looking to the West for guidance. Democracy as an idea somehow possesses a measure of autonomy in the popular mind from attitudes toward Western civilization. This discovery casts cold water on the claims by some analysts in the West that democratic ideas are indivisible and must always be juxtaposed against the values of non-Western cultures. As the history of French, Japanese, Mexican, or Botswanan democracy demonstrates, countries can build democratic institutions without turning into facsimiles of the United States. Our data hint that a similar process of nativization of the idea of democracy may be starting in Russia.

Table 2.7. Attitudes toward the Idea of Democracy and Preferred Political System for Russia, Classified by Position on Westernization of Russia, 1999–2000

Idea/position	*Position on Westernization of Russia (percentage)*			
	Imitate the West	*Selectively borrow from the West*	*Follow a unique path*	*Don't know*
The idea of democracy[a]				
Support it	69	76	52	35
Against it	6	10	28	4
Don't know	25	13	20	60
Preferred political system[b]				
Unreformed Soviet system	15	15	36	39
Reformed Soviet system	39	43	38	32
Current political system	8	16	9	5
Western democracy	15	13	5	5
Other response or don't know	23	13	11	20

Note: Percentages may not add to 100 due to rounding.
[a] N = 1,919 weighted cases.
[b] N = 1,846 weighted cases.

POPULAR ATTITUDES TOWARD THE COMPONENTS OF DEMOCRACY

Substantively, the word "democracy" means different things to different people. It has been used to describe everything from the city-states of Greek antiquity to the pre-1990 German "Democratic" Republic. Soviet ideology was never rhetorically antidemocratic. In the new Russia, Boris Yeltsin's appropriation of the term to describe his reforms and his allies—the "democrats" versus the "communists"—served to muddy and distort, if not to discredit, the term. Support of democratic ideas correlates in many modern countries with support for liberal and democratic procedures, but not always and not neatly.[13] To fully appreciate people's attitudes about democracy, therefore, requires us to deal with some specific institutions and folkways of democracy.

When disaggregated into specific components (see table 2.8), endorsement of democratic institutions and practices is higher in Russia than the already considerable support for democracy as a global concept. Regarding what is by most definitions the *sine qua non* of democracy—competitive elections—Russians, by a lopsided majority, believe in them. Eighty-seven percent of survey respondents in 1999 answered that it was important to them that the country's leaders be popularly elected; a paltry 9 percent said it was not important. In addition, when asked about citizen responsibilities, 86 percent fully agreed or agreed that it is the duty of each citizen to vote in elections; 6 percent disagreed or completely disagreed. These figures help explain why voter turnout in Russian national elections has hovered around two-thirds, except for the dip in the parliamentary elections and referendum of December 1993.

Elections, of course, are not the only ingredient of a consolidated democracy, and citizen approval of them in Russia could possibly be a legacy of the Soviet era, since leaders back then were "elected" as well, albeit in elections with a single name on the ballot slip.[14] Russian voters, it so happens, espouse many other attributes of the democratic polity that did not exist in Soviet times. By expansive margins, they concur in a number of the classic freedoms enshrined in a liberal democracy (table 2.8). And, unlike some of the other responses to questions about democracy in the abstract, fewer than 5 percent of survey respondents in 1999 found it impossible to answer these survey items. More than 85 percent of those polled reckoned that the freedom of one's convictions, free expression, and freedom of the mass media were important to them. Seventy to 75 percent found free choice of place of residence and religious freedom to be important. In only one domain—freedom to travel abroad, which most Russians cannot act on for financial reasons—did less than a majority (40 percent) agree with the importance of the freedom.

For this bundle of civic and personal freedoms, the incidence of support is so high in Russia that it runs through all groupings within the population and cuts across expressions of support for particular regimes. So, for example, 94 percent of the advocates of a Western democracy, 91 percent of the supporters of the current political system, and 90 percent of the supporters of a reformed Soviet system agree with the importance of elections—but so do 78

Table 2.8.   Importance of Rights and Freedoms to Russians, 1999

	Importance to the respondent (percentage)		
Right or freedom	*Important*	*Not important*	*Don't know*
Freedom to elect the country's leaders	87	9	4
Freedom to have one's own convictions	87	9	4
Freedom of expression	87	10	3
Freedom of the press, radio, and television	81	14	5
Free choice of place of residence within the country	75	22	3
Religious freedom	70	26	4
Freedom to travel abroad	40	56	4

Note: Interviews before 1999 parliamentary election (N = 1,919 weighted cases).

percent of those who say they prefer Russia to have a Soviet-type regime, as it existed before *perestroyka*.

Regarding more complex liberal and democratic precepts, support among Russians does not come so close to unanimity, but the levels are often, nonetheless, impressive. On checks and balances and the constitutional separation of powers—rather demanding concepts—a majority of Russians favor a divided and federalized government. Cultural theorists and Kremlin propagandists often assert that the Russian people want a strong president to head their government, unconstrained by other political actors. In fact (see table 2.9), Russians seem more comfortable with a division of power between the president and parliament. In response to the question whether the president or parliament should be stronger, the largest number of respondents take a middle position, recommending that the executive and legislative branches have equal power. This result is somewhat unexpected given the low reputation Russia's parliament enjoys. In our questions about trust in institutions, the Federal Assembly ranked near the bottom, well below the most trusted (the army and the Russian Orthodox Church). In favoring the norm of separation of powers while ranking the actual parliament so low, Russian citizens evince a sophisticated grasp of some facets of democratic government. Nor do they want to assign the federal government in Moscow unbridled power

Table 2.9.   Opinions on the Balance among Russian Political Institutions, 1999

Question/Answer	Percentage
Who should have more power in the central government, on a five-point scale "where 1 denotes that the President should have much more power than Parliament and 5 denotes that Parliament should have much more power than the President?"	
1 (President much stronger)	17
2	8
3 (President and Parliament equal in power)	45
4	7
5 (Parliament much stronger)	16
Don't know	8
Distribution of decision-making power between Moscow and the regions	
Everything should be decided in Moscow	5
Most questions should be decided in Moscow	10
Some questions should be decided in Moscow and some in the regions	53
Most questions should be decided in the regions	23
Everything should be decided in the regions	6
Don't know	2

Note: Interviews before 1999 parliamentary election (N = 1,919 weighted cases). Percentages may not add to 100 due to rounding.

over regional governments (table 2.9). Again, when asked if the center or the regions should have more power, the lion's share of respondents gravitated to the neutral answer of some power to the center, some power to the regions.

Even highly unpopular actors and organizations are recognized as necessary units in a fully functional democratic system. Political parties enjoy the lowest level of trust among all of Russia's institutions and organizations. Yet, when asked how necessary political parties are in making the Russian political system work, many more of our respondents answered that they were necessary than asserted that they were unnecessary (see table 2.10). By a smaller margin, more people agreed than disagreed with the statement that competition among political parties makes the polity stronger. If Russians are willing to accept political parties—entities deemed to be inept, marginal, and ineffective in other polls—as a necessary evil of democracy, then gut knowledge of democratic theory and practice among Russians may be deeper than we tend to assume.

Another question on which Russians face vexing choices is that of law and order. The Soviet heritage, combined with the blossoming of crime and corruption in the 1990s, might well bias them against the rights of the accused and in favor of an iron-hand approach to crime. As table 2.11 illustrates, though, Russian views on this fraught issue are mixed, with liberal views hav-

Table 2.10. Attitudes toward Political Parties, 1999–2000

Question/Answer	Percentage
Necessity of political parties in Russia, on a five-point scale "where 1 means that political parties are necessary to make our political system work and 5 means that political parties are not needed in Russia."	
1 (Parties are necessary to make our political system work)	32
2	21
3	20
4	8
5 (Parties are not needed in Russia)	10
Don't know	10
Agreement with statement, "Competition among various political parties makes our system stronger."	
Fully agree	4
Agree	35
Indifferent	17
Disagree	24
Completely disagree	6
Hard to say	13

Note: Interviews after 1999 parliamentary election (N = 1,846 weighted cases). Percentages may not add to 100 due to rounding.

ing the edge over illiberal views but the latter far from unrepresented in the population. As the top panel of the table tells us, more Russian citizens are willing to let some criminals go free in the name of preserving individual rights than are unwilling to support such a principle. The margin is 45 percent favoring safeguards for the rights of the accused to 29 percent opposed, with the rest neutral or undecided. In the bottom panel, we see a liberal majority on the allied question of the need to defend society's rights even if some innocent people need to be imprisoned. Almost 60 percent contest this assertion, and fewer than 20 percent uphold it. Support for this idea requires a subtle understanding of the rule of law, which one might suspect not to be widespread in current-day Russia.[15] We should expect the poor performance of the legal system to undermine support for the idea of the rule of law. A sizable minority manifests highly illiberal attitudes, but the overall distribution is not consistent with the thesis that Russians in general yearn for law and order no matter what the consequences.

Arguably, the grossest violations of human rights in Russia are now taking place in Chechnya, where federal troops were reintroduced, and heavy fighting resumed, several months before the first and second waves of our election survey.[16] We know from other research that mass support for Putin's handling of the war was high—nearly 60 percent—from the incursion in September 1999 to the election campaign a half-year later, and that many voters were

Table 2.11. Attitudes toward Law and Order, 1999–2000

Question/Answer	Percentage
Agreement with statement, "The rights of the individual must be defended even if guilty people sometimes go free."	
Fully agree	9
Agree	36
Indifferent	17
Disagree	25
Completely disagree	4
Don't know	9
Agreement with statement, "The rights of society must be defended even if innocent people sometimes are imprisoned."	
Fully agree	3
Agree	15
Indifferent	15
Disagree	47
Completely disagree	12
Don't know	8

Note: Interviews after 1999 parliamentary election (N = 1,846 weighted cases). Percentages may not add to 100 due to rounding.

attracted to Putin because of his vigorous prosecution of the military effort.[17] But support for the war against the Chechen guerrillas is a different issue than identification with Putin's stated objective in the war, which is to keep Chechnya within the Russian Federation regardless of the cost. Our survey results found public opinion on Chechnya polarized, with a substantial group favoring an all-out effort to keep Chechnya within the federation, another willing to let it separate, and the remainder unsure what the solution might be. On a five-point scale where value 1 denotes keeping Chechnya "at all costs" and 5 allowing it to leave Russia, 45 percent of our survey respondents in the winter of 1999–2000 were strongly or moderately in favor of keeping Chechnya and 33 percent in favor of ceding it independence (see table 2.12). Although nationalist and racist motivations are not absent in the Russian electorate, especially among ethnic Russians, they fail to predict the attitudes of many citizens even on this highly emotive question.

Table 2.12. Attitudes toward the Chechnya Problem, 1999

Position on five-point scale	Percentage
1 (Keep Chechnya at all costs)	33
2	12
3	14
4	6
5 (Let Chechnya leave Russia)	27
Don't know	8

Note: Interviews before 1999 parliamentary election (N = 1,919 weighted cases).

DEMOCRACY VERSUS ORDER

Many theorists of democracy address the potential tradeoff between democracy and social order. Russians often relate one to the other, and surveys done in Russia sometimes probe the tensions between the two values, finding that large majorities, if forced to choose, will opt for order over democracy. On the basis of such results, many analysts assert that there is a prevalent thirst for dictatorship and a rejection of democracy within Russian society today. In internal Russian debates, proponents of autocracy, be they businessmen who want more decisive economic reform or generals who want a more muscular foreign policy, cite polling data to bolster their claims that authoritarian rule is popular with common citizens. If the majority crave order and are willing to surrender democracy to achieve this end, then autocratic policies would be legitimate.[18]

The philosophical logic behind such arguments is, in our view, flawed. Order and democracy should not be thought of as two poles on a continuum.

To imply in a survey question that there is a natural tradeoff between them, and that more of one necessitates less of the other, presents the respondent with a false dichotomy.

As a practical matter, the Russian respondents in our surveys have some conception of the logical trap, as the information laid out in table 2.13 indicates. When asked to react to the bald statement that democracies "are not any good at maintaining order," our informants were divided (see table 2.13). Slightly more disagreed or completely disagreed with this statement than fully agreed or agreed. Nor are Russian citizens unanimous in adopting the clichés often heard about the ineptitude of democracies in coming to decisions and executing economic reform. When asked if democracies "are indecisive and have too much squabbling"—a standard question wording that makes it easy for the respondent to agree—more disagree with this statement (41 percent) than agree (34 percent). Russians may very well believe that their own government is indecisive and squabbles too much, but they do not automatically make this assumption about democracy in the abstract. On the more specific relationship between democracy and economic progress, Russians are dubious of the assertion that democracies are bad for the economy. Forty-nine percent of our respondents disagreed with the proposition that in a democracy "the economic system runs badly," as against 18 percent in agreement. Again, because we know that Russians have ample reason to be disgruntled with their economy and the state of their democracy, this outcome points to a rather refined awareness of how democracy and the economy should interact and might interact under conditions more benign than those in Russia. Knowledge of the successful record of the Western mar-

Table 2.13.   Attitudes toward Possible Tradeoffs between Democracy and Order, 1999–2000

Statement	Position (percentage)					
	Fully Agree	Agree	Indifferent	Disagree	Completely Disagree	Don't Know
Democracies are not any good at maintaining order	4	28	19	31	4	15
Democracies are indecisive and have too much squabbling	6	28	12	36	5	13
In a democracy, the economic system runs badly	3	15	17	44	5	15

Note: Interviews after 1999 parliamentary election (N = 1,846 weighted cases). Percentages may not add to 100 due to rounding.

ket democracies probably informs this attitude. Table 2.13 intimates that a Pinochet-style dictatorship in the name of market reform would not be wildly popular.

Our survey work also indicates that, whatever their outlook on the general and abstract notion of democracy, Russians' willingness to forgo concrete rights and protections for greater order is lower than much previous discussion has let on. When asked what they actually are prepared to relinquish, Russians volunteer a variety of reactions, frequently telegraphing that they want order to be buttressed but are reluctant to give up much to accomplish it.

Table 2.14 sets forth responses to a multi-item question put to survey respondents in the run up to the State Duma election of December 1999. The preamble read, "Today in Russia there is a lot of talk about the need to bring about order in the country. Are you prepared or not prepared to support the following measures to that end?" The one underpinning of a democratic system that a majority would compromise to achieve more order was the political party system. Almost 70 percent were prepared to ban certain parties, while fewer than 20 percent opposed this egregiously antidemocratic act. These numbers are cause for concern about democratic liberties, although one would have to qualify it by being aware that there are undemocratic parties and movements in Russia that, were they to exist in the United States, most Americans would probably want to proscribe. On no measure other than the banning of some parties is there a majority of Russians on the side of the restriction. A plurality would support elimination of free trading in U.S. dollars. On the three remaining issues—limitations on foreign travel, the introduction of censorship, and the declaration of a state of emergency—a majority of our respondents came out against the possibility. The largest majority in the data is that opposed to a state of emergency in which

Table 2.14. Attitude toward Measures "To Bring About Order in the Country," 1999

	Percentage Response		
Measure	Support	Oppose	Don't Know
Ban certain political parties	69	18	13
Do away with free exchange of the dollar	44	39	16
Limit the freedom to enter and exit the country	35	50	15
Introduce censorship of the press and television	32	53	16
Declare a state of emergency	10	76	14

Note: Interviews before 1999 parliamentary election (N = 1,919 weighted cases). Percentages may not add to 100 due to rounding.

individual rights would be suspended wholesale. In similar fashion, our interview subjects staunchly opposed military rule in Russia, despite the fact that the army is the state institution in which by far the greatest number of them have confidence.

WHO ARE THE FRIENDS OF
DEMOCRACY IN RUSSIA?

Democracy is not yet a consensus value in Russia. As the raw proportions clearly demonstrate, Russians are anything but unanimous in their political preferences. A spectrum of practical options running from constitutional democracy to Stalinism is, to say the least, broad—beyond the comprehension of the median citizen of any Western nation. Political values, in all their variation and quirkiness, are not randomly distributed across the face of the Russian population. As in most other developing countries, attachment to democratic values generally rises with indices of social modernization, so that persons who are better educated, have higher incomes, work in higher-status occupations, and live in more urbanized environments are appreciably more likely to favor a democratic regime than the poorly educated, the lower-paid, those in blue-collar work, and the residents of villages and small towns.

But the strongest correlation revealed by our data is with a demographic characteristic that is not, strictly speaking, part and parcel of modernization— namely, with the *age* and associated generational experience of the citizen.

A perfect illustration is furnished by preferences with regard to regime type (see table 2.15). To be sure, the data testify to the enormous staying power of aspects of the Soviet worldview. In all age groups, the most appealing political system for Russians is either a reformed Soviet system or, for those seventy and older, an unreconstructed Soviet-style regime. Over and above that conservative center of gravity, there are significant gradations by genera-

Table 2.15.   Preference for Political System, by Age Group, 1999–2000

	Age Group/Percentage Response					
Preferred political system	*18–29*	*30–39*	*40–49*	*50–59*	*60–69*	*Over 69*
Unreformed Soviet system	10	20	21	29	36	45
Reformed Soviet system	36	40	46	46	41	29
Current political system	23	17	10	8	9	8
Western democracy	15	13	8	8	5	4
Other response or Don't know	15	11	14	10	9	14

Note: Interviews after 1999 parliamentary election (N = 1,846 weighted cases). Percentages may not add to 100 due to rounding.

tion. Nearly half of men and women over the age of sixty-nine in 1999 preferred an unreformed Soviet political system; among those younger than thirty, that proportion was 10 percent. Almost 40 percent of survey respondents between eighteen and twenty-nine favored either a Western democracy or the current political system; this fraction declined to 12 percent among individuals in their seventies and eighties. To put it simply, the longer a Russian lived with the Soviet dictatorship, the more likely he or she is to still cling to Soviet political values. The seventy-year-old was born before the Great Patriotic War (World War II), came of age under Stalin, and never saw a more liberal politics in action until the verge of retirement. The twenty-five-year-old was born in the 1970s, encountered the Gorbachev reforms in his grade school years, and was an adolescent when Yeltsin swept away the rule of the Communist Party at the beginning of the 1990s. The differing beliefs of those prototypical individuals reflect differing biographical experiences.

The generational factor also shines through with respect to opinions concerning individual liberties, although less starkly than for regime type. Older Russians are less likely on every measure of liberties to adopt a permissive attitude (see table 2.16). The steepest gradient is on foreign travel, something few older Russians ever had the chance to do: 62 percent of persons aged eighteen to twenty-nine would object to curtailment of that right, as opposed to 29 percent of those in their seventies and eighties. On one political question (censorship), the divergence between the oldest and the youngest voters is quite large (28 percentage points); but on banning suspect parties and invoking a state of emergency it is less pronounced (9 percentage points and 18 percentage points between the extremes, respectively).

Another vital source of attitudinal variation on democracy has to do with economic fulfillment and personal well-being, and their inverses, economic frustration and personal malaise. In 1999 our interviewers asked a straightfor-

Table 2.16.   Opposition to Repressive Measures to Bring About Order, by Age Group, 1999

	Age Group/Percentage Response					
Measure	*18–29*	*30–39*	*40–49*	*50–59*	*60–69*	*Over 69*
Ban certain political parties	21	17	21	19	15	12
Do away with free exchange of the dollar	53	49	41	36	30	19
Limit the freedom to enter and exit the country	62	60	53	51	41	29
Introduce censorship of the press and television	64	57	58	54	42	36
Declare a state of emergency	81	82	78	78	71	63

Note: Interviews before 1999 parliamentary election (N = 1,919 weighted cases).

ward retrospective question about experience in the decade of change Russians had just undergone: "In general, did you win or lose as a result of the reforms carried out in the country in the 1990s?" The self-perceived losers far outnumbered the winners. Some 70 percent of our respondents said they had lost out to some degree; a trifling 6 percent said they had won to some degree; and a substantial minority, 17 percent, said they had won some and lost some; the rest were undecided. One could hardly think of a sharper gauge of the failure of economic and socioeconomic reforms to improve the lot of ordinary Russians.

What is most pertinent to our discussion is the consonance between individual contentment and attitudes toward democratization and regime type. Table 2.17 portrays but one of the many interconnections that can be traced. It shows in no uncertain terms that interest in more democratic and liberal political arrangements is strongly associated with personal experience with the results of (mainly economic) reform. Among Russians who feel they have won or mostly won because of reforms, about 60 percent empathize with either the current political system or with Western democracy; only 6 percent of them want a return to Soviet rule and about one-third would prefer a humanized Soviet system. When we look at Russians at the bottom end of the welfare yardstick, the relationships are reversed: about 70 percent prefer either a neo-Soviet regime or a reformed Soviet regime, and support for the current system or Western democracy slides to 15 or 20 percent.

Table 2.17.   Preferred Political Regime by Personal Experience with Reforms of 1990s, 1999 (percentages)

	Response by Percentage				
Preferred Political System	*Won*	*Mostly Won*	*Won Some and Lost Some*	*Mostly Lost*	*Lost*
Unreformed Soviet system	6	4	19	25	30
Reformed Soviet system	32	28	36	43	45
Current political system	38	33	19	10	9
Western democracy	18	26	14	11	5
Other response or Don't know	6	9	12	12	12

Note: Question about personal experience in interviews before 1999 parliamentary election; question about preferred political system in interviews after election (N = 1,846 weighted cases). Percentages may not add to 100 due to rounding.

THE PUTIN ELECTORATE: DEMOCRATS OR AUTOCRATS?

The second Chechen war has been popular with Russian citizens. Public backing for the war has remained steady at roughly 60 percent even as casualties have mounted.[19] Undoubtedly, this popular groundswell translated into positive ratings for Vladimir Putin as a political leader. Opinion soundings conducted in the fall of 1999, after his appointment as prime minister, underlined that voters were most obliged to Putin for accepting responsibility for the security of the Russian people. He looked like a leader who was taking charge during an uncertain time and making good on his pledge to provide stability and safety. By the end of 1999, the time Yeltsin made him acting president and heir presumptive, he enjoyed an extraordinary 72 percent approval rating. The glow remained untarnished until the presidential election of March 26, 2000, which Putin won in one round.[20] Many analysts have cited this correlation between support for the war and support for Putin as a sign that his supporters yearn for nothing but order, a mighty state, and a strong-armed leader. Some posit that his election as president proves that Russians place no value on democracy. How, after all, could advocates of democracy cast their ballots for a man who made his career in the KGB, one of the most repressive organizations of the Soviet era? In comparative context, Putin's conquest of power bears some resemblance to the dictatorial Thermidor that has ensued from other revolutions in the modern era.[21]

Putin may indeed evolve into the Napoleon or Stalin of the Second Russian Revolution, but he will not take that path because his followers are pressing him to do so. The fact is that his supporters in the presidential election possessed political views in the mainstream of Russian society, meaning that they support some core principles of democratic governance.

Table 2.18 crosses selected issue positions with the votes cast in March 2000 for the winner, Putin; for the runner-up, Gennadiy Zyuganov, the nominee of the Communist Party of the Russian Federation; and for the third-finishing Grigoriy Yavlinskiy, the leader of the liberal Yabloko Party. On support for the ideal of democracy, 68 percent of those who reported in the third wave of our survey that they had voted for Putin gave a positive answer to the question, or several percentage points above the national average. On this score, Putin supporters were noticeably more pro-democratic than Zyuganov supporters though less pro-democratic than those who voted for Yavlinskiy. On the most appropriate regime for governing Russia, Putin voters—like the majority of Russians—were nostalgic for the defunct Soviet system, but not nearly as much as Zyuganov voters. The modal response for Putin voters was to favor a reformed Soviet system; for Zyuganov voters, it was an unreformed Soviet system; and for Yavlinskiy voters, it was the current political system. Putin voters were about one-fourth as likely as Zyuganov voters, although about twice as likely as Yavlinskiy voters, to approve of an unreformed Soviet system. On specific democratic practices and liberal norms, such as support for competitive elections and freedom of religion, travel, and expression, Putin voters were consistently at or above the national average in support of these measures, while Zyuganov voters were consis-

Table 2.18. Composition of the March 2000 Presidential Vote, by Position on Selected Political Issues

Issue/Position	Putin Voters	Zyuganov Voters	Yavlinskiy Voters
The idea of democracy[a]			
Support	68	50	80
Oppose	15	31	12
Don't know	17	19	9
Preferred political regime[b]			
Unreformed Soviet system	12	50	7
Reformed Soviet system	38	41	28
Current political system	31	3	30
Western democracy	9	2	22
Other response or don't know	11	4	13
The problem of Chechnya[c]			
1 (Keep Chechnya at all costs)	42	38	29
2	13	8	14
3	15	15	22
4	5	6	8
5 (Let Chechnya leave Russia)	17	20	17
Don't know	9	13	10

Note: Percentages may not add to 100 due to rounding.
[a] Interviews after 2000 presidential election (N = 1,506 weighted cases).
[b] Interviews before 1999 parliamentary election (N = 1,506 weighted cases).
[c] Interviews after 2000 presidential election (N = 1,506 weighted cases).

tently below average and Yavlinskiy voters above average. On Putin's signature issue, the war in Chechnya (table 2.18), Russians who voted for him were more inclined than Zyuganov or Yavlinskiy voters to take an unyielding line on retention of the republic within Russia (positions 1 and 2 on the five-point scale), but the difference was not pronounced, and one Putin voter in four took a neutral stance or could not answer. Putin voters were 9 percentage points more likely than Zyuganov voters, and 12 percentage points more likely than Yavlinskiy voters, to oppose Chechen independence.

CONCLUSION

Assuming that for centuries on end Russian culture was in the main antidemocratic and antiliberal, the 1990s may represent a significant mutation of that culture in only ten short years. The rapidity of this shift in attitudes makes a striking contrast to the slowness with which the parallel change in political institutions has proceeded. Comparative scholars throughout the 1970s and 1980s portrayed the process of democratization as a top-level affair, a bargain between elites that resulted in new democratic institutions.[22] These democratic institutions then helped to change society in a more democratic and liberal direction. The Russian case brings to mind a quite different dynamic: the people have assimilated democratic values faster than the elite has negotiated democratic institutions.

In cross-national perspective, the distribution of attitudes toward democracy within the Russian population is not so very different from many other countries in transition. Aggregate satisfaction with democracy in Russia is in fact lower than in most transitional countries. It is comparable to mass opinion in countries such as Zimbabwe, which experienced democratic erosion after initial successes in replacing dictatorship with democracy.[23] As in Zimbabwe, bitter disappointment with the practicalities of democracy has not yet produced a rejection of the ideals of democracy.

This is not to deny that the gap between dissatisfaction with the reality of Russia's government and receptivity to democratic principles is unhealthy for the long-term development of liberal democracy there. Experiences elsewhere suggest that this kind of disparity is fertile soil for the growth of anti-democratic alternatives.[24]

Nor can one have much faith that Russian democrats would rally to defend the ineffective institutions already in place. Scholars have insightfully argued that citizens must venerate and be willing to fight for democracy if it is to be sustained.[25] Veneration of democracy and the resolve to defend it are in short supply in Russia. Should Putin eventually attempt to reinstall an overt dictatorship, he may meet little open resistance, at least initially. Although Russians did mobilize on the streets and at the workplace to challenge the authority of the Soviet state a decade ago, there is scant willingness to make sacrifices for democracy in post-Soviet Russia, a decade after the high-water mark of democratization. Pro-democratic interest groups and mass movements are weak and disorganized, institutional checks are fragile, and Western leverage is marginal. Surveys conducted by other scholars show that popular resistance is unlikely should an authoritarian coalition reemerge within Russia.[26] Of course, we will only know whether society is prepared to defend democratic practices only after the fact—once those holding state power have already transgressed the rules of the game. If the state moves to impose authoritarian rule, the current balance of forces favors it, not society.

At the same time, our data suggest that the infliction of a full-blown dictatorship would not be an easy task. Would-be destroyers of democracy in Russia would first have to articulate an alternative model for organizing the polity. Adam Przeworski calls this condition the "organization of counter hegemony: collective projects for an alternative future."[27] Any attempt to put forward such a project would have to reckon with the fact that a majority of

Russians continue to agree with Winston Churchill: flawed though it may be, democracy is still a superior system to the alternatives.

There still exists the possibility for improvement in the practice of democracy and growth of procedures that resonate with the ideas of democracy. To the extent that mass support for democratic governance jars with the actuality of political life since 1991, the best remedy for the populace's disillusionment with Russian democracy is for the leaders of the country to start behaving more like democrats and less like elected tsars. To the extent that support for democracy varies by age, some improvement can be expected to occur naturally with the biological succession of generations, absent a catastrophe. And to the extent that support for democracy increases with individuals' sense of well-being and personal welfare, well-conceived economic reforms that actually make Russian life better, not worse, can also be expected to nudge democratization along.[28]

The chasm between democratic attitudes and inadequately democratized institutions also may offer a lesson for policymakers in Russia and the West committed to promoting democracy. The old formula for democracy was, "Get the institutions right, and the people will follow." The new formula should be, "Represent the will of the people within the state, and the institutions will follow." For years, democracy assistance programs have provided technical assistance for the crafting of democratic institutions, including support for democratic electoral laws, constitutions, courts, and political parties. The approach was top-down. If the rules, laws, and procedures were democratic, then society eventually would be remade by these "right" rules into the "right" kind of citizens—democrats.[29] The burden thus was on newly designed institutions to change society. A decade after this strategy was put into effect, it may no longer be applicable. Russian society seems more transformed—more democratic, in its own way—than the political structures governing it. The problem of undemocratic institutions remains. In thinking of new ways to promote humane governance, therefore, program managers would be well advised to consider projects that empower society. The more influence pro-democratic elements in Russia's society have over the development of political institutions, the better the chances that these institutions will become genuinely democratic.

NOTES

Reprinted with permission from *Post-Soviet Affairs* 18, no. 2, pp. 91–121. © V. H. Winston & Son, Inc., 360 South Ocean Boulevard, Palm Beach, FL 33480. All rights reserved.

    1. Vserossiiskii Tsentr Izucheniya Obshchestvennogo Mneniya (VTsIOM), *Ot*

mennii k ponimaniya: Obshchestvennoe mnenie—2000 (Moscow: VTsIOM, December 2000), 68.

2. Robert V. Daniels, "Russia's Democratic Dictatorship," *Dissent* (Summer 2000): 10.

3. Masha Lipman, "Blackout in Russia," *Washington Post*, January 23, 2002; Department of State, Office of Research, "Russians Ready for a Course Change, Glad Putin Is at the Helm," *Opinion Analysis*, no. M-206–00 (December 7, 2000): 4; Interfax, "Two Thirds of Russia Do Care about TV-6-Pollsters" (citing poll conducted by the Public Opinion Foundation), January 24, 2002.

4. Ted Gerber and Sarah Mendelson, "How Russians Think about Human Rights: Recent Survey Data, *PONARS Policy Memo*, no. 221 (December 2001): 73.

5. Nikolai Biryukov and Viktor Sergeyev, *Russian Politics in Transition: Institutional Conflict in a Nascent Democracy* (Brookfield, Vt.: Ashgate Publishing, 1997), 3.

6. Seymour Martin Lipset, "The Social Requisites of Democracy Revisited," *American Sociological Review* 59, no. 1 (February 1994); Samuel Huntington, "After Twenty Years: The Future of the Third Wave," *Journal of Democracy* 8, no. 4 (October 1997); and Russell Bova, "Democracy and Liberty: The Cultural Connection," *Journal of Democracy* 8, no. 1 (January 1997).

7. Robert Tucker, "Sovietology and Russian History," *Post Soviet Affairs* 8, no. 3 (1992), Nikolai Biryukov and Victor Sergeyev, *Russia's Road to Democracy: Parliament, Communism and Traditional Culture* (London: Edward Elgar, 1993); Jonathan Steele, *Eternal Russia: Yeltsin, Gorbachev and the Mirage of Democracy* (Cambridge, Mass.: Harvard University Press, 1994); Don Murray, *A Democracy of Despots* (Boulder, Colo.: Westview Press, 1996); Tim McDaniel, *The Agony of the Russian Idea* (Princeton, N.J.: Princeton University Press, 1996); Gregory Feifer, "Utopian Nostalgia: Russia's New Idea," *World Policy Journal* 16, no. 3 (Fall 1999); Boris Kagarlitskii, "The Traps of 'Westernism' and the Blind Alleys of 'Nativism': The Political Culture of Post-Soviet Pseudodemocracy," *Russian Politics and Law* 38, no. 3 (May/June 2000); Zbigniew Brzezinski, "The Primacy of Culture and History," *Journal of Democracy* 12, no. 4 (October 2001).

8. *The Economist*, July 3, 1999, 43.

9. Stephen Cohen, *Failed Crusade: America and the Tragedy of Post-Communist Russia* (New York: Norton, 2000), 48.

10. Eugene Husky, "Political Leadership and the Center-Periphery Struggle: Putin's Administrative Reforms," in *Gorbachev, Yeltsin & Putin: Political Leadership in Russia's Transition*, ed. Archie Brown and Lilia Shevtsova (Washington, D.C.: Carnegie Endowment for International Peace, 2001; Masha Lipman and Michael McFaul, "'Managed Democracy' in Russia: Putin and the Press," *Harvard International Journal of Press/Politics* 6, no. 3 (Summer 2001); "Russia's Hybrid Regime," *Journal of Democracy* 12, no. 4 (October 2001); Grigorii Yavlinskiy, "Going Backwards," *Journal of Democracy* 12, no. 4 (October 2001); Michael McFaul, "Russia Under Putin, One Step Forward, Two Steps Backward," *Journal of Democracy* 11, no. 3 (July 2000).

11. Larry Diamond, *Developing Democracy: Toward Consolidation* (Baltimore, Md.: Johns Hopkins University Press, 1999).

12. Michael McFaul, "*Russia's Unfinished Revolution: Political Change from Gorbachev to Putin* (Ithaca, N.Y.: Cornell University Press, 2001), chapter four.

13. Diamond, *Developing Democracy.*

14. Stephen White, Richard Rose, and Ian McAllister, *How Russia Votes* (Chatham, N.J.: Chatham House, 1997), chapter one.

15. Ronald Pope, "The Rule of Law and Russian Culture—Are They Compatible," *Demokratizatsiya* 7, no. 2 (Spring 1999).

16. Human Rights Watch, *Welcome to Hell: Arbitrary Detention, Torture, and Extortion in Chechnya* (New York: Human Rights Watch, October 2000).

17. Peter Rutland, "Putin's Path to Power," *Post-Soviet Affairs* 16, no. 4 (October/December 2000): 322–24.

18. T. I. Kutkovets and I. M. Klyamkin, *Russkie Idei* (Moscow: Institut Sotsiologichogo Analiza, 1997).

19. See the website of the Foundation for Public Opinion at www.fom.ru.

20. Agenstvo Regional'nykh Poloticheskikh Issledovanii (ARPI), *Regional'nyi Sotsiologicheskii Monitoring*, no. 49 (December 10–12, 1999): 39.

21. Vladimir Mau and Irina Starodubovskaya, *The Challenge of Revolution: Contemporary Russia in Historical Perspective* (Oxford: Oxford University Press, 2001), 338.

22. Guillermo O'Donnell and Philippe Schmitter, *Transitions from Authoritarian Rule: Tentative Conclusions About Uncertain Democracies* (Baltimore, Md.: Johns Hopkins University Press, 1986).

23. Michael Bratton and Robert Mattes, "Africa's Surprising Universalism," *Journal of Democracy* 12, no. 1 (January 2001): 109.

24. Diamond, *Developing Democracy.*

25. Barry Weingast, "The Political Foundations of Democracy and the Rule of Law," *American Political Science Review* 91, no. 2 (June 1997).

26. James L. Gibson, "A Mile Wide but an Inch Deep: The Structure of Democratic Commitments in the Former USSR, *American Journal of Political Science* 40, no. 2 (May 1996).

27. Adam Przeworski, *Democracy and the Market: Political and Economic Reforms in Eastern Europe and Latin America* (Cambridge: Cambridge University Press, 1991): 54–55.

28. Adam Przeworski, Michael Alvarez, Jose Antonio Cheibub, and Fernando Limongi, *Democracy and Development: Political Institutions and Well-Being in the World, 1950–1990* (Cambridge: Cambridge University Press, 2000).

29. Michael McFaul and Sarah Mendelson, "Russian Democracy—A U.S. National Security Interest," *Demokratizatsiya* 8, no. 3 (Summer 2000).

Chapter Three

Putin, the Duma, and Political Parties

Thomas F. Remington

The contrast between the Yeltsin and Putin presidencies is nowhere more visible than in president-parliament relations. Whereas President Yeltsin never commanded a majority of votes in the Duma, Putin's legislative record is filled with accomplishments. Even on the most controversial issues—land reform, political parties, ratification of START—the president and government have won majorities. By comparison, Yeltsin faced a hostile Duma that came close to passing a motion of impeachment in 1999. To get his legislation through, Yeltsin bullied the deputies with threats of decrees and dissolution and wooed them with material inducements. On a number of issues, unable to win passage of his preferred legislation, Yeltsin simply allowed legislation he supported to die, permitting the legal vacuum to be filled by regional acts or government regulations, or by issuing a decree (*ukaz*). Putin, however, has enjoyed consistent support in both the State Duma and the Federation Council, and has established an accumulating record of successes in enacting an ambitious legislative agenda.

Under Russia's constitution, the Duma must approve draft legislation before it can be signed into law. There are certain categories of legislation that the Federation Council must consider, and it can consider any bill if it takes it up within two weeks of passage by the Duma. The Federation Council's vetoes of legislation, however, can be overridden by the Duma. The two chambers can also override a presidential veto by a concurrent two-thirds vote. Therefore, if the president wants to enact a law, he must obtain the consent of a majority of members of the Duma. The president can enact some measures by decree—in cases where a law is not already in force—but even then, experience has shown that a law is more stable and therefore more authoritative than a decree, which can be more easily reversed. Putin has preferred to operate by the normal legislative process, in contrast to President Yeltsin, who often relied on presidential decrees (*ukazy*) to enact important policy changes, particularly from 1992–94. Under Putin, the number and importance of presidential decrees has continued to decline.

Thanks to a relatively reliable base of support in the Federal Assembly, Putin's administration and the government have been enacting a far-reaching program of reform legislation. Putin spelled out his policy priorities explicitly in his messages to parliament in 2000 and 2001. In 2000, among other items, he called for a flat income tax rate, lower taxes on profits, and a lower social tax, firm protections on property rights, less intrusive regulation of business, banking reform, and other measures to liberalize economic activity. In his April 3, 2001, message, he went into still more detail about his legislative priorities. He emphasized the need for good-quality legislation that would replace petty administrative interference with business tax reform and appealed to parliament to stop passing budget-busting laws:[1]

> Bureaucratic rule making (*vedomstvennoe normotvorchestvo*) is one of the chief brakes on the development of entrepreneurship. A bureaucrat is used to acting according to an instruction which, after one or another law has come into force, often is inconsistent with the law itself, but yet for years is never rescinded. The government, ministries and departments should, finally, take radical measures with respect to bureaucratic regulation—even going so far as to eliminate the whole body of departmental regulations in cases where there are already federal laws of direct force in place.
>
> Moreover, many times it has been pointed out that any law should be secured both organizationally and materially. However, in practice, we have an entirely different picture. The Federal Assembly continues, unfortunately, to pass laws, for the implementation of which it is essential to go back again to the federal budget that has been passed and the budget of the Pension Fund. I consider such decisions, even when they are motivated by the most noble intentions, as politically irresponsible. We are long overdue for a systematization of legislation that would permit not only taking into account the new economic realities, but also to preserve the traditional branches which have been dangerously "washed away" in recent years. . . .
>
> This year the government has prepared a package of laws on debureaucratization and minimization of administrative interference by the state into the affairs of enterprises. It is necessary to work to further reduce the list of licensed forms of activity. It is necessary energetically to put order into other spheres where there is excessive state interference. . . .
>
> Today our strategic priority is a rational and just taxation of natural resources, the main wealth of Russia, of immovable property, a consistent lowering of the taxation of non-rent income, and the final liquidation of turnover taxes. The government in the immediate future will complete the consideration of these issues and, as the chairman of the government just reported to me, in three or at most four weeks, he will introduce a package of laws to this effect to the parliament. We must continue customs reform. Naturally, the customs code must conform to the norms of the WTO, the joining of which remains our priority.

The task of parliament is to bring Russian legislation into conformity with the norms and regulations of the World Trade Organization. . . .

In addition, it is necessary to speed up the adoption of a new law on privatization, a law which will set clear and transparent rules for selling and obtaining state property and will permit us to end, once and for all, the speculation on the theme of "the sale of Russia."

He also called for reform of the pension system, a new Labor Code to free up labor markets, and stronger intellectual property protection.

Any suspicion that Putin's annual messages might have been window dressing for Western and liberal audiences that bore little relation to his actual policy goals was dispelled by the far-reaching legislative agenda that he submitted to the parliament, especially in 2001. In 2001 alone, the Duma enacted (after years of controversy) a Land Code permitting the free ownership, purchase, and sale of land (a major overhaul of the pension system providing, among other things, for a system of private pension plans to supplement state insurance); a new Labor Code giving employers greater discretion to dismiss workers without trade union consent; comprehensive tax reform, including a low flat income tax rate, a unified tax for all social assistance funds, a lower excise tax, a lower profits tax, a lower rate on transactions in hard currency, a new sales tax, and a lower tax on production-sharing agreements; a series of bills overhauling the judicial system that included the expansion of the jury trial system; reform of the Civil Code that liberalized inheritance rights; a set of reforms lowering the regulatory burden for business, including laws on the registration of businesses, licensing of businesses, regulation of stock companies, money laundering, and three laws on banking reform; and a law on the regulation of political parties that imposed stiff membership requirements on political parties and prohibited purely regional parties. None of these bills could have passed the old Duma. The agenda reflects Putin's commitment to making Russia a far more stable and orderly society under firm Kremlin management and with a legal and economic climate favorable to investment and growth. This chapter will now review Putin's strategy for dealing with parliament. It will address his relations with both chambers, and the means by which he has built up his support in each. It will examine the process by which legislation is developed and enacted by parliament, investigating relations between the presidential administration and the government, and the executive branch and the factions in parliament in deciding on the legislative agenda. It concludes by exploring the implications of Putin's strategy for passing his legislative agenda for the development of Russia's constitutional framework in the future. I argue that Putin's success rests upon constant bargaining and compromise, both within the executive branch and between the executive branch and the parliament. Like his predecessors, Putin has traded off organizational rights to political parties in return for parliamentary support of his power and program. We should expect, therefore, that a more institutionalized relationship of reciprocal dependence between the Duma and the government will result based on the gradual consolidation of a system of political parties.

BUILDING THE KREMLIN'S MAJORITY

Conquering the Duma

From the very beginning, Putin demonstrated his mastery of parliamentary tactics in dealing with the third Duma, which convened in January 2000. His adroit manipulation of interfactional negotiation resulted in a temporary alliance between the Unity faction—whose members were elected on the Unity party list in December 1999—and the communists, which was joined by a group of single-member district independents called People's Deputy. Unity was a hastily constructed coalition of pro-Kremlin politicians that had achieved overnight success in the Duma election through their association with the popular Putin, whereas the communists (Communist Party of the Russian Federation) were hard-line opponents of the Kremlin and its policies. Controlling a bare minimum majority in the Duma, this odd alliance succeeded in electing communist Gennadii Seleznev to the speakership and in allocating the committee chairmanships among themselves. Factions excluded from the arrangement—the Fatherland/All-Russia coalition (OVR), Yabloko, and the liberal SPS—walked out in protest and refused to return to the Duma for three weeks.[2] But the communists' triumph was ephemeral. Quickly it became apparent that they had very little power within the Duma. Their committee chairmanships did not include any of the committees with jurisdiction over the main policy issues that were politically important to them or to Putin: they did not control the defense, security, foreign relations, budget, legislation, property, or banking committees. Nor could they determine the majority, as they had done in the two previous Dumas. In 1994–95 and again 1996–99, the communists were the dominant faction by virtue of the interaction of two crucial advantages: their size and their cohesiveness. In the first two Dumas it became extremely difficult to form a majority that did not include the communists. As the pivotal faction, they could usually dictate the terms on which they would join a majority coalition. Now, in the third Duma, they were marginalized, despite holding the speakership and ten committee chairmanships. Their role as the pivotal faction was taken over by Unity. Unity had nearly as many members as the communists (eighty-nine initially for the communists, eighty-one for Unity), and a level of voting discipline that rivaled the communists, but they also had one additional crucial advantage: direct access to the Kremlin. Unity became the Kremlin's majority-maker in the Duma, and the Duma's major intermediary with the Kremlin. Given the asymmetry in constitutional powers between president and parliament, it became clear that Unity's strength and cohesiveness gave the Kremlin the ability to form majorities around nearly any bill it wanted to pass.[3]

The Federation Council

Putin's strategy in the upper chamber of the parliament has been equally effective. The law that he succeeded in getting passed in both chambers in the summer of 2000 gave him a secure base of support in that chamber as well.[4] Under the new method for naming members, the Federation Council is made up of members chosen by the chief executives and the legislatures of the eighty-nine territorial units of the federation. Previously, the chamber's members were the chief executives and chief legislative officials of the regions who held their seats ex officio. The new members generally lack independent resources and tend to be susceptible to the influence of the presidential administration. By the beginning of 2002 the changeover was complete.

The immediate goal of the reform seems to have been Putin's desire to reduce the status of regional governors. As members of the upper house of parliament, they had a direct role in federal lawmaking, and excellent opportunities to bargain with federal executive agencies, trading votes for special benefits for their regions. As members of parliament, they also enjoyed full immunity from arrest and prosecution—a significant privilege. Putin's reform stripped them of their ex officio status as members of parliament, although it gave them the opportunity to send full-time representatives to Moscow to serve as their lobbyists and spokespersons. As we shall see, the new members have turned out to be far more faithful to the Kremlin's interests than to those of the governors who sent them.

The "Coalition of the Four"

Table 3.1 indicates the breakdown of members of the Duma factions as of September 2001 by electoral mandate type. (Note that the figures do not reflect all changes in Duma membership and faction membership as of that time, so should be taken as approximations.) It shows that factions vary in the electoral backgrounds of their members: the communists are relatively balanced between party list and single-member district (SMD) deputies, whereas factions such as LDPR, Yabloko, and even Unity are highly dependent on their list contingents for their membership.[5] Groups such as People's Deputy and Russia's Regions are entirely made up of SMD deputies, except for a few deputies elected on other parties' lists, who have changed factional affiliation since their election.[6] The agrarians would also be an all-SMD

Table 3.1. Duma Factions by Electoral Mandate Type, September 2001

Faction	N, %[a]	SMD	Party List	Total
CPRF	N	35	49	84
	%	41.70	58.30	100.00
APG	N	22	20	42
	%	52.40	47.60	100.00
LDPR	N	0	12	12
	%		100.00	100.00
Rus Reg	N	35	6	41
	%	85.40	14.60	100.00
Nar Dep	N	53	0	53
	%	100.00		100.00
Yabloko	N	3	15	18
	%	16.70	83.30	100.00
Unity	N	17	63	80
	%	21.30	78.80	100.00
OVR	N	15	28	43
	%	34.90	65.10	100.00
SPS	N	8	28	36
	%	22.20	77.80	100.00
Not in faction	N	8	4	12
	%	66.70	33.30	100.00
	Total	196	225	421

[a] N = Number; % = percentage of faction.

group, but the communists seconded some of their members to them to bring the group up to the strength required for registration.

The varying electoral composition of different factions directly affects the ability of the pro-Kremlin forces to command a voting majority in the Duma. The coalition supporting Putin and the government consists of Unity and three allied factions—People's Deputy, Russia's Regions, and OVR. Since spring 2001, this coalition has gone so far as to form an organizational structure for coordinating positions on major legislation, but faces difficulties in imposing voting discipline. Unity and OVR are factions formed on the basis of deputies elected on the Unity and OVR party lists, plus deputies who won single-member district races and chose to affiliate with those factions. People's Deputy and Russia's Regions are, technically speaking, not factions, but groups; groups are formations that are not based on successful list parties, but rather comprise deputies elected in single-member districts who did not have other party affiliations. Groups that can claim at least thirty-five members can register for the same rights and status as party factions, so both groups and factions will sometimes be referred to here (as they often are in the Duma) as factions when speaking of Duma political formations generally. But an important distinction between groups and factions in practice is that groups, precisely because they are formed out of single-member district members—usually without a party affiliation, and for the purpose of providing such members with political teammates—tend to be much less cohesive in voting than party factions. Therefore Unity, which boasts a high level of voting discipline even in comparison with other party factions, has a difficult time holding its coalition partners in line on divisive votes. If the coalition of the four vote cohesively, they can command a majority of votes; when they are joined (as they usually are) by Zhirinovsky's small LDPR faction, the majority is more secure, and when SPS supports the item, the coalition can afford to lose some defectors. This insurance is needed because the coalition cannot count on disciplined voting within People's Deputy and Russia's Regions, especially on matters where their members feel strong pressures from their constituencies.

Unity faces a different problem with OVR. OVR was led in the Duma until recently by Yevgeny Primakov, whom Putin evidently regarded as a rival and a threat. OVR tended to adhere to an independent line in Duma voting until it agreed formally to join the Unity coalition in the Duma. Even then, it indicated that it would maintain its own line and would decide whether to side with Unity on a vote-by-vote basis. Therefore Unity has had some difficulty in forming and maintaining its majority coalition. Deputies cannot be blackmailed into voting discipline by the threat that defection from the party program will lead to the collapse of the government: there simply is no parliamentary responsibility for maintaining a government in power in Russia as there is in a true parliamentary system. Given the dependence of pro-government deputies in the Duma on the presidential administration for material benefits and electoral assistance, the possibility that they might bring about the dissolution of either the government or the Duma through a vote, no confidence is too remote to give faction leaders any leverage to use against straying members. Moreover, the government can look for a majority by building agreements with other factions, bypassing its ostensible Duma allies. Still, leaders of the pro-government forces have some leverage. Faction leaders can and do threaten members who defect on key votes with exclusion from the faction, although this is a weak sanction; it may mean, however, that the errant deputy will lose the Kremlin's administrative assistance at the next election. The pro-government factions have enough bargaining resources that when the government needs their support on particular pieces of legislation, they can bargain for concessions. Consequently, there is a reciprocal interest on the part of the executive and the pro-executive factions in building a more institutionalized relationship. The government's objective is to consolidate its influence so that the bargains are less costly and support more reliable; Unity and People's Deputy both aspire to expand their influence (and access to the Kremlin) by regularizing the coalition arrangement so that they can count on the votes of all four factions in the coalition and minimize its dependence on other factions for votes. People's Deputy has competed with Unity to be the Kremlin's favorite partner, looking to win benefits by positioning itself as a more viable electoral force than Unity in future parliamentary elections. OVR's price for joining the coalition appears to be the Kremlin's willingness to ally itself with Moscow's mayor, Yuri Luzhkov. Russia's Regions' interest, to the extent that so loosely organized a group can share a common interest, appears to be to obtain what policy and election benefits it can from joining the coalition rather than opposing it. However, there is so little voting discipline within the group that it brings rather little bargaining leverage to the table.

The first hints that the Duma was moving toward a more majoritarian pattern of governance was the tactical alliance created by Unity, the communists, and People's Deputy in January 2000. Following the Kremlin's strategic direction, they found that they commanded the minimum necessary number of votes in the Duma and could divide up the lion's share of the office benefits that came with majority status. This trio represented the three largest factions in the Duma; by uniting, they represented the smallest number of factions as well as the smallest number of deputies that could have controlled a majority. Their alliance represented a sharp departure from the traditions of proportional representation that had previously governed the distribution of committee chairmanships, and of course a still greater departure from the parity principle used to form the Council of the Duma. Other factions protested at the violation of these practices. The coalition of Unity, CPRF, and People's Deputy was short-lived, however. It was evidently intended at keeping Primakov from winning the speakership and at co-opting the communists by giving them numerous but largely nominal leadership offices. It left Unity free to forge other tactical alliances on an issue-by-issue basis. This Unity proceeded to do, always closely adhering to the Kremlin's legislative goals and strategies.

Over 2000 and 2001, Unity was on the winning side of nearly all major votes, but its partners varied. Sometimes Unity allied with the factions of the left (the communists, the agrarians, and some of OVR), and on other issues its partners were SPS and Yabloko. The pivotal member of nearly every winning coalition, Unity delivered the president and government a string of victories, but at a price. The government had to make concessions on a number of policy fronts in order to win passage of its highest-priority legislation, such as the modifications to the 2001 and 2002 budgets, and tax reform. On land reform, the government simply jettisoned the provisions that would have legalized the buying and selling of agricultural land as a condition for winning passage of this landmark law. (As table 3.2 shows, it passed in second reading with 253 votes, 27 more than the bare minimum required.) The convergence of interests of the government and the key pro-government factions in the Duma led to their efforts to create a more durable alliance structure that would lower the bargaining costs of building a majority.

The coalition began outside the Duma in April 2001 when Luzhkov, as head of Fatherland (one part of the electoral coalition of Fatherland and All-Russia, whose joint list produced the Duma faction OVR), joined with Minister of Emergency Situations Sergei Shoigu, as head of the Unity movement, in announcing that they were forming a united party. They held a meeting with President Putin the same day, reporting that the president supported the idea. Several days later, their Duma factions joined with People's Deputy and Russia's Regions in forming a "coordination council" that would harmonize the positions of the factions in passing legislation. The head of the Unity faction, Vladimir Pekhtin, observed that their goal was to "unify the efforts of deputies of the center and thus to facilitate the accelerated passage through the Duma of decisions necessary for ensuring stable economic growth."[7] The head of the Russia's Regions faction, Oleg Morozov, went further in describing the goal of the new council. Eventually, he said, they intended to form a government of the parliamentary majority.[8] Together, the coalition of the four commanded 234 members at the time of its formation—enough to pass ordinary legislation if all members voted cohesively, although not enough to pass constitutional laws, which require 300 votes.

Since its formation, the coordinating council has been active, although it is far from exercising the disciplined voting power that a majority coalition in a parliamentary democracy would normally exhibit. The fall term began with sparring over the 2002 budget between the Duma and the government. The coalition of the four demonstrated its potential by preempting the usual committee deliberations and negotiating separately with the government over the shape of an acceptable compromise. After a series of meetings between the finance ministry and the four factions, the government and the coordinating council announced that they had reached a compromise that would enable the four pro-government factions to support the budget in first reading. The government, with a show of reluctance, agreed to raise its estimate of revenues for 2002 by another 123 billion rubles, thus allowing the four factions to direct additional spending into electorally profitable directions: pensions, defense, regional aid, industrial investment, and highway construction.[9] Four days later the budget passed the vote in first reading with 262 affirmative votes. Unity, People's Deputy, OVR, and Russia's Regions voted by overwhelming margins in favor of the bill. Clearly, the deal with the government satisfied the coalition members; their support in turn made it more advantageous for other factions to join them than to oppose the bill. Most of the SPS and Yabloko deputies reportedly supported the budget, while LDPR, CPRF,

Table 3.2. Voting on Key Votes by Faction (percent voting "Yes" in each faction)

Vote No.	Date	Subject	Total "Yes"	CPRF	APG	LDPR	Rus Reg	Nar Dep	Yabloko	Unity	OVR	SPS	Indep
V34970	22-Feb-2001	Profits tax, 2nd reading	233	0.000	0.000	1.000	0.578	0.831	0.944	0.952	0.205	0.737	0.467
V34990	22-Feb-2001	Tax on securities, 2nd reading	226	0.012	0.000	1.000	0.422	0.542	0.778	0.940	0.659	0.763	0.400
V37580	22-Mar-2001	State regulation of foreign trade, 2nd reading	213	0.977	0.977	0.417	0.778	0.169	0.389	0.000	0.523	0.053	0.267
V38000	4-Apr-2001	Single tax-agreemt commiss report	253	0.965	0.953	0.083	0.711	0.831	0.000	0.024	0.795	0.000	0.533
V39910	18-Apr-2001	Use of atomic energy, 2nd reading	244	0.465	0.512	0.917	0.467	0.695	0.000	0.843	0.591	0.000	0.467
V40020	18-Apr-2001	Environmental protection, Art. 50, 2nd reading	230	0.384	0.419	0.917	0.467	0.644	0.000	0.831	0.591	0.000	0.533
V40080	18-Apr-2001	Special ecological programs, 2nd reading	267	0.488	0.558	1.000	0.378	0.763	0.000	0.916	0.818	0.026	0.533
V41860	26-Apr-2001	Tax Code part 2, Chap 23, 2nd reading	269	0.000	0.000	1.000	0.733	0.712	1.000	0.916	0.977	0.921	0.600
V42850	23-May-2001	Production-sharing agreements, 2nd reading	275	0.128	0.140	0.833	0.756	0.644	1.000	0.952	0.818	0.921	0.467
V44260	24-May-2001	Political parties, 2nd reading	261	0.035	0.116	0.917	0.800	0.949	0.889	0.964	0.977	0.079	0.467
V44570	6-Jun-2001	Principles of org of power in subjects, 2nd reading	250	0.884	0.791	0.000	0.689	0.220	1.000	0.024	0.795	0.895	0.467
V44710	6-Jun-2001	Law on *militsiia*, 2nd reading	235	0.012	0.163	1.000	0.756	0.949	0.722	0.976	0.477	0.105	0.400
V45610	13-Jun-2001	Basic guarantees of elec rights, 2nd reading	289	0.895	0.953	0.583	0.711	0.610	0.889	0.060	0.932	0.711	0.467
V46700	14-Jun-2001	Social development of rural settlements, 2nd reading	236	0.953	1.000	0.000	0.689	0.610	0.000	0.000	0.818	0.000	0.533

ID	Date	Description											
V47170	15-Jun-2001	Take up Land Code on floor	254	0.000	0.000	1.000	0.378	0.797	0.944	1.000	0.864	1.000	0.133
V47250	15-Jun-2001	Give floor to Gref for Land Code debate	251	0.000	0.000	0.917	0.356	0.746	0.944	1.000	0.818	0.974	0.467
V47310	15-Jun-2001	Land Code, 1st reading	236	0.000	0.000	1.000	0.333	0.542	0.944	0.988	0.818	1.000	0.267
V48630	21-Jun-2001	Political parties, 3rd reading (2nd try)	238	0.000	0.000	1.000	0.444	0.949	0.944	0.988	0.977	0.026	0.467
V48830	21-Jun-2001	Media law, 2nd reading (2nd try)	223	0.012	0.000	1.000	0.689	0.932	0.000	0.952	0.864	0.026	0.400
V49110	21-Jun-2001	Procedure for considering Labor Code	247	0.023	0.000	1.000	0.378	0.712	0.889	0.940	0.932	0.921	0.267
V51840	4-Jul-2001	Nadezhdin amendment (sets term limits for governors), 2nd reading	240	0.930	0.977	0.167	0.133	0.119	1.000	0.012	0.932	0.974	0.400
V52090	4-Jul-2001	Money laundering, 2nd reading	237	0.035	0.000		0.578	0.864	1.000	0.976	0.977	0.211	0.467
V52230	4-Jul-2001	Rates for calculating individual pensions, 2nd reading	230	0.012	0.000	1.000	0.400	0.881	1.000	0.964	0.977	0.000	0.400
V53370	6-Jul-2001	Minerals tax, 2nd reading	266	0.012	0.000	1.000	0.467	0.915	0.944	0.976	0.864	0.921	0.467
V54800	11-Jul-2001	Licensing business, 2nd reading	289	0.047	0.000	1.000	0.733	0.949	0.778	1.000	0.932	0.974	0.600
V55400	12-Jul-2001	Law on police (agreement comiss version)	236	0.163	0.326	1.000	0.689	0.966	0.778	0.964	0.023	0.053	0.667
V56710	13-Jul-2001	State pensions, 1st reading	255	0.000	0.000	0.917	0.556	0.678	0.722	0.988	1.000	0.816	0.533
V59270	14-Jul-2001	Land Code, 2nd reading	253	0.000	0.000	1.000	0.489	0.627	0.944	0.976	0.932	0.947	0.400
V60990	27-Sep-2001	Procuracy, 1st reading	242	0.233	0.349	0.000	0.556	0.593	0.944	0.976	0.114	0.947	0.533
V61300	28-Sep-2001	2002 budget, 1st reading	259	0.023	0.023	0.083	0.711	0.966	0.778	0.988	1.000	0.474	0.467

and the agrarians opposed it.[10] The procedure for handling the budget was reminiscent of the majoritarian efficiency with which the issue of the distribution of leadership posts had been settled in January 2000, but the core of the majority bloc now was the pro-government coalition of the four.

Voting cohesion among the members of the coalition has been growing, but is not usually as high as in the budget bill's case. Analysis of a number of important votes this year indicates that on close votes Unity can usually count on a majority of People's Deputy members but not Russia's Regions or OVR. Table 3.2 lists the breakdown by faction of support for thirty major votes this year. All are votes where fewer than 65 percent of the Duma voted on the winning side and all are items of high salience for the government and Duma. They concern issues such as tax policy, land reform, imports of nuclear wastes, regulation of political parties, electoral reform, federal relations, labor relations, and the budget. Unity was on the winning side in twenty-four of the cases (80 percent), but more striking is the high level of voting discipline: in nearly all cases, at least 90 percent of its members voted on the same side. OVR was relatively cohesive as well; 80 percent of the time its members could call upon at least three quarters of its members to vote the same way. The other two partners were far less unified. People's Deputy could deliver three quarters of its membership less than half the time and Russia's Regions could muster 75 percent agreement only 20 percent of the time.

Table 3.3 indicates how closely factions were aligned with one another on these thirty votes. Using a simple "party voting" measure, where the position taken by a simple majority (50 percent plus one) of the members of a faction is taken as the position of the faction, each faction's position is correlated with that of every other faction. Majorities of Unity and People's Deputy voted together twenty-seven of thirty times, so Pearson's r, the coefficient of correlation, between their positions is .66. LDPR voted the same way as Unity twenty-six of thirty times, so the coefficient is .64. People's Deputy and LDPR were the most consistent voting partners of Unity on these votes: neither OVR nor Russia's Regions was nearly as frequent a voting ally with Unity; both in fact voted against Unity more often than they voted with it. The communists and Unity never voted the same way, so the coefficient of agreement is a perfect −1.0. Unity and SPS voted differently almost as often as they voted together. Clearly, the coalition of the four had a considerable distance to go before it could command a consistent and cohesive voting majority. It was therefore in the interests of Unity and People's Deputy to improve the coordination of the four core members of the government's majority, and equally so for the government.

In April 2002, the pro-Kremlin coalition of centrist factions flexed their muscles with another show of majoritarian clout. They demanded a redistribution of committee chairmanships, the firing of the head of the parliament's staff (whom they accused of favoring the communists), and the dismissal of

Table 3.3. Interfactional Agreement Correlations on Thirty Key Votes, February–September 2001

		CPRF	APG	INDEP	LDPR	RR	PD	YAB	UNITY	SPS	OVR
CPRF	PC	1									
	Sig. (2)										
APG	PC	0.8292	1								
	Sig. (2)	0									
INDEP	PC	0.0364	0.0987	1							
	Sig. (2)	0.8487	0.6039								
LDPR	PC	−0.6407	−0.4886	−0.0987	1						
	Sig. (2)	0.0001	0.0061	0.6039							
RR	PC	0.2691	0.071	0.2789	−0.3752	1					
	Sig. (2)	0.1505	0.7093	0.1356	0.041						
PD	PC	−0.6667	−0.5528	0.2182	0.5528	−0.0673	1				
	Sig. (2)	0.0001	0.0015	0.2467	0.0015	0.724					
YAB	PC	−0.3152	−0.5584	−0.3268	0.202	−0.0053	0.0788	1			
	Sig. (2)	0.0897	0.0013	0.078	0.2845	0.9778	0.6789				
UNITY	PC	−1	−0.8292	−0.0364	0.6407	−0.2691	0.6667	0.3152	1		
	Sig. (2)	0	00.8487	0.0001	0.1505	0.0001	0.0897				
SPS	PC	−0.0334	−0.1914	−0.1166	0.1914	−0.1458	−0.0891	0.5898	0.0334	1	
	Sig. (2)	0.8609	0.311	0.5393	0.311	0.4483	0.6397	0.0006	0.8609		
OVR	PC	0.1961	0.2365	−0.1712	−0.0148	−0.345	−0.1307	−0.2164	−0.1961	0.0262	1
	Sig. (2)	0.299	0.2082	0.3657	0.9382	0.0655	0.491	0.2508	0.299	0.8907	

Note: N = Number of key votes. PC = Pearson correlation; Sig. (2) = Sig. (2-tailed).

the speaker himself. Speaker Seleznev—a moderate communist who had long since been co-opted by the Kremlin—managed to hold on to his job, but the head of the staff was replaced with a member of the pro-Kremlin camp and there was a massive reshuffling of committee chairmanships. Duma insiders interpreted the episode as having to do with preparations for the 2003 parliamentary elections: Unity and its allies wanted to secure control of the organizational resources of the Duma (its communications and staff) to help them mount their election campaign, and they wanted to deny these resources to the communists, who in the past had run their parliamentary election campaigns from the Duma.

Remaking the Federation Council

Putin's strategy for winning firm control of the Federation Council was quite different. The law reforming the method by which its members were selected provided a gradual transition to the new system. All the former governors and legislative chairs were to rotate out of the chamber by the end of December 2001, but could decide on the optimal timing of their departure in order to arrange for their replacement. By October 31, 2001, nearly half (eighty-five) of the members were newly appointed delegates and by early 2002, nearly all the new members had been selected. The new members were to be full-time legislators, and many were experienced in regional and federal-level politics. As soon as the rotation began, most of the new members positioned themselves as allies of President Putin and challenged Egor Stroev for leadership. By December, the new pro-Putin caucus replaced Stroev with one of their members, Sergei Mironov (a longtime associate of Vladimir Putin's from St. Petersburg). In early 2002, the new members had taken control of the chamber, reorganizing the committee system and putting Putin loyalists in key leadership positions.

As more and more new members entered the chamber in 2001, they began demonstrating their desire to support the president in a series of high-profile issues. Demonstrations of the pro-presidential bloc's voting strength came on three pieces of legislation where the previous Federation Council had for the most part been opposed to passage and where members were under some pressure from their home regions to block the bills or at least hold out for more favorable terms. These were the law on political parties, the law on appointments of chiefs of police, and the Land Code. All three showed how the reform of the Federation Council had given Putin the opportunity to bring a majority of the new members under the Kremlin's influence. In the case of the law on parties, members of the old Federation Council had been strongly opposed to the provision that bans regional parties—but the new Federation Council handily passed the bill on June 29.[11] The law on appointments of heads of regional branches of the MVD amended the old law by providing that the president had to clear appointments with the regional governor (a practice which had also been followed under the late Soviet regime, when an oblast first secretary had the right to veto the appointment of a police chief in his region). The new law did not require the consent of the affected governor. The Federation Council rejected the law and called for sending it to an agreement commission. The agreement commission version made only a slight concession to the governors, providing that the governors' opinion needed to be taken into account when the president made the appointment. With this minor modification, the Federation Council passed the bill on July 20 with 103 affirmative votes.[12] Finally, the Federation asserted its voting clout by voting cohesively for the Land Code on October 10, delivering 103 votes in favor of passage despite pressure from many governors to oppose it.[13] (Two members of the Federation followed their governors' lines and voted against the bill, and were threatened with expulsion from the group.) Notwithstanding the predictions of Chairman Stroev and other observers that these measures would be defeated by the Federation Council, the Federation group's cohesion and loyalty to the Kremlin ensured victories for these bills.[14]

Thus in both chambers, President Putin had helped to engineer the formation of organized caucuses through which the presidential administration and government could bargain for their major legislative priorities, trading off privileged access to the Kremlin in return for reliable voting support.

Rationalizing Policy Development

One reason that President Putin has been so effective in passing legislation reflecting his policy goals is that he has dramatically improved the efficiency of the policymaking processes in the executive branch itself. One indication of this is the close coordination between the two components of the executive in Russia, the presidential administration and the government. Under President Yeltsin the administration and government had not competed so much as they had divided responsibility; the president's staff tended to focus on political strategy and national security issues, leaving the development of much of the country's economic policy to the government, particularly after the initial wave of reform in the early 1990s had subsided.[15] As soon as Putin assumed the presidency, however, he began to organize a process for developing policy proposals that could be submitted to the Duma as draft legislation. He called upon think tanks to which he had ties from his service in St. Petersburg, including the "Center for Strategic Planning" (Tsentr strategicheskikh razrabotok) headed by German Gref. Gref's center became a key part of policy planning and development, sufficiently independent of the executive branch to be able to call upon experts and public figures as needed, but enjoying close access to Putin. One crucial aspect of the center's effort was to coordinate policy planning with the government. Government officials in a number of agencies, including those responsible for social welfare, were opposed to the liberal thrust of much of the Putin/Gref economic policy. For the most part Putin's team succeeded, however, in preventing them from blocking his policy initiatives by forming tacit alliances with sympathetic committees in the Duma. For one thing, government officials were brought into the working groups drafting much of the legislation, with the result that much of the legislative program was slow to form. For another, control of the key Duma committees in charge of the Putin team's priorities—budget, taxation, deregulation, judicial reform, pension reform, land reform, labor relations, and the like—was for the most part in the hands of the pro-Putin factions. A telling instance of the importance of committee jurisdiction control for the progress of the legislation once submitted to the Duma was the turf fight for control of the Land Code. In May, the pro-Kremlin factions succeeded in transferring jurisdiction over this legislation from the agriculture committee, which had been firmly controlled by the agrarian faction (allied closely with the communists) to the committee on property and privatization, whose chairman is a Unity deputy. Once the transfer occurred, the bill took the liberal form that the Kremlin desired and was quickly reported out for floor action.[16]

Putin made Gref himself minister for economic development and trade, with a broad mandate for shepherding through the economic reforms. Gref continued to head the Strategic Planning Center on an honorary basis and to draw upon its expertise and legislative drafting. Gradually Gref expanded his influence within the government, carefully lining up support from both executive branch departments and important organized social interests. He cultivated close ties with the Russian Union of Industrialists and Entrepreneurs (RUIE, headed since 1991 by Arkadii Vol'skii), and encouraged it to submit its proposals on economic and social policy. The RUIE became an important source of influence and advice on tax policy, deregulation, and pension policy, for instance. Other government officials pursued a similar strategy of consultation with important affected social interests in developing legislation. Minister of Labor and Social Policy Alexandr Pochinok helped to broker an agreement between the Employers' Association and FITUR (the Federation of Independent Trade Unions of Russia, the major umbrella association representing organized labor) over the terms of a new labor code. On judicial reform, deputy head of the presidential administration Dmitri Kozak headed a working group of judicial specialists in drafting a comprehensive reform of judicial institutions. Here, however, the Kremlin was unable to forge consensus on the part of affected interests: the procuracy and the Council of Judges, the major interest group representing the bench, have strongly opposed the new measures, and worked to find allies among the left wing of the Duma. On some issues, the government retreated, on others it succeeded in finding mutually acceptable compromises, and on still others it proceeded with its plans despite opposition. Notable was the skill of the Kremlin managers in developing consensus within the executive branch and between the executive branch and major social actors, before submitting legislation to the Duma. It is not only due to the Kremlin's reliance on loyal members of parliament, therefore, that it has been so successful in passing its legislative program, but also due to careful preparatory working in minimizing opposition from within the state bureaucracy and important external interests.

Putin has drawn upon other resources in policymaking as well. The Security Council played the central role in drafting some of the important policy initiatives on federal relations in 2000, including the law reforming the method of selection of Federation Council members and the creation of the seven federal super-districts with appointed presidential plenipotentiaries. It also developed the ominous "information security doctrine" in the summer and fall of 2001, which laid the foundation for a sweeping definition of the state's national security interests in the sphere of the media and telecommunications. The procuracy has been used to harass and intimidate open opponents, striking particularly at organizations and individuals associated with Boris Berezovsky and Vladimir Gusinsky. More recently, Putin's administration has attempted to form a kind of overarching state umbrella organization to manage relations with all NGOs, although the president retreated from its initial conception and instead opted for a quasi-corporatist arrangement involving state recognition of social associations and institutionalized consultations. The law on parties, which Putin pushed through parliament with remarkable speed, is a good example of Putin's vision for Russia's political system. It indicates that he seeks to make the political arena more orderly, more regulated, more manageable, and less fragmented, although not to shut down political contestation entirely.

Under this law, which Putin signed in July 2001, only parties can run candidates in elections and there are tight restrictions on organizations seeking to register as parties. A party must have at least 10,000 members, and these must be distributed throughout the country so that there are branches with at least 100 members in each of at least half the country's eighty-nine regions. Parties that fall below this membership threshold can be disqualified. Parties may not be created on an occupational, gender, ethnic, religious, or social group basis. The law further stipulates that parties *must* run candidates in presidential, parliamentary, and regional elections and that if they fail to do so sufficiently often, their registration can be withdrawn. In short, the new law imposes very stringent conditions on electoral politics. Very few of Russia's currently existing parties will survive the new rules and it is likely that the number of parties competing in the 2003 parliamentary elections will fall drastically. Putin's model of a political system appears to be one in which a pro-Kremlin party dominates the political system, with weak opposition parties on its right and left to provide safe outlets for political dissent.

Putin's approach to policymaking thus combines paternalistic and authoritarian elements with democratic neocorporatism, and it appears that his preferred model would be a state possessing relatively firm controls over the political arena and a market-oriented economic system operating under clear and well-enforced laws. His skill so far in enacting the legislative foundation for such a system suggests that he may achieve his goals.

CONCLUSION

President Putin is hardly the first leader since Russia began shedding its communist regime to create a new institutional framework by bargaining off organizational rights to organized political interests in return for their support of his policies and power. Mikhail Gorbachev took the first steps by opening up the country to competitive elections in 1989 and allowing the plethora of informal political movements to channel their energies into contests for seats to the new USSR parliament that convened in that year. Once organized as parliamentary caucuses, he allowed them formal rights within the parliament and often called upon them for information and support. Likewise Yeltsin extended the practice of institutionalizing political factions within the interim RSFSR parliament in 1990–93, giving them wider formal rights in return for their support of his chairmanship. Later his successor as chair, Ruslan Khasbulatov, went so far as to form a "Council of Factions" in the parliament, which he used when he needed to find a majority for a difficult decision. This experience in turn formed the basis for the new party-run model of governance in the Russian State Duma, itself the product of an electoral system that Yeltsin decreed into existence that gave half the seats in the Duma to candidates elected from party lists in a federation-wide electoral district. At each point, the leader sought to consolidate his own power by granting procedural, organizational, and electoral rights to partisan groups in parliament, whose leaders gained leverage thereby in attracting followers and invoking discipline. As a result, party development in Russia's parliament has outpaced party development in the country at large. The effect has been to regularize policymaking and give parliament a far greater opportunity to form majorities and speak with a collective voice than would be expected if parliament's development depended mainly on the far slower pace at which civil society has been forming.

Therefore we should expect that Putin's strategy of building support within each chamber of parliament by building up institutionalized party organizations—a defined four-faction majority coalition in the Duma and a pro-Putin majority caucus in the Federation Council—will have consequences for the future. One clear direction of development is suggested by the continuing demands by the coalition of the four in the Duma to build a government of a parliamentary majority. The all-parties governance system in the past meant that no one faction bore any particular responsibility for either the maintenance or the policies of the government—even the previous "party of power," Our Home Is Russia. If there is to be a stable pro-Kremlin majority coalition in the future, it will stake further claims to influence over the government, especially if it does well in the 2003 parliamentary elections. Putin is undoubtedly too powerful and popular for the current coalition of the four to have much chance of pressing its case for now. If Putin weakens, however, and if the coalition succeeds in establishing reliable voting discipline, its ability to bargain for more rights for itself in determining the composition of the government will increase. The leaders of the pro-Putin party have already been moving in this direction. Speaking to a congress of the "United Russia" party in April 2002, one of the party's cochairs declared that the party wants "to ensure a direct tie between the president and the people, bypassing all the bureaucratic barriers" and would claim the right to demand the removal of government ministers who are not coping with their jobs.[17] While this was mainly pious rhetoric (at present, United Russia is so dependent on the Kremlin that it would never challenge Putin directly over a government appointment), it reflected a universal trend of development: once parties are given the opportunity to mobilize electoral support and win majorities in parliament, they demand a share of executive power. This has been the pattern in France's semipresidential Fifth Republic; it is no less applicable to Russia as well.

One lesson from the record of the past decade in Russia's post-communist transition is that the institution-making that has resulted from short-term bargains between self-interested political leaders, at junctures when each side has something to offer and something to gain from agreeing on a new institutional arrangement, has been surprisingly long lasting.[18] Where new institutions have been produced by the stroke of a pen, as has frequently occurred, they have short shelf lives. But when actors have been in situations where they must negotiate with one another in order to obtain a preferred outcome, the result has been new institutions that last—and have serious and often unpredictable consequences for subsequent political development.

NOTES

1. Following are my translations from the published versions of the president's message, as posted to the presidential website at www.president.kremlin.ru/events.

2. OVR stands for "Fatherland–All Russia" and was the parliamentary party made up of deputies elected on the Fatherland-All Russian party list. In the Duma,

OVR takes a generally centrist and pro-government position and in 2002 joined with Unity in forming a new pro-Kremlin party called "United Russia."

Yabloko is led by liberal economist Grigorii Yavlinskii and espouses democratic principles with a strong social democratic orientation. It has been very critical of many of Yeltsin's policies and continues to criticize many of Putin's policies.

SPS (The Union of Rightist Forces) is a strongly pro-market, pro-democratic party calling for policies that will stimulate business activity and economic growth, and deepen Russia's integration into the international economy. It supports some but not all of Putin's policies.

3. On the relations between Kremlin and Duma under Yeltsin and Putin, see Thomas F. Remington, "Putin and the Duma," *Post-Soviet Affairs* 17, no. 4 (November/December 2001): 285–308; idem, " 'Taming Vlast': Institutional Development in Post-Communist Russia," in *A Decade of Post-Communism: The Fate of Democracy in the Former Soviet Union and Eastern Europe,* ed. Donald Kelley (Fayetteville: University of Arkansas Press, forthcoming); idem, "Coalition Politics in the New Duma," in *Elections, Parties and the Future of Russia: The 1999–2000 Elections,* ed. Vicki Hesli and William Reisinger (Cambridge: Cambridge University Press, forthcoming); idem, "The Evolution of Executive-Legislative Relations in Russia Since 1993," *Slavic Review* 59, no. 3 (Fall 2000): 499–520.

4. The bill reforming the method for selecting Federation Council members was initially rejected by the Federation Council on June 28, 2000. The chamber later passed a slightly modified version of the bill, however, on July 26, 2000, after an agreement commission made up of members of the two houses found a mutually acceptable compromise version of the plan.

5. The Liberal Democratic Party of Russia (LDPR) is the party led by Vladimir Zhirinovsky, a bombastic figure who has made a reputation for adopting extreme chauvinistic public stances. In its actual behavior in the Duma, his small faction is known for its faithful subservience to the Kremlin.

6. Russia's Regions and People's Deputy tend to be loyal to the Kremlin in their actual parliamentary behavior. But because both are made up of members elected in single-seat district races, their members often defect from the pro-Kremlin line when strong local interests pressure them to vote against the government.

7. www.polit.ru (accessed April 17, 2001).

8. www.polit.ru (accessed April 18, 2001).

9. www.polit.ru (accessed September 24, 2001).

10. www.polit.ru (accessed September 27 and 28, 2001).

11. A. N. Medushevskii, "Federal'nyi konstitutsionnyi zakon 'O politicheskikh partiiakh,' " on the website of the Institute of Law and Public Policy, October 31, 2001, at www.ilpp.ru/bulletin/.

12. P. A. Kravchenko, "Federal'nyi zakon 'O vnesenii izmenenii i dopolneniia v stat'I 7 i 9 Zakona Rossiiskoi Federatsii 'O militsii' (odobren Sovetom Federatsii na 75-m zasedanii)," on the website of the Institute of Law and Public Policy, October 31, 2001, at www.ilpp.ru/bulletin/.

13. www.polit.ru (accessed October 10, 2001).

14. The Federation group also made shrewd use of the provision in the constitution by which the Federation Council is not required to consider all pieces of legisla-

tion that pass the Duma. It is only required to take up bills on certain subjects, such as budgeting, taxation, and federal relations. In the case of the three controversial bills legalizing the import of spent nuclear fuel, which were widely opposed by regional and environmental interests, the Federation group simply allowed two of the bills to bypass the chamber and go straight to the president for his signature.

15. The recent collective memoir by Yeltsin's political advisors, *Epokha Yel'tsina*, provides extensive detail on the way the president's administration dealt with the government in policymaking. It is striking that the president allowed the government to take the lead in developing most of the country's economic and fiscal policy, sometimes agreeing to the government's requests for a decree to lend clout to a decision, in other cases ignoring Yeltsin's expressed wishes. See G. A. Satarov et al., *Epokha Yel'tsina: Ocherki politicheskoi istorii* (Moscow: Vagrius, 2001).

16. www.polit.ru (accessed May 17, 2001).

17. www.polit.ru (accessed April 25, 2002).

18. Cf. Thomas F. Remington, *The Russian Parliament: Institutional Evolution in a Transitional Regime, 1989–1999* (New Haven, Conn.: Yale University Press, 2001); Michael McFaul, *Russia's Unfinished Revolution: Political Change from Gorbachev to Putin* (Ithaca, N.Y.: Cornell University Press, 2001).

Part Two

STATE AND SOCIETY

Chapter Four

Putin and the Media

Masha Lipman and Michael McFaul

PUTIN'S WEAK SPOT

Since becoming president on January 1, 2000, Vladimir Putin has made a remarkable imprint on Russian economic, political, and foreign policy. As discussed in other chapters in this book, Putin cannot be considered a preserver of the status quo. He already has initiated real changes in many arenas. His reform agenda regarding economic issues is truly radical, grand, and sweeping.[1] Putin has made clear his intention of tackling the hard structural reforms needed to make Russia a growing market economy. Regarding foreign policy, Putin also infused new vigor into the pursuit of Russian national interests. Better than his predecessor, Putin understands the limits of Russian power. Nonetheless, Putin has reaffirmed Russia's status as an important actor on the international stage. Putin has reenergized economic reform at home and foreign policy abroad while still maintaining a 70 percent approval rating from his citizens.[2]

Putin also has changed the dynamics of political reform in Russia. But in contrast to economic and foreign policy, democratization has moved in a negative direction. Before Putin became president, Russian democratic institutions were already weak and unconsolidated[3] and have eroded further under his tenure.[4] Putin's policy changes in the political sphere have served to consolidate his own power, emasculate alternative centers of power within the Russian polity, and limit the influence of individual and social actors that oppose state policy.

Most unappealing has been Putin's indifference to human rights in Chechnya.[5] Russia had the right to defend its territorial integrity in the summer of 1999 when Chechen fighters invaded Dagestan. If the initial use of force may have been justified, the conduct of the Russian campaign since then is not. Wars are always brutal, but Russian actions in Chechnya have routinely been

63

inhumane, while Russian neglect of displaced persons as a result of the war, estimated to be more than 400,000 people, has been disappointing.[6] The harsh prosecution of Putin's crusade against Chechen "bandits" has inspired more fanaticism within Chechnya and made Russia less secure.

Also on Putin's watch, the State Security Service (FSB) has stepped up harassment of targeted human rights activists, environmental leaders, and Western nongovernmental organizations and religious groups and their Russian affiliates. New guidelines on foreign contacts for academics have even been published (though without being enforced), and even a few academics have been charged with espionage.[7]

Alternative power centers within the state have been weakened as well. Putin's allies invented a new party, Unity, to compete in the 1999 parliamentary elections.[8] Its capture of almost a quarter of the popular vote helped to make the State Duma much more cooperative with the president. Subsequently, the Kremlin orchestrated a merger of Unity with Fatherland, its vehement foe during the 1999 parliamentary election.[9] The merger has made the Duma even more of a rubber stamp for Putin's policies. Putin's so-called reform of the upper house of parliament, the Federation Council, has gravely weakened this once important check on presidential power—a body once elected and now appointed. Plans for reasserting Moscow's authority throughout the regions of Russia have been less successful, but there is an unmistakable tilt toward the center.[10]

Putin's antidemocratic proclivities have been most starkly exposed in his approach to the nongovernment-controlled media. The Russian state has arrested, intimidated, and even pushed into exile journalists Andrei Babitsky and Anna Politkovskaya for reporting the "wrong" news about Chechnya. The elimination of Media-MOST, the biggest privately owned media group in Russia and owner of the NTV television network, most dramatically demonstrates Putin's intolerance of criticism. The government-supported campaign against TV-6, the network to which a large number of NTV's staff migrated, has further underscored Putin's resolve to muzzle the press as an independent check on his political power.

The end of anarchy in certain spheres should not be equated with the end of democracy. Changes in some state institutions were needed after Yeltsin, and not all of Putin's reforms in the political sphere have been antidemocratic. For instance, Putin's proposals for legal reform—whereby the powers of prosecutors will be trimmed and jury trials will be introduced nationwide—are progressive in spirit and may strengthen democracy in the long run.[11] Over time, a growing economy that produces a wealthier citizenry also might deepen democratic institutions.[12] In the short term, however, the consequences of Putin's rise to power have been bad for Russian democracy and Russian democrats. And a leading indicator of a free society, and independent media, has moved the fastest and farthest in the negative direction.

The process of creating and sustaining Russian media not controlled by the state has never been only about democracy or politics. Those most involved in Russia's independent media outlets at the national level were never the most passionate defenders of democracy and human rights themselves. Rather, they were profit seekers with questionable business ethics and controversial political agendas.[13] Their involvement, coupled with the specific economic context of post-Soviet Russian media, has served to cloud the cleavages between good and evil in the struggle for a free and independent press in Russia. Even after failing to identify "white hats" or "Sakharovs" in defense of Russia's independent media, we still conclude that the nature of Putin's policies has severely undermined one of Russia's most important democratic achievements of the last decade—a critical and independent press that acted, in some small way, as a check on state power. While Russia's media tycoons themselves may not have been ardent advocates of a free and independent press, their media outlets offered an alternative view, different from that of the state. Putin could have disciplined or brought to justice Russia's oligarchs without destroying their media empires, but he did not. Instead, the Kremlin's exuberant campaign to crush these oligarchs also has squelched the free press in Russia by eliminating this alternative voice. The erosion of this vital institution will have long-term negative consequences for the future of Russian democracy.

PUBLIC/PRIVATE SPHERES IN
POST-COMMUNIST RUSSIA

For most of this century in Russia, there was little space for political, economic, or social life independent of the state. The Soviet regime aimed to manage the economy, monopolize political activity, control the media, and destroy all independent associational life—and very nearly succeeded. To the extent that organized social or economic groups did exist outside of the family, they were atomized, apolitical, or illegal. At the same time, the Soviet system crowded private life with myriad social, political, and press organizations that mimicked their counterpart organizations in the West in name, but in practice helped to control society.

In the late 1980s, Gorbachev began to liberalize the Soviet political system. In the name of *glasnost*, Gorbachev allowed several newspapers, literary journals (the so-called "thick" journals), and weekly magazines greater editorial license to criticize the Soviet system, especially its past. Gorbachev's *glasnost* gave birth to a new generation of independent-minded journalists and commentators. During the peak years of *perestroika*, writers at *Moscow News*, *Argumenty i Fakty*, *Ogonyok*, and *Izvestiya* were ahead of the political class and civil society in leading the charge for democratic reform.[14] While still enjoying the economic benefits of state subsidization, new independent newspapers such as *Nezavisimaya gazeta*, *Kuranty*, and *Kommersant'* appeared for the first time. Liberalization of television was much slower. Only in the spring of 1991 did the Russian government succeed in compelling the Soviet state to give Russia its own television station, RTR.[15] Yet, the general trajectory of more pluralism had even begun to penetrate electronic media by the end of the Soviet era. Significantly, however, the state—be it the Soviet Union or the Russian Republic—still owned or subsidized every major media outlet in Russia before the collapse of the Soviet Union in December 1991.[16] In other words, a paper like *Moscow News* could not have survived without assistance from the federal or local government. But because the state's leader, Gorbachev, tolerated a critical press, *Moscow News* from the "left" and *Den'* from the "right" could publish moderately critical articles of Gorbachev and his government without fear of closure.

After the collapse of Soviet communism and creation of an independent Russian state, Boris Yeltsin's reforms created new space for independent political, social, and economic activity. The first decade of post-communism in Russia was a period of freedom for the press, though the causes of this freedom were many. Yeltsin, at some fundamental level, appeared to value an independent press. He never intervened to mute criticism of himself or his government. Rhetorically, he lauded Russia's independent and critical media as an achievement of his democratic reforms. Early in his tenure, the Yeltsin government drafted and succeeded in passing some very progressive laws on freedom of the press. At the same time, during most of the early Yeltsin years leading up to the 1996 presidential campaign, Yeltsin and the press were allies against a common threat—a communist comeback.[17] This alliance likely was forged with no normative commitment to loftier principles of democracy, as the Yeltsin government was also weak. Fighting many political and economic battles simultaneously, the Russian state simply did not have the capacity to control the media. Even the state's own media—such as ORT, Russia's largest and most watched television network—was de facto controlled by a private actor, Boris Berezovsky.

Market reforms initially helped to stimulate still further the growth of media outlets not controlled by the government, including, first and foremost, television.[18] NTV, the first private television network, started by Vladimir Gusinsky in 1993, provided a source of information that was truly independent of the government and that reached beyond Moscow.[19] Defying government threats to its license, NTV earned its credentials as a serious news organization when it provided critical coverage of the first Chechen war. NTV also achieved a new level of post-Soviet professionalism, quality, and style that its rival channels, ORT (channel one) and RTR (channel two), lacked. News anchor Evgeny Kiselev became a national celebrity by producing and hosting *Itogi*, a Sunday night talk show on politics. Before starting

NTV, Gusinsky already had begun to publish his own daily newspaper, *Segodnya*. He also bought a stake in a popular radio station, *Ekho Moskvy*, and later founded a weekly magazine, *Itogi*, published in partnership with *Newsweek*, making Media-MOST a media powerhouse.

Other financial tycoons followed in Gusinsky's wake, believing that the media, especially television, was an important political tool.[20] Through an inside deal arranged by the Kremlin, Boris Berezovsky acquired part ownership and de facto control of ORT, Russia's largest television network.[21] Berezovsky also obtained a major stake in a smaller channel, TV-6. Moscow's mayor, Yuri Luzhkov, and his financial empire, founded TV-Tsentr primarily as a campaign tool for his (aborted) presidential bid in 2000. Russia's small group of financial houses and oil and gas companies also gobbled up most of Russia's national newspapers.[22]

From afar, Russia's oligarchs may have appeared to be buying "private" media outlets and establishing independent media empires. Of course, these outlets were biased, but at least they were private entities, which offered an alternative view to the state.[23] Yet even a decade after the collapse of communism, the space for genuinely independent economic or political activity from the state was still very limited. The state—or more aptly in Russian, *vlast* (the power)—was still the 800-pound gorilla in many sectors of Russian political and economic life. While the weakness of the Russian state was apparent in some sectors such as health, education, and security, the state was still a dominant actor in some strategic sectors including the media. The Russian federal state was still the majority shareholder in ORT and owned 100 percent of RTR, while regional heads of administrations still controlled the major television networks in their regions and subsidized most print media. For periods in the 1990s, the state, and especially the Russian federal state under Yeltsin, did not exercise its property rights, creating the false sense of "independence" for some state-owned media outlets.

In contrast to ORT, RTR, TV-Tsentr, and many of Russia's national newspapers, Gusinsky's Media-MOST was the most financially independent media company in the 1990s. Different from other major media assets, Gusinsky's empire was not a privatized Soviet-era enterprise, but created from scratch, meaning the state did not initially own shares in his companies. But even Gusinsky acquired his initial capital from connections with the Moscow city government (his Most Bank served as the city's banker for years), then obtained additional control over Channel 4, on which NTV broadcast, as a reward for his cooperation with Yeltsin during the 1996 presidential election.[24] He then offered an equity stake to Gazprom, a largely state-owned gas company, to finance his expansion plans. Gusinsky also secured loans from several sources, including Gazprom and CS-First Boston.[25] Before the Russian financial crash in August 1998, Gusinsky's business plan and debt-to-equity ratios looked ambitious, but within reason. The crash, however, slashed the advertising market by two-thirds, from approximately $540 million to $190 million.[26] The crash also made Gusinsky's dollar-denominated debts significantly more expensive, compelling him in November 2000 to surrender more equity to Gazprom to retire some of these debts. This transfer of shares made Gazprom—or more specifically Gazprom's subsidiary, Gazprom Media—a 46 percent shareholder, and left Gusinsky's Media-MOST with 49.56 percent of shares in NTV, with the balance, 4.44 percent, owned by an American investment company, Capital Research and Management Group.

Like any other sensible director of an ailing enterprise in Russia, Gusinsky pursued foreign investment as a strategy to avoid state control.[27] Although the details of the proposed deal remain murky, Ted Turner and a group of Western investors appeared ready to buy out Gusinsky's stake in NTV.[28] Turner's only condition was that the Russian government agree that it would not interfere in the business or editorial affairs of NTV. Despite efforts from even the U.S. State Department, Putin never agreed to such an arrangement. He and his government resisted because NTV's problems were never just financial. They were also political.

GUSINSKY VERSUS PUTIN: A POLITICAL AND PERSONAL VENDETTA

NTV's editorial line regarding the Russian government has vacillated considerably over the last several years. During the first Chechen war (1994–96), NTV reporters covered the war from within Chechnya. Although Russian federal commanders tried to limit coverage and denied reporters access to Russian troops, Russian journalists and NTV reporters in particular eventually exposed the brutal and ineffective military campaigns.[29] The coverage had a profound effect on Russian public opinion. By January 1995, only 16 percent of the Russian populace supported the use of force in Chechnya, while 71 percent opposed the war.[30] Opposition to the war fueled general disapproval of Yeltsin's presidency. A full 70 percent of those polled disapproved of Yeltsin's performance as president in September 1994, growing to 80 percent by January 1995.[31] To secure Yeltsin's re-election in 1996, his campaign officials believed that they had to end the war.[32] Thus, in April 1996, Yeltsin announced a cease-fire.

During the 1996 presidential campaign, NTV reversed course and supported Yeltsin in his re-election bid. In doing so, NTV joined forces with nearly every major media outlet in the country not controlled by the Communist Party in supporting Yeltsin. NTV's general director, Igor Malashenko, blurred the lines between the campaign and the media when he joined the Yeltsin re-election team without resigning from his television post. In providing unabashedly positive coverage for Yeltsin and very critical reporting of Zyuganov during the campaign, NTV reporters as well as journalists working for Gusinsky's *Segodnya* newspaper and his new weekly, *Itogi* (which began publication just before the presidential election), explained that they were protecting Russian democracy, and in particular, their survival as an independent media. If the communist Zyuganov became president of Russia, they argued that they would all be closed down.[33] For journalists concerned with preserving their independence, this election was considered a life-or-death matter. Yeltsin won, and the specter of government seizure of nongovernmental media was postponed (ironically until the next election).

After the 1996 presidential election, Gusinsky expected a payoff for his help during the campaign. Indeed, soon after the election he acquired full control of Channel 4 for NTV. He also hoped to acquire Svyazinvest, a telecommunications company that would dovetail nicely with his business interests in media.[34] Unlike the other oligarchs, Gusinsky did not acquire a major asset through the corrupt loans-for-shares programs. Now he believed it was his turn, especially after his helpful work during the 1996 presidential election.

In the auction of Svyazinvest, Deputy Prime Minister Anatoly Chubais decided to change the old, corrupt rules of oligarchic privatization established under the loans-for-shares program, and instead offered up Svyazinvest to the highest bidder.[35] Before Svyazinvest, competitive bidding had never occurred. Instead, every previous auction of a major company was an inside deal. Gusinsky was incensed that Chubais was now trying to change the rules, but went ahead and made a bid anyway. Gusinsky teamed up with Boris Berezovsky and the Alfa group to raise the capital to acquire the company, but another team of investors, headed by rival oligarch Vladimir Potanin and his Western partner, George Soros, outbid Gusinsky by $16 million ($1.87 billion to $1.71 billion).

Chubais was elated with the process.[36] Gusinsky was furious and insinuated that Chubais had provided information about Gusinsky's bid to Potanin. Deploying his media as his weapon, Gusinsky set out to destroy Chubais and his reformist government. Berezovsky joined the battle and put his ORT—Russia's largest national television network—into action to besmirch Chubais and his allies.[37] Muckraking campaigns, encouraged by Berezovsky and Gusinsky, produced some embarrassing results for Chubais and his associates, including most damagingly a book contract for the Chubais group that paid five authors $90,000 each to write chapters for a book on privatization.[38] As a result of the book scandal, three of Chubais's closest associates were forced to resign from their government posts. Eventually Chubais himself had to leave.

After the Svyazinvest scandal, NTV became increasingly critical of Yeltsin and his government, focusing in particular on corruption within the Kremlin's inner circle. NTV once again provided the only critical coverage of the second Chechen war as it unfolded in the fall of 1999. This second war, however, was much more popular than the first military intervention, prompting Kremlin loyalists to call NTV an unpatriotic, pro-fascist (because they called the Chechen guerrillas fascists), pro-Western organization, which reported Russian military atrocities without devoting any coverage to violations of human rights carried out by Chechen guerrillas. Vladimir Putin, then prime minister, was offended personally by NTV's coverage and made his opinions known both to his colleagues in the government and to Gusinsky personally.[39]

In the run-up to the December 1999 parliamentary election, NTV did not support the government's candidates, but gave much free airtime and positive coverage to opposition political parties, such as Fatherland and Yabloko. At the time, Fatherland leader Yevgeny Primakov was considered the only politician who might be able to seriously challenge Putin in the 2000 presidential elections. To their credit, especially compared to the other national television networks, NTV news editors allotted huge chunks of prime time to debates between parties and discussions among voters. Yet, NTV did not endorse the Kremlin's party, Unity, in the parliamentary race nor back Putin in the March 2000 presidential election. Putin took notice.

After his landslide win in March 2000, Putin began to articulate a new approach toward the press and democratic institutions—one that differed qualitatively from that of Boris Yeltsin. Of course, Putin endorsed the notion of a free press and the importance of democracy in principle. He repeatedly pledged allegiance to freedom of the press; he readily admitted that freedom of the press is absolutely necessary in a modern society, and that if Russia aspires to become a modern society it must ensure that the press is free. Yet, his statements and speeches also revealed a poor understanding of these concepts and a lack of respect for their importance in the operations of the Russian state, economy, and society. In his first annual address (*poslanie*) to the members of the Russian parliament in July, Putin hinted of his mistrust of the press, claiming that "sometimes [the media] turn into means of mass disinformation and tools of struggle against the state."[40] The Doctrine of Information Security issued several months later made it clear that state-owned media must dominate the information market, since only the state can provide the citizens of Russia with *objective* information about what goes on in Russia. The doctrine also pledged to battle disinformation coming from abroad.

When faced with crises that required action, Putin made clear his real attitude toward the disloyal press. Radio Liberty correspondent Andrei Babitsky was the first journalist to experience the wrath of Putin when Russian security services secretly arrested him in Chechnya and kept him incommunicado for several weeks. In March 2000, when Babitsky's whereabouts were still unknown, Putin claimed that Babitsky "worked directly for the enemy—for the bandits."[41] Putin made it very clear that there could be only one truth about the Chechen war. To publicly express an alternative view was considered traitorous. The following year, Anna Politkovskaya, a Russian journalist critical of Russia's military campaign in Chechnya, also came under pressure from the state and felt compelled to leave the country.

Putin also vehemently denounced those who criticized the way he and his government handled the crisis caused by the sinking of the Kursk submarine in August 2000. In an interview on RTR on August 23, 2000, Putin did not conceal his strong feelings toward his critics, asserting that they were responsible for the destruction of the Russian state, army, and the navy.[42] It is against this background of statements and actions about the press by Putin that the campaign against NTV must be understood. Although NTV's financial woes made the company vulnerable, the state's campaign against the channel was simply *another* example of what happens to a news organization when it gets in the way of the Kremlin.[43] There was certainly a pragmatic desire by Kremlin officials (especially those responsible for Putin's re-election) for wanting to take control of the third-largest television network in the country and the only privately owned national channel. But Putin's personal hatred for Gusinsky and his "traitorous" opinions about the Chechen war should not be underestimated. According to Putin's definition of state interests, Gusinsky was the enemy of the state and therefore Putin's personal enemy.

Putin was too savvy and too concerned with his image in the West to be directly involved or to simply shut down NTV by force. Instead, those leading the campaign to seize NTV and dismantle Media-MOST pursued several different strategies over several months. One of these strategies was to threaten Gusinsky personally. The idea was to use the prosecutor's office to bring criminal charges against Gusinsky, intimidate him, and thus silence his media. The implementation of this criminal variant began with a raid on Gusinsky's media office building in May 2000 by masked, gun-toting men who burst in under the pretext of a search. Gusinsky and his people were accused of various crimes, but no convincing evidence was ever presented, and the cases fell apart soon thereafter. In the months that followed the first raid, affiliate offices of Gusinsky's corporation were raided and searched dozens of times, proceedings were opened and closed, Gusinsky's employees were interrogated and their apartments were searched. Eventually, in June, Gusinsky himself was arrested and then released three days later, but placed under house arrest.[44] A month later, on July 20, 2000, Gusinsky agreed to sign a secret deal to sell his controlling stake in Media-MOST to Gazprom in return for his freedom. (His freedom was guaranteed in the notorious Protocol 6 signed by Minister of the Press Mikhail Lesin.) Six days later, Gusinsky signed the sales deal, was released, and immediately fled the country. Three of his closest associates soon followed him in exile, since they, too, feared arrest. Soon thereafter, information about the sale and the secret protocol became public. Gusinsky denounced these agreements as null and void, since they had been signed under duress. Thereafter, Gusinsky and Gazprom began negotiating again about debts and equity.

This ploy did not work. NTV continued to operate, and its coverage of Putin and his government was as critical as ever. Realizing that a strategy of intimidation through criminal charges had failed, the Kremlin began devoting greater attention to the "business variant." The raids, interrogations, and threats of further criminal investigations continued. In parallel, however, Media-MOST's largest creditor, Gazprom, moved to assert control over NTV. The largest stakeholder in Gazprom is the Russian federal government. A meticulous litigation campaign ensued. According to a Russian weekly magazine *Kommersant-Vlast'*, for a period of two years, a court hearing involving Media-MOST was held every 4.3 days.[45] Finally in April, Gazprom succeeded in changing the management. On April 3, 2001, Gazprom convened a shareholder's meeting in which a slight majority—Gazprom (46.0 percent) plus Capital Research (4.44 percent) or 50.44 percent—agreed to remove NTV's old management. Alfred Kokh, the executive director of Gazprom's affiliate, Gazprom-Media, became chairman and Boris Jordan, a former American investment banker, assumed the role of general director in place of Kiselev.[46]

Yet even this strategy did not work completely. Led by Kiselev, the old NTV staff asserted that the shareholders' meeting was unlawful. Their petitions to the courts to stop the takeover were at the time heard, but then quickly reversed, demonstrating that the courts were not neutral arbitrators in this drama. Nonetheless, Kiselev and his supporters refused to leave, maintained a twenty-four-hour vigil in their offices, and continued to broadcast protest programming. Strikingly, a public demonstration in Moscow in defence of NTV that weekend attracted 20,000 people, the largest showing of public activism for democracy since 1993. The following weekend, another 15,000 people showed up. It looked like the old NTV was winning the struggle for public opinion. And yet, national polls suggested that "only four percent of the public regarded the NTV takeover as a state attempt to limit media freedom."[47]

Frustrated by the continued drama of the standoff and worried that the Turner investment might actually take place, the Kremlin's surrogate, Gazprom, adopted more aggressive tactics. In the predawn hours of April 14, the new managers assumed their offices at NTV's headquarters, accompanied by a newly hired security service. In response, the old NTV staff split allegiances. Kiselev and several dozen journalists and anchors went to TV-6, a channel owned by Berezovsky, who by this time also had left Russia for fear of arrest.

Others stayed behind to work for the "new" NTV, which has continued to broadcast but with a falling viewership.[48]

The assault against nongovernmental media did not end with NTV. In the earlier debt negotiations between Gusinsky and Gazprom, Gusinsky relinquished a stake in each of his media assets, including his publishing house, Seven Days, which published *Segodnya* and *Itogi*. By the beginning of the year, Gazprom had enough shares in Seven Days to conspire with the president and shareholders of that publishing house to close *Segodnya* and oust the entire staff of *Itogi*. They did so on April 17, 2001. Like NTV, *Itogi* continues to be published, but with an entirely new editorial orientation. The first cover story of the new *Itogi* featured soccer, with no mention in the magazine of what had transpired the week before. *Newsweek*, of course, withdrew from the partnership with Seven Days, fully supporting the original staff of *Itogi*.[49]

Putin apologists claim that he played no role in this "merger and acquisition." And that is the point. If he really cared about freedom of the press, he could have stopped this gross violation of democracy with one public statement. But he did not intervene. He broke his silence only once—during German chancellor Gerhard Schroeder's visit to Russia a few days after Gazprom changed the NTV management. On this occasion, he once again confirmed his adherence to freedom of the press, but added that "I do not think, I, under these conditions, have the right to interfere in this conflict between different economic players."[50]

His inaction revealed his real attitude toward the media not controlled by the government. Journalists can be free and independent just as long as they do not get in the way of the president and his agenda.

A LUTA CONTINUA: TV-6

The "restructuring" of NTV and *Itogi* and the closing of *Segodnya* did not mean the end of all media independent of the government. Nor did this seizure of NTV's assets mean that all national television fell under the control of the government. Kiselev, the new director general of TV-6, and his associates from NTV tried to make TV-6 a genuinely national television network with an editorial line independent of the Kremlin. Before Kiselev and his NTV colleagues assumed editorial control of TV-6, the station was an entertainment channel that targeted a young, non-news-watching audience. Given the station's previous reputation and limited technological reach within Russia, many believed that the NTV renegades would eventually fade from prominence. By the fall of 2001, however, the former NTV team had managed to fully transform the channel's programming, turning it into a serious television business with highly professional news content. They launched a few successful programs, and were the first to produce a very popular "reality TV" program in Russia.

The very existence of TV-6, and especially its rapid and successful development, was extremely exasperating and humiliating for the Kremlin. The exiled oligarch, Boris Berezovsky, maintained his 75 percent share in the network and continued to finance the station from abroad. Although Berezovsky had little influence or say in the editorial policy of TV-6, he continued to make anti-Putin statements from exile, calling Putin a dictator and suggesting that he was also a criminal. Berezovsky even hinted that he had evidence linking the Russian government to the apartment bombings in September 1999.[51] Berezovsky also financed human rights organizations and a liberal opposition party, and vowed to invest more energy and money in undermining the current Russian regime. Vladimir Gusinsky, though not a formal owner of TV-6, also loomed large behind the scenes. He maintained contact with the journalists who had left NTV after the takeover, and continued to raise issues of freedom of the press in Russia in the West. Even from abroad, Berezovsky and Gusinsky kept up their efforts to taunt the Kremlin. Given the time and effort already spent to eradicate the defiant tycoons, the sustained "presence" of both Berezovsky and Gusinsky within Russia infuriated the Kremlin. When traveling abroad, Putin was constantly embarrassed as Western journalists hounded the Russian president about media issues. Even President Bush felt compelled to raise the issue during his first summit with Putin in the United States in November 2001.

The combination of TV-6 successes and Putin's continued annoyance with Gusinsky and especially Berezovsky eventually prompted the Russian state to act against TV-6 as well. The weapons deployed were similar to those used against NTV. Like the NTV case from the previous year, the attack against TV-6 was disguised as a "business affair." A minor TV-6 shareholder, Lukoil-Garant, a pension fund controlled by the giant oil company Lukoil, which is loyal to the Kremlin, applied to the arbitration court seeking to liquidate TV-6.[52] Lukoil-Garant owned only 15 percent of TV-6. Yet, the pension fund made the request for liquidation in accordance with a very arcane Russian law, which states that any shareholder, including a minority shareholder, can request the liquidation of a company if its net assets are lower than its minimum authorized capital. In other words, a minority shareholder can close down a company that has failed to make a profit in the last three years, which was indeed the situation at TV-6 between 1998 and 2000. The law, which had never been invoked, would have liquidated most Russian firms. Even the pro-Kremlin Duma recognized the folly of this law and annulled it at the end of 2001. Lukoil-Garant issued its request for liquidation in May 2001, but the proceedings dragged on throughout the summer, creating the false expectation that no court would recognize the obviously political suit. In late September 2001, however, the Moscow arbitration court ruled that TV-6 must be liquidated. In fact, TV-6 had turned a profit by 2001, largely due to the vigorous efforts of the old NTV team. Thus, the court's decision exposed the true political nature of the case.

Disappointingly, the vast majority of Russian public paid no attention to the campaign against TV-6. Interested viewers understood that TV-6 was being attacked by the Kremlin for political reasons. Even some Kremlin supporters would not argue with Kiselev's statement that "this is an absolutely obvious political thing."[53] Yet, few seemed to care.[54]

Public appeals, demonstrations, or work-ins, therefore, were not options for the TV-6 staff. Instead, they resorted to their only course of action—the courts. In late November, the arbitration court once again confirmed the decision to liquidate TV-6, but on December 29, the last working day of 2001, the federal arbitration court overturned the lower court's decision.[55] A rare television appearance by Boris Yeltsin strengthened the counteroffensive. In a prime-time interview with a popular political anchor on the government channel (RTR), Yeltsin said firmly that TV-6 should not be liquidated. Even the Bush administration weighed in. U.S. State Department spokesperson Richard Boucher stated in early January 2002 that "We continue to urge Russian officials to ensure that TV-6 gets a full fair hearing and ensure that press freedom and the rule of law can be best served by keeping TV-6 on the air."[56]

The triumph of TV-6 and its defenders was short lived. On January 4, the first working day of 2002, a member of the Supreme Arbitration court publicly criticized the federal arbitration court's decision of December 29. On January 11, the lower court (which was ordered by the federal court to reconsider its earlier decisions) reconfirmed TV-6's liquidation. In sharp contrast with normal practice, the court acted swiftly in conducting its review of the case. TV-6's staff refused to give up. Allegedly, Minister of the Press Mikhail Lesin called the TV-6 management on January 11, 2002, to offer them a deal. TV-6 would become the property of its journalists under the condition that neither Berezovsky nor Gusinsky would be among the shareholders. This call was reportedly followed by another, from Alexander Voloshin, the head of Putin's administration and one of Yeltsin's former aides. Voloshin allegedly advised TV-6 management to accept Lesin's offer. Berezovsky endorsed the idea, stating that it was his intention to "preserve a TV channel independent of the state, of the Kremlin. If this requires presenting the shares as a gift to journalists, I will do that as well."[57] At the same time, Berezovsky denounced the arbitration court's decision in January to dissolve TV-6 and pledged to fight the court's decision at the next level, the Constitutional Court.[58] Kiselev also vowed to fight on, hinting that the company had not yet exhausted all of its legal and political resources.[59] Putin finally broke his silence on this drama and offered the TV-6 staff governmental support. Thus, the TV-6 team faced the dilemma of either becoming yet another government-controlled media outlet or going out of business. They ultimately refused to take up the government's offer, and on January 22, 2002, TV-6 went off the air. The shutdown of TV-6 reverberated throughout the country, since 156 regional affiliates also lost their main source of programming that same day.[60] On channel six, where TV-6 used to broadcast, sports programming filled the void.

Immediately after closure, the TV-6 team began looking for a way to get back on the air. The government announced that it would hold an auction for the rights to broadcast on channel six on March 27, 2002, so Kiselev decided to construct an offer. In February, a dozen prominent business tycoons with close ties to the Kremlin formed a consortium to finance a new TV-6. According to Kiselev, obtaining the support of these loyalists and abandoning Gusinsky and Berezovsky was the only strategy for survival left for his team of journalists. In the run-up to the March tender, Kiselev brought on new, unexpected allies to join his new company—Media-Socium—to insure victory. Most amazingly, former Prime Minister Yevegny Primakov and Arkady Volsky, the chief of the Union of Industrialists and Entrepreneurs, joined the Media-Socium team, allegedly at the request of government officials who were negotiating with Kiselev about the future of the channel. Both men have stronger loyalties to the Kremlin than Kiselev, prompting many commentators to conclude that Kiselev had sacrificed editorial independence for the chance to be on the air once again.[61] After Media-Socium won the tender, Primakov stressed the need for "self censorship" for the new company to succeed.[62] On June 1, 2002, the renamed TVS, owned by Media-Socium, began broadcasting on channel six.[63]

CONCLUSION

In the wake of the tragedy of September 11, President Putin made a powerful pro-Western move. He joined ranks with the United States in its struggle against terrorism because he saw it as a chance to integrate Russia in the Western community of states. This was a shrewd analysis and a brave and decisive move. To lean westward, Putin cut against the interests and inclinations of some of his most important supporters within Russia.[64]

Unfortunately, there appears to be no causal relationship between Putin's new Western tilt in foreign policy and his democratic practices at home. The campaign against NTV and then TV-6 are not isolated incidences. Even after September 11, the Russian state has continued to squelch critical voices and undermine democratic practices.

Russia, nonetheless, still has media outlets that are not controlled by the state. Smaller cable television networks, though mostly devoid of political content, are still in operation, and regional television networks have begun to sprout. In Moscow, several privately owned newspapers are in circulation, private radio stations are in business, and a small number of private political websites are still in operation.[65] *Ekho Moskvy* continues to broadcast, even if the status of the station is still precarious. The ousted staff of *Itogi* has reorganized and secured funding to publish a new weekly magazine, *Ezhenedel'ny Zhurnal*. The new weekly's first issue was published in January 2002. Yet, after the dismantling of the Media-MOST empire, the takeover of NTV, and the dissolution of TV-6, the balance between state media and private media has become clearly skewed in favor of the government. After all, 90 percent of Russian citizens reported in a poll conducted last year that their main source of political news was television, and today all television channels with a national reach are under varying degrees of government control.[66] The Kremlin's success, albeit after a protracted struggle, in shutting down critical media outlets at the national level may embolden regional heads to take the same action against regional media critics, who are already small in number and weak in resources.[67] Another consequence of the campaign against Media-MOST, NTV, and TV-6 is self-censorship. Journalists and political commentators realize that there are real risks in going too far in criticizing the government. Some have decided to quit the profession altogether.

The blow to Russian democracy more generally cannot be underestimated. Competitive elections cannot occur without a pluralist and independent press. Corruption cannot be fought without a free press. Elected government officials cannot be held accountable to their constituents without a free press. And ultimately, Russia cannot become a normal European country without a free press. Putin continues to believe that these developments at home do not impact his foreign policy mission abroad. He has stated numerous times that he wants to see Russia become a full member of Western institutions, such as the G8, NATO, and the European Union. These organizations, however, do not accept applications from nondemocracies.

Is there a future for independent media in Russia? Of course. Most important, a robust economy with a growing middle class will create propitious conditions for the emergence of new, privately owned media companies. Without question, NTV's financial problems, especially after the August 1998 financial crash, made the company more vulnerable. The next NTV-like project will have a greater chance to succeed when profits can be made and sustained in a more vibrant economy.[68]

However, a growing economy and a better business plan will not be enough. The destruction of Media-MOST revealed several other conditions necessary for a free press in Russia. First, Russia also must develop an independent and uncorrupt judiciary that can defend not only state interests but minority shareholders rights as well. When push finally came to shove, Gusinsky and his colleagues had no legal means to defend their interests within

Russia because no court would stand up to the pressure of the state. In even starker fashion, the same was true for TV-6.

Second, at least in the near future, an independent media in Russia can only develop if the leadership in the Kremlin believes in the norms of free press and democracy more generally. For the foreseeable future, the state will continue to have enormous power over private, societal activity in Russia. The state, therefore, must be supportive or at least indifferent toward the development of independent media. In the wake of Putin's latest campaign, Gorbachev's tolerance of and Yeltsin's commitment to an independent media is striking. Putin continues to aver publicly his support for a free press. He also has stated repeatedly that the people of Russia must learn to live without relying on the state. In most sectors of the economy, he is a believer in the market and the individual. Yet, when it comes to the media, he continues to promote a larger, not smaller, role for the state. His lack of press conferences and his comparison of journalists to intelligence officers also underscore his ignorance of the role that a free press plays in a democratic polity.

Third, an independent press in Russia needs popular support. In a poll conducted in 2000, an overwhelming number of Russian voters—79 percent—answered that they considered freedom of the press to be important.[69] Yet, few of these supporters of a free press believed that destruction of Media-MOST was such an issue.[70] A large plurality showed indifference to the campaign against TV-6. A solid 39 percent understood that the campaign against TV-6 was political, yet they did not seem to be bothered by that fact.[71] In fact, an amazing 70 percent of respondents in this same poll believed that Putin was an advocate of democratic change.[72] These struggles were understood, following the Kremlin spin, as either a business dispute or a battle between a corrupt oligarch and the state, whose leader, Putin, still enjoyed amazingly positive approval ratings.

Gusinsky, of course, is no Andrey Sakharov. Like all other oligarchs in post-communist Russia, he most likely bent the rules and relied on rents from the state (the Moscow city government) to amass his fortunes. But Gusinsky's media empire was not destroyed because of past improprieties. Until Russian society values and is willing to defend an independent press as a basic institution of democracy, future media critics of the state will find it difficult to stay in operation. Until then, Putin will continue to consolidate his "managed democracy." Elections will occur, multiple parties will compete for office, and several television channels will broadcast separate news programs, but real societal control over the state will remain minimal.

NOTES

A portion of this chapter originally appeared as "'Managed Democracy' in Russia: Putin and the Press," *Harvard International Journal of Press/Politics* 6, no. 3 (Summer 2001): 117–28.

1. For relatively similar assessments from a set of analysts that has often disagreed about the Russian economy, see Jacque Sapir, "The Russian Economy: From Rebound to Rebuilding," *Post-Soviet Affairs* 17, no. 1 (2002): 1–22; James Millar, "The Russian Economy: Putin's Pause," *Current History* 100, no. 648 (October 2001): 336–42; and Anders Aslund, *Building Capitalism: The Transformation of the Soviet Bloc* (Cambridge: Cambridge University Press, 2001).

2. In January 2002, the Center for the Study of Public Opinion (VTsIOM) asked Russians if they fully approved or disapproved of the president's activities. Seventy-five percent fully approved. Throughout 2001, Putin averaged this same level of approval. See www.polit.ru/printable/4699009.html.

3. On the weakness of Russian liberal institutions, see chapter nine of Michael McFaul, *Russia's Unfinished Revolution: Political Change from Gorbachev to Putin* (Ithaca, N.Y.: Cornell University Press, 2001).

4. For overviews, see Michael McFaul, "The Power of Putin," *Current History* (October 2000): 307–14; and "Russia Under Putin: One Step Forward, Two Steps Backward," *Journal of Democracy* 11, no. 3 (July 2000): 19–33.

5. Human Rights Watch has doggedly documented these human rights violations. See their publications, "Now Happiness Remains: Civilian Killings, Pillage, and Rape in Alkhan-Yurt, Chechnya," *Russia/Chechnya* 12, no. 5D (April 2000): 1–33; "February 5: A Day of Slaughter in Novye Aldi," *Russia/Chechnya* 12, no. 9D (June 2000): 1–43; "The 'Dirty War' in Chechnya: Forced Disappearances, Torture, and Summary Executions," *Russia* 13, no. 1D (March 2001): 1–42; "Burying the Evidence: The Botched Investigation into a Mass Grave in Chechnya," *Russia/Chechnya* 13, no. 3D (May 2001): 1–26; and *Welcome to Hell: Arbitrary Detention, Torture, and Extortion in Chechnya* (New York: Human Rights Watch, 2000).

6. This figure is cited in Sarah Mendelson, "Russia, Chechnya, and International Norms: The Power and Paucity of Human Rights?" *NCEEER Working Paper*, July 17, 2001, 11.

7. The successful appeal of treason charges against the environmental activist, Aleksandr Nikitin, fueled hope that the courts were becoming more autonomous. Nikitin himself was optimistic. Nikitin's release, however, was followed by the conviction of Grigory Pas'ko, a journalist accused of treason for publishing in the Japanese press information about the dangerous dumping of nuclear waste by Russian nuclear submarines.

8. Timothy J. Colton and Michael McFaul, "Reinventing Russia's Party of Power: "Unity and the 1999 Duma Election," *Post-Soviet Affairs* 16, no. 3 (Summer 2000): 201–24.

9. On the battles between these parties, see Michael McFaul, Nikolai Petrov, and Andrei Ryabov, eds., *Rossiya v izbiratel'nom tsikle 1999–2000 godov* (Moscow: Moscow Carnegie Center, 2000); and Michael McFaul, "Russia's 1999 Parliamentary Elections: Party Consolidation and Fragmentation," *Demokratizatsiya* 8, no. 1 (Winter 2000): 5–23.

10. Eugene Huskey, "Political Leadership and the Center–Periphery Struggle: Putin's Administrative Reforms," in *Gorbachev, Yeltsin & Putin: Political Leadership in Russia's Transition*, ed. Archie Brown and Lilia Shevtsova (Washington, D.C.: Carnegie Endowment for International Peace, 2001), 113–42.

11. If progressive in spirit, the actual practice of legal reform has been strikingly disappointing. Under Putin, the role of the prosecutor's office has grown tremendously. Putin's administration has relied heavily on this office to threaten and eliminate adversaries.

12. Adam Przeworski, Michael Alvarez, Jose Antonio Cheibub, and Fernando Limongi, *Democracy and Development: Political Institutions and Well-Being in the World, 1950–1990* (Cambridge: Cambridge University Press, 2000).

13. David Hoffman, *The Oligarchs: Wealth and Power in the New Russia* (New York, Public Affairs, 2002).

14. On the emergence of civil society in the USSR, see M. Steven Fish, *Democracy from Scratch* (Princeton, N.J.: Princeton University Press, 1993); and Geoffrey Hosking, *The Awakening of the Soviet Union* (Cambridge, Mass.: Harvard University Press, 1991).

15. Control over television was such a major issue for Russia's anticommunist forces before the collapse of the Soviet Union. One of the biggest demonstrations in downtown Moscow in 1991 was devoted to demanding a Russian television station. On Yeltsin's efforts to gain control of RTR, the Russian station, see Ellen Mickiewicz, *Changing Channels: Television and the Struggle for Power in Russia* (Oxford: Oxford University Press, 1997), 92–97.

16. Some political parties had their own newspapers and a few small newspapers associated with human rights organizations published newspapers and newsletters with support from Western foundations. But the circulation of these kinds of publications was a tiny fraction of the state-controlled newspapers.

17. Michael McFaul, *Russia's 1996 Presidential Election: The End of Polarized Politics* (Stanford: Hoover Institution Press, 1997).

18. Mickiewicz, Changing Channels.

19. On the channel's creation, see the detailed account in chapter seven of Hoffman, *The Oligarchs*.

20. Floriana Fossato, "Russia: Changes Sweep Through Two TV Networks," *RFE/RL*, November 5, 1997.

21. The Russian Public Television (ORT) gained control of the first national television channel in Russian through a presidential decree (no. 2133) on November 29, 1994, and began broadcasting on April 1, 1995. In the company's charter, fourteen organizations are listed as shareholders, including state institutions such as the State Property Committee of Russia, the Ostankino Russian State Television, and Radio Broadcasting Corporation, as well as private companies such as Menatep, National Kredit, and Stolychny banks; Gazprom; and Berezovsky's own company Logovaz. See *Russian Public Television: Collection of Constituent Documents* (Moscow: ORT, 1995), 18. The private companies that purchased 49 percent of the new company faced no competition for their purchase. Logovaz owned 8 percent of the shares, while the share of the state owners totaled more than 50 percent. Nonetheless, Berezovsky used side payments and bribe to gain control of the company's operations and editorial policy. See Paul Klebnikov, *Godfather of the Kremlin: Boris Berezovsky and the Looting of Russia* (New York: Harcourt, 2000), 159–61.

22. Mark Whitehouse, "Buying the Media: Who's Behind the Written Word?" *Russia Review* (April 21, 1997): 26–27; and Oleg Medvedev and Sergei Sinchenko,

"The Fourth Estate—Chained to Banks," *Business in Russia*, no. 78 (June 1997): 38–43.

23. On the distorting influences of private ownership on editorial lines, see Laura Belin, "Political Bias and Self-Censorship in the Russian Media," in *Contemporary Russian Politics: A Reader*, ed. Archie Brown (Oxford: Oxford University Press, 2001), 323–44.

24. Hoffman, *The Oligarchs*.

25. In Protocol 3, signed by Gusinsky and Gazprom-Media General Director Alfred Kokh on July 20, 2001, to authorize the transfer of Gusinsky's assets to Gazprom-Media (a protocol that Gusinsky later renounced), six different companies   CS First Boston, Gazprom, Gazprombank, the city of Moscow, Vneshtorbank, and Eksimbank B are listed as creditors. An initial CS-First Boston loan of $211 million, due in March 2000, was taken over by Gazprom when Gusinsky failed to pay. The next CS-First Boston debt for $262 million was due in July 2001. The other non-Gazprom debts are not due until 2003 and 2009 respectively.

26. Celestine Bohlen, "Defining a Free Press: The Unique Evolution of Russian TV," *New York Times*, April 29, 2001, section four, 4.

27. Gusinsky had wanted to secure foreign investors long before, which is why Capital Research was given an equity stake in his company.

28. Andrew Higgins, "Turner Sets Investment in Russia's Media-MOST," *Wall Street Journal*, January 22, 2001, A16.

29. Anatol Lieven, *Chechnya: Tombstone of Russian Power* (New Haven, Conn.: Yale University Press, 1998); and John Dunlop, *Russian Confronts Chechnya: Roots of a Separatist Conflict* (Cambridge: Cambridge University Press, 1998).

30. Fond obshchestvennoe mnenie (FOM), as quoted in *Segodnya*, January 28, 1995, 3. These numbers remained constant throughout the war. A fall 1995 poll conducted by FOM revealed that only 10 percent of the population supported the intervention, while 69 percent opposed. Fond "Obshchestvennoe mnenie," *Obshchestvennoe mnenie nakanune vyborov-95*, 3 (Moscow: October 25, 1995), 15.

31. Vserossiiskii Tsentr Izucheniya Obshchestvennogo Mneniya (VTsIOM) poll, as quoted in *Segodnya*, January 17, 1995, 2.

32. McFaul, *Russia's 1996 Presidential Election*.

33. In frequent interaction with Russian journalists during the 1996 campaign, the authors heard this justification.

34. Like Gazprom, Svyazinvest had been created from hundreds of smaller entities to make it a viable private entity. It is the largest telecommunications company in Russia.

35. Chrystia Freeland, *Sale of the Century: Russia's Wild Ride from Communism to Capitalism* (New York: Crown Business, 2000); Hoffman, *The Oligarchs*, 433.

36. Hoffman, *The Oligarchs*, 437.

37. For details of the campaign, see Hoffman, *The Oligarchs*, 439–42.

38. The $450,000 was leftover funds from the 1996 campaign. The book contracts were a way to launder the money back to those who had been involved in the campaign. Chubais admitted to the scheme.

39. Vladimir Gusinsky, address at the National Press Club, Washington, D.C., May 3, 2001.

40. The speech can be found at www.president.kremlin.ru/events/200007.html.

41. *Kommersant*, March 10, 2000.

42. See his even more emotional statements quoted in *Kommersant-Vlast'*, no. 34, August 29, 2000.

43. NTV officials even dispute the company's alleged financial problems. See Chris Renaud, Finance and Strategic Director, Media-MOST, "NTV Had No Financial Crisis," *Wall Street Journal Europe*, April 30, 2001.

44. Putin, in Germany at the time, claimed that he could not reach his chief prosecutor on the phone and argued that the prosecutors were acting independently of the state. Yet, in a press conference, he displayed perfect knowledge of Gusinsky's credit history, exposing how intimately he was involved with the case.

45. *Kommersant-Vlast'*, April 10, 2001.

46. Kokh eventually resigned and Jordan replaced him. Jordan stated that his main objective as the new director was to prepare the Gazprom's media assets for sale. See Andrei Zolotov, "Jordan, Dybal to Organize NTV Sell-Off," *St. Petersburg Times*, October 30, 2001.

47. Floriana Fossato, "The Russian Media: From Popularity to Distrust," *Current History* 100, no. 648 (October 2001): 343.

48. On certain issues such as Chechnya, the new NTV has provided more critical coverage of the Russian government than ORT or RTR, but the channel in no way resembles the old editorial line or qualitative journalism of the old NTV. See Peter Baker, "On NTV, Kremlin Is in Softer Focus," *Washington Post*, June 27, 2001, A18.

49. At the time of this writing, *Ekho Moskvy* remains independent and on the air but fully at the mercy of Gazprom and its head Boris Jordan. In the meantime, the *Ekho Moskvy* team won a bid for a new frequency. Their victory was seen as an unexpected concession made by the Kremlin as a minor compensation for more important crackdowns on media freedom, such as the closure of TV-6 that took place shortly thereafter. The head of *Ekho Moskvy*, Aleksei Venediktov, claims that his team would quit *Ekho Moskvy* and move to the new frequency as soon as Gazprom-Media has effectively taken over.

50. *Moscow Times*, April 10, 2001, 3.

51. Interview with Boris Berezovsky in *Gazeta Daily*, January 31, 2002, 3, translated and distributed by the *Federal News Service*. Later, Berezovsky produced an investigative documentary shot by French journalists who put together evidence that the Russian Federal Security Service (FSB) was involved in the terrorist attacks of September 1999. The movie was shown in the West, and even though copies of it were brought to Moscow all national TV channels refused to show it. See Patrick Tyler, "Russian Tycoon's Bombshell: Can It Be?" *New York Times*, February 13, 2002, A12.

52. Again, like the NTV assault, Putin himself was not personally involved. Yet, Putin had met with the CEO of Lukoil, Vagit Alekperov, shortly before the case was filed. Given the magnitude of the case, it is hard to believe that the two did not discuss the issue.

53. "Press Conference with TV-6 Director General Yevgeny Kiselyov," Radisson Slavjanskaya Hotel, November 27, 2001, translated transcript provided by *Federal News Service*.

54. When asked about their reactions to the closing of TV-6, the biggest segment of the population—38 percent—expressed no emotion one way or another. See the VTsIOM poll results from January 25–28, 2002, as published at www.polit.ru/print-able/469009.html.

55. Sharon LaFraniere, "TV Station Spared Closure in Russia," *Washington Post*, December 30, 2001, A22.

56. Quoted in "Russian TV Station Ordered to Close," *Associated Press*, January 11, 2002. U.S. Ambassador to Russia, Alexander Vershbow, also spoke out in defense of TV-6. See "US Ambassador Concerned at TV's Independent Fate in Russia," *Interfax*, December 3, 2001.

57. "Interview with Boris Berezovsky," *Izvestya*, January 9, 2002, 1–2; quoted here from the translated transcript provided by the *Federal News Service*. See also "Kiselev zayavlaet o gotovnosti TV-6 k kompromissu s vlast'u," *Interfax*, January 8, 2001.

58. "Berezovskii nameren otstaivat' YV-6 v Konstitytsionnom sude," at www .ng.ru (accessed January 11, 2002).

59. "High Arbitration Court Rules That TV-6 Must Be Liquidated," *MonitorCA Daily Briefing on the Former Soviet States 7*, no. 8 (January 11, 2002).

60. Sabrina Tavernise, "Russia's Regional TV Stations Suffer as Nationwide Broadcaster Stays Dark, *New York Times*, January 28, 2002.

61. See Virginie Colloudon, "Plus Ça Change," and Laura Belin, "Has Kiselev Stepped on the Same Rake?" in *RFE/RL Political Weekly* 2, no. 10 (April 2, 2002).

62. Ivan Chelnok, "Self-Censorship to Contribute to Democracy," *Gazeta.ru*, March 29, 2002.

63. Michael McFaul, "Putin's Risky Westward Turn," *Christian Science Monitor*, November 9, 2001.

64. For details on these groups, see Michael McFaul, "U.S.-Russian Relations After September 11th," testimony before the subcommittee on Europe of the House Committee on International Affairs, February 27, 2002.

65. Even the Internet is being reined in. Using complicated licensing procedures, the Russian state has threatened to close Internet access providers that support websites critical of the government. For example, Rostelecom, a company in which the state is the largest shareholder, temporarily shut down Memonet, an Internet provider to the popular political websites Inopressa.ru and NTV.ru. At the same time, the Russian government plans to build a $200-million Internet portal, Electronic Russia, to provide "proper" information about Russia.

66. The poll was conducted by Timothy Colton and Michael McFaul, in cooperation with DEMISCOPE. A total of 1,919 voters were interviewed between November 13 and December 13, and 1,842 of them were reinterviewed after the Duma election, between December 25 and January 31. A third wave, reinterviewing 1,748 first- and second-wave respondents, was completed in April–May 2000, soon after the March 2000 presidential election.

67. In the provinces, the methods of submission are much rawer; flagrant violations of the law more common. In January 2002, for instance, in Lipetsk, a group acting allegedly with the blessing of the governor simply seized the assets of a local television station. They met no resistance. On the struggle of others, see Sabrina Tav-

ernise, "In Siberia, Serious TV News Fights to Survive," *New York Times*, March 4, 2002.

68. Video International's monopoly over the advertising market in Russia will also have to be loosened, but this too can happen with real, sustained economic growth.

69. See the chapter by Timothy J. Colton and Michael McFaul in this book.

70. *Strana.ru*, April 27, 2001.

71. Office of Research, Department of States, "Russian Not Alarmed by Threats to Free Speech," No. M-2-02, January 8, 2002.

72. See the VTsIOM poll results from January 25–28, 2002, as published at www .polit.ru/printable/469009.html.

Chapter Five

Putin's Anticorruption Reforms

Virginie Coulloudon

From the end of World War II until the late 1980s, Soviet lawyers, investigators, and prosecutors have repeatedly exposed political and economic corruption in the Soviet Union, characterizing it as a disease linked to the nature of the communist system. Corruption, as they pointed out, was a highly political issue, not mere bureaucratic deviance, and eradication of this "infectious epidemic" was impossible under a single-party regime. The fact that these experts themselves were arrested by Soviet authorities and consequently exiled as dissidents was a testament to the accuracy of their observations.[1] While the Communist Party of the Soviet Union (CPSU) was in power, Western Sovietologists and Soviet dissidents tended to consider the "disease" of corruption a temporary pathology caused by society's difficulty in accepting the overwhelming role of the party in their lives. Interestingly enough, both dissidents and Soviet officials believed that reform of the state apparatus was enough to eliminate corruption.

Despite these expectations, corruption did not disappear together with the Soviet regime. Neither was the August 1991 coup a turning point for systems of patronage. On the contrary, collusion between the public and private spheres has continued to grow and has become one of the major issues in post-Soviet political and economic development. Today's Russian political leadership proclaims that it has become a vital priority to "clean" the state from "corrupt" elements, and state officials, together with Vladimir Putin, have adopted the well-known terminology of "active offensive on crime" and "onslaught on corruption."[2] Eradication of corruption is now on the agenda of leaders from all the parties in the political spectrum. Yet, instead of opening a debate and reflecting on the different forms and functions of contemporary corruption, Russian officials focus mostly on individuals, using anticorruption campaigns as political weapons, and failing to build a consensus on this sensitive issue.

Since Vladimir Putin became president, there has been great skepticism concerning his willingness to fight crime. Does Putin truly mean what he says? What is his personal motivation? Is he really trying to establish the rule of law, or is he more concerned with eliminating political opponents and winning popular support? "Corruption serves as a convenient brush with which to tar opponents," writes one critic. "When it suits the state, guilt can be manufactured on demand."[3] Such skepticism is, of course, the result of Putin's professional background and the negative perception many in the West have of the former KGB officer. Is Putin really "Mr. Clean?" Many observers seem to doubt it.[4] How will Putin be able to balance between promises to establish the rule of law, without undermining his own allies? At first glance, it seems that legal charges, audits, and arrests under Putin have been extremely selective, with law enforcement clearly targeting the media and the diamond industry.[5] However, a closer analysis of Putin's struggle against endemic corruption, as well as that of his predecessors, show that there has been little difference between his initiatives and those of earlier Soviet and post-Soviet leaders.

This chapter examines three different types of anticorruption campaigns launched by the federal authorities under Yeltsin and Putin, and highlights the sequence of these campaigns. It also exposes the negative consequences of these anticorruption campaigns, which were implemented without prior debate. It shows the discrepancy that exists between the structural causes of corruption and the political incentives of most anticorruption campaigns. This discrepancy has progressively distorted the nature of these crusades and tarnished the image of the state, including its leaders. In addition, this chapter examines judicial reform in Russia and discusses to what degree it is an efficient tool to fight corruption in its current incarnation.

THE MULTIFACETED
ANTICORRUPTION CAMPAIGN

Anticorruption campaigns are far from a new phenomenon. In prerevolutionary Russia, they were aimed primarily at high-ranking corrupt officials who had exceeded their power. Under the Soviet regime, Stalin, too, charged several officials of bureaucratic malfeasance, embezzlement, and bribery. These campaigns were traditionally directed against a handful of individuals who were accused of misusing their positions. They helped preserve the apparent morality of the czarist court and of Bolshevik ideology, and therefore kept the system intact. They also provided for a kind of balance within the system: they maintained the existing hierarchy and distribution of power within the state and party, while they prevented high-ranking officials from overindulging in bribes or, as was said in Russia, from "taking more than befitted their rank."[6]

In the late 1970s, while at the head of the powerful KGB, Yuri Andropov appeared to be the first high-ranking official seriously interested in launching a large-scale anticorruption campaign. Since then, all successive Russian top leaders have systematically adopted "the struggle against corruption" as a political instrument, although their reasons have differed. The three key motivations are (1) the struggle for power, (2) the need to build an image of incorruptibility or "a clean state," and (3) the need to restructure the state and launch a reform strategy.

Putin faces a critical challenge in maintaining a firm grip on power while he pursues a strident anticorruption initiative. However, as this chapter will show, his efforts do not mark a major break with the past. Surprisingly enough, since Andropov, all Russian leaders have launched these three types of anticorruption campaigns in identical order and have relied on the same sequence of incentives to justify them. In so doing, they have developed a particular style of governance that has been unchanged for the last thirty years, encompassing both Soviet and post-Soviet Russia. Putin, since he came to power as head of the Federal Secret Service (FSB, the successor to the KGB), then prime minister and acting president, also used anticorruption campaigns for the same reasons.

The Struggle for Power

For the past thirty years, anticorruption campaigns have been used in Russia both to gain and to preserve political power. Opponents and newly elected heads of state have resorted to gathering compromising material, and even to falsifying evidence, in order to tarnish the image of their political opponents.

Under CPSU General Secretary Leonid Brezhnev, corruption was a direct consequence of the centralized and planned economy and of the systematic shortage of raw materials and goods that resulted from it. Lacking raw materials, cement, or any other essential good gave industrial managers no choice but to buy them on the black market in order to meet plan targets set by the State Planning Ministry (GOSPLAN). The black market demanded cash, and in a noncash economy, the only way to obtain hard currency was by falsifying data[7] or paying real salaries to fictitious workers or "dead souls." It also meant bribing the political leadership to avoid government audits and to negotiate better resource allocation. Such a system of organized corruption was often perceived by Soviet industrialists and the political elite as a consequence of the planned economy and the concomitant absence of market economy and of private property.[8]

Soviet industrialists often distinguished between corruption undertaken to meet plan targets, which involved deliberate transgression of laws, and corruption for personal gain. The actors themselves created a sharp divide between rule evasion and bribery undertaken to ensure the survival of a plant, on the one hand, and self-enrichment on the other. Workers, in turn, often forgave self-enrichment when economic results were satisfactory. In such a context, corrupt industrial managers felt no remorse for their behavior, although they were perfectly aware that it was illegal. If they knew that they were breaking the law, they also believed their actions to be within the framework of what they understood as the norm, in compliance with party discipline and the people's interests.

The Soviet Union constituted one colossal public sector and, because access to those resources was not regulated by legislation, any civil servant or party official—just by doing his or her job—was engaging in, and could be accused of, corruption. But not everyone was pilloried and, even if they were, not all accusations of corruption were treated the same way. The difference lay in the discretionary power of the authorities. Andropov, for example, eager to reimpose discipline within the party structures, resorted to fear and intimidation. In the process, he also got rid of political opponents and strengthened his own team.

Relying on the power of the KGB and his own network of protégés, Andropov collected compromising materials that showed how high-ranking officials were involved in gift giving. But not all were accused of misusing their power and overindulging in bribes. Andropov launched a large-scale anticorruption campaign that led to the arrest and trials of numerous regional CPSU first secretaries, as well as Interior Ministry officials, all tied to General Secretary Leonid Brezhnev, including his son-in-law. As it turned out, all those arrested were politically close to Brezhnev. Conversely, those officials who helped Andropov gained in political clout within the almighty Politburo. Among Andropov's protégés were Mikhail Gorbachev, who would later become CPSU general secretary, then president of the Soviet Union; Eduard Shevardnadze, currently president of Georgia; and Heydar Aliyev, currently president of Azerbaijan.

Does this mean that Andropov's people were "clean" and had managed to make a brilliant career without belonging to corrupt networks? Considering that they came to professional maturity in the Soviet system, it would be hard to conclude that they had never played according to the rules of gift giving and rule evasion. However, Andropov's anticorruption campaign served as a vehicle for his acquisition and consolidation of political power, as witnessed by his 1982 appointment as general secretary after Brezhnev died. Furthermore, Andropov's rise to power marked a shift in the usual paths for a political career. Andropov maintained patronage networks, but demonstrated that the "struggle against corruption" could be part of a political strategy to destroy the client-patron alliances of his opponents.

All politicians since Andropov have repeated this pattern as part of their effort to seize power. Although not all of these campaigns were as successful as Andropov's, they have nonetheless become a widespread political instrument in Russia. Yeltsin relied on the team of special investigators headed by Telman Gdlyan and Nikolai Ivanov to collect compromising information on Gorbachev, Politburo member Yegor Ligachev, and other major political figures at the union level.[9] Similarly, in post-Soviet Russia, most of Yeltsin's opponents resorted to accusations of corruption to discredit the head of state and his entourage in the hope that this would help undermine Yeltsin's regime.[10]

Interestingly enough, with the exception of Brezhnev, who did not realize that his power was being eroded by Andropov's campaigns and was physically too weak to impose a strategy of defense on his own team, all Soviet and Russian leaders who were accused of corruption responded with the same weapon. These countercampaigns had a twofold objective: First, they were undoubtedly meant to eliminate political rivals and potential contenders. Second, they contributed to demonstrating the strength of the ruling team and consolidating the elite in power.[11]

During his tenure as head of the FSB, while he was working in Yeltsin's administration, Putin too relied on the rhetoric of anticorruption policy to protect Yeltsin's family members and close associates involved in various scandals.[12] During one corruption scandal, known as the Mabetex affair,[13] he openly sided with the main protagonist, Pavel Borodin, who had brought him into the Kremlin in 1988. Mabetex was a Swiss-based contracting company,[14] which was selected to renovate the White House, the former headquarters of the Russian Supreme Soviet, after the bloody events of October 1993. Under another contract, Mabetex was entrusted with the renovation of Yeltsin's apartment in the Kremlin. Mabetex vice president Viktor Stolpovskikh was also the head of Mercata, the contracting company that would later transform the Russian president's *Ilyushin* jet into a flying hospital.[15] Backed by Prime Minister Yevgeny Primakov, General Prosecutor Yuri Skuratov accused the head of the Kremlin chancellery, Borodin, a man close to Yeltsin, of insider dealings and misappropriation of public funds.[16] Since then, former prosecutor General Yurii Skuratov has repeatedly argued that Putin had been chosen as Boris Yeltsin's heir precisely because he had represented no threat to Yeltsin's patronage networks. He has maintained that Putin's appointment demonstrates a lack of political will at the top echelons of power to combat corruption. Skuratov's statements seemed to be confirmed by the Kremlin's behavior during the presidential campaign. When the presidential administration felt politically threatened by Luzhkov's political ambitions, Putin asked for a financial and tax audit of Inteko, a company run by Luzhkov's wife, Yelena Baturina. This operation resulted in accusations of embezzlement and tax evasion, putting Luzhkov, then a potential contender in the 2000 presidential election, in a difficult position.

Although this pattern was obviously inefficient and most of these politically motivated campaigns eventually fell through, Putin fell into the same trap. For example, Putin answered the "war of *kompromat*" (compromising material) and the attacks from the Media-MOST holding company, which had financed the electoral campaigns of both Moscow Mayor Yuri Luzhkov and parliamentary leader Grigoriy Yavlinskiy, by releasing compromising material aimed at Media-MOST. Four days after Putin was sworn in, the FSB and the tax police raided the headquarters of the Media-MOST Group, Russia's biggest media holding, headed by Vladmir Gusinsky.[17] The Kremlin justified its decision to crack down on one of the most powerful oligarchs by claiming that Media-MOST was suspected of tax evasion. The raid was reportedly successful: not only did the FSB announce it had found evidence of tax irregularities, but law enforcement agencies also claimed that they had discovered eavesdropping devices that Gusinsky and his associates were allegedly using against the government. Not surprisingly, Media-MOST denied the Kremlin's allegations and argued that the raid was "politically motivated."[18] Eventually, Gusinsky also was cleared of all charges. He immigrated to Spain and sold his shares in Media-MOST.

To be sure, during his electoral campaign, Putin had repeatedly promised to free Russia from the power of the oligarchs. In January 2000, the presidential administration had even proposed to set up a new agency to combat corruption.[19] But as we have just seen, the Kremlin was then preparing for a presidential election by launching a campaign against corruption aimed at shaping a "clean" image for the new team in power while eliminating potential political rivals.

Building an Image of Incorruptibility

Once having won elections and undermined the credibility of their rivals, Russian leaders have relied on the same instrument of anticorruption campaigns to distinguish themselves from their predecessors and forge an image of cleanness and incorruptibility, in an effort to secure political support from the part of the population.

During his tenure as head of the FSB, Vladimir Putin made the struggle against corruption one of his favorite themes. He upgraded the FSB Economic Security Department by creating new subdepartments responsible for the security of industrial and transport facilities, for the banking sector, and for the struggle against smuggling and drug trafficking. In November 1999, during his tenure as prime minister, Putin announced that the Interior Ministry would lead a consortium of law enforcement agencies in a battle to reduce the shadow economy, end capital flight, and prevent criminal groups from penetrating the government.[20] However, none of these moves helped him build an image of probity, neither for the Yeltsin regime nor for himself. In

December 1999, when Putin became acting president following Yeltsin's resignation, public opinion focused more on his decree guaranteeing "immunity from criminal and/or administrative prosecution" and "lifetime full
security services" to Yeltsin and his family than on the anticorruption measures he had adopted previously.[21]

After the presidential election, in March 2000, anticorruption campaigns
continued to be used as a political instrument to build an image of incorruptibility while, at the same time, to get rid of political opponents. The most
visible and widely publicized aspect of Putin's anticorruption reform was his
crackdown on the oligarchs and regional governors—it was selective, calculated, and highly profiled. In waging a war against these powerful figures,
Putin seemed to be in a win-win situation: this cause found great support on
the part of Russian public opinion and Putin consolidated his power while
getting rid of political opponents.[22] Reactions in the West have reflected the
inherent confusion over the Kremlin anticorruption campaigns. On the one
hand, international lending institutions, frustrated with Russia's cronyism,
applauded the Kremlin's anticorruption efforts and its claim that the "dictatorship of law" in Russia was in the interest of the U.S. and other Western
powers. On the other hand, following the arrest of press magnate Vladimir
Gusinsky, the U.S. House of Representatives adopted a resolution criticizing
Putin for his crackdown on the media.[23]

While trying to clean up the image of his regime, Putin's team has failed to
launch a genuine debate on the structural causes of corruption. Systematically
referring to a far too vague concept—corruption—and targeting anticorruption campaigns against immediate political opponents have aggravated the
political risk of looking just like the old state.

Restructuring the State

The third type of anticorruption campaign is focused toward bureaucracy and
the reorganization of state structures, a common goal of all newly elected
rulers. In this regard, Putin was no exception. Soon after he became president, the chairman of the Anticorruption Commission of the State Duma,
former Interior Minister Sergei Stepashin, developed the following seven-
step agenda to fight against corruption and economic crime. At the same
time, Stepashin claimed that his program was genuinely aimed at restructuring the state and reforming the bureaucracy:[24]

1. Reform of government finance:
   a. New budget code "based on transparency of all financial flows in the
      country"
   b. Open budget hearings on both the federal and regional levels
   c. Reform and audits of the state purchasing system

    d. Tax reform: better tax administration, equal enforcement, elimination of arrears

    e. Attack corruption in privatization (but not deprivatization)

    f. Information transparency

2. State administrative reform

    a. Better checking of qualifications for officeholders

    b. Regular rotation of officials into new positions

    c. Disclosure of financial interests

    d. Reduced bureaucracy

    e. Improved pay to prevent corruption

3. Deal with monopolies

    a. Introduce competition

    b. Examine monopolies in energy, the telephone system, state banking services

    c. Improve financial reporting and management accountability

4. Reduce economic regulations and barriers to the market

    a. Limit regulations and authority of controlling entities where they exist simply to solicit bribes

    b. Streamline documentation and paperwork

    c. Assure consumer rights

    d. Improve the judicial system

5. Support for civil institutions

    a. Anticorruption campaign in the media

    b. Support for journalists who uncover crimes

    c. Legal education of the population

6. Support for reform in the private sector

    a. Business code and ethics

    b. Procedures for financial reporting

7. Legislative reform of the law enforcement agencies

    a. Study and change laws that may encourage corruption

    b. Modernize the agencies in terms of technology and personnel, to expand expertise

    c. Stop the use of state funds in private financial organizations

    d. Create law on international cooperation for purposes of investigation and extradition

On paper, this reform appears to be indeed structural and aims at improving the state decisionmaking process. However, the way the reform has been carried out confirms a tendency to implement short-term political strategies, which are aimed at individuals.

    A few months after this reform was made public, Stepashin again used the pretext of reinstalling order and discipline to regain control over some of the key corporations, such as the electricity monopoly UES (Unified Energy System) or the gas monopoly Gazprom. He then declared that the audit of UES had showed "serious problems related to the privatization process." To be sure, Stepashin immediately added that his institution planned to closely examine the audit before officially referring it to the president. By allowing news agencies to cite him on this particular issue, Stepashin nevertheless demonstrated that the state was still willing to regain control over some strategic enterprises even after Putin met with twenty-one of its representatives and reassured them that the privatization process would not be reexamined.[25]

During the entire summer of 2000, the presidential administration repeatedly referred to systematic tax evasion and bribery to justify the creation of new bureaucratic agencies. In July, it was considering setting up a financial intelligence agency that would monitor all financial flows; in addition, the Kremlin was reportedly working on a decree to give the Federal Tax Police extra powers.[26] The result was to spread fear among businessmen. In an interview published on the eve of the meeting, Unified Energy Systems chief Anatoly Chubais suggested that "medium-sized businesses have been sending alarm signals that are changing into signals of panic."[27]

Likewise, Putin raised the issue of tax evasion on the part of many Russian governors to justify the creation of seven new federal districts. These districts were aimed at reinforcing the presidential administration's control over the 89 regions of the Russian Federation. In July 2000, the Tax Ministry set up interregional audit departments in each of the new districts to monitor the regions' compliance with federal tax law and supervise the activities of the regional tax collecting agencies. Russia's Tax Minister Gennady Bukaev made it clear that none of the current heads of the regional tax departments would be chosen for the job as it would violate the essence of the reform. In other words, the Kremlin suggested that only personnel chosen at a federal level would be able to impose control over the regional branches of the ministry and genuinely struggle against corruption and tax evasion.[28]

Improving the efficiency and the coherence of the state's decisionmaking process, reinforcing discipline among civil servants at both the federal and local levels, and struggling against corruption, more precisely against misappropriation of public funds and tax evasion, were all used as a pretext to reform the state. Interestingly enough, during his presidential campaign, Putin repeatedly stressed that what his country needed most was a "paternalistic leader" and a "vertical state," in which discipline predominated.[29] In so doing, the Kremlin seemed to not realize that centralization of the state's decisionmaking and cadres policy could lead to the establishment of a new patron-client relationship between the Kremlin and some regional governors, thereby maintaining the patronage system.

JUDICIAL REFORM IN RUSSIA

Judicial reform in Russia stands as another example of how the struggle against corruption can be used to implement structural reforms. However, here again, successive failures have tarnished the image of the state in the eyes of the population.

The History of Judicial Reform

As paradoxical as it may appear at first glance, the history of post-Soviet judicial reform began in 1990 when a new group of People's deputies was elected. Independence and sovereignty of the Russian Federation were declared and that included the judicial system. On October 24, 1991, following Yeltsin's initiative, the Supreme Soviet of the Russian Federation, the highest legislative body of the country at that time, approved a program of judicial reform that focused on several crucial decisions: the abolishment of capital punishment for nonviolent crimes[30] and the creation of a constitutional court to balance the power of the executive branch.

The judicial reform was intended to show the Kremlin's political will when it came to democratizing the country. First, Russian citizens were given the right to complain to the court against the decisions and actions by officials they believed to be illegal. Second, in 1992, a law on the status of judges brought structural changes. In the first years of Yeltsin's regime, it was important to promote independence of the judiciary from the political power. Therefore, the Kremlin decided that judges would be appointed for life and made them more independent from the central government. In fact, this decision had the unforeseen consequence of encouraging bribery among judges who were ready to "buy" their appointment (the law was eventually changed in 2001). Also, in 1992, arbitration courts were created, not only to offer a judicial instrument to business, but also to balance conflicts between enterprises and state bodies. Finally, in 1993, international law and provisions of treaties with the participation of Russia and the former Soviet Union were recognized as an essential part of national legislation. Two years later Russia ratified the European Convention on Human Rights and acknowledged the jurisdiction of the European Court located in Strasbourg.

With regard to criminal law, in 1992, every person detained by militia or arrested received the right to appeal to a judge. Then, in 1993, a law was adopted that obliged judges to exclude illegally obtained evidence. Also in 1993, the Supreme Soviet of the Russian Federation approved the Law on Jury Trial despite the Prosecutor General's reluctance. Jury trials were implemented in nine regions of the Russian Federation and took jurisdiction over all cases in regional courts involving criminal cases: murders, terrorism, corruption, bribery, abuse of power, treason, crimes against justice, etc. Since then, jury trials have been involved in approximately 400 cases concerning 850 defendants each year. One interesting statistic is worth noting: in 2000, 16 percent of the defendants pleaded not guilty in jury trials. Before they were implemented, the share of defendants declared innocent used to be less than 0.5 percent.[31]

Today the Russian judiciary consists of three branches: a Constitutional Court with nineteen Constitutional judges; arbitration courts with 2,500 judges; and courts of general jurisdiction with 16,700 judges. This last branch includes the Supreme Court of the Russian Federation, eighty-nine regional courts, approximately 2000 district courts, and 16,700 judges. Eight percent of judges' positions are vacant. More than one third of the Russian judges were at one time either police officers, investigators, or public prosecutors.[32]

Although the steps undertaken in the area of judicial reform may appear impressive at first glance, there is still a lot to do before Russian citizens enjoy a fair, quick, and impartial trial. To make judges genuinely independent from political power, they must, first, receive higher salaries and rely on a transparent budget, and second, free themselves from the pressure court chairmen can exert on them.

While in 2001 the Justice Ministry received only half of its budget from the federal authorities, it was still an improvement, considering that in previous years Russian courts had obtained only one third of their budget. Being unable to count on a predictable budget, Justice Ministry officials could not make allocation decisions until the money was actually in hand. This systematic shortage of financial resources, undoubtedly, leaves room for informal decisionmaking mechanisms and, here again, for corruption of Ministry officials in charge of allocating resources. Besides, regional courts depend more and more on local authorities' willingness to pay for their electricity, furniture, and stationery bills. Such an unstable situation leaves even more room for bribing local authorities susceptible to offer additional nonministerial resources. Although gift giving is forbidden by the Constitution, most of the regional courts depend on their good relationship with local authorities, not only to erase debts, but also to maintain their premises in a decent state. Inevitably, such a situation encourages de facto bribery and patron-client networks.

Corruption is endemic in regional courts. With a monthly salary of approximately US$150, judges cannot afford to be independent, neither from local authorities, nor from court chairmen. Regional court chairmen therefore have tremendous power. For example, they can dismiss judges in their court system. Many of them do it quite arbitrarily and this situation, again, does encourage gift giving and bribery. To balance the court chairmen's authority and to protect their rights, judges are allowed to turn to councils of judges, but here too, corruption often prevails, as court chairmen are the ones who have the last word. In this situation, the last places where judges can turn to avoid corruption networks are human rights associations and NGOs, such as former human rights activist Lev Ponomarev's group, which has organized demonstrations against the unlawful dismissal of many Russian judges.[33]

As a result of the unequal power relationship, which reigns in regional courts and often leads to arbitrary decisions from the part of court chairmen, informal decisionmaking mechanisms continue to play a major role in many cases. In an effort to avoid having their decision overturned, judges maintain informal contacts with individuals such as public prosecutors, court chairmen, and Supreme Court judges. The outcome of criminal cases is often decided informally between the judge and the court chairman, even before the trial starts. This often means that court procedures and process become meaningless. Complaints of professional misconduct by Russian judges have increased from 4,000 in 1995 to 18,000 in 2000. There are three main grounds for these complaints: delays in court proceedings; serious violations of law and human rights; and rudeness.[34]

In his annual address to the nation, Putin proclaimed judicial reform to be a national priority. He said that judicial efficiency was crucial to the smooth development of the economy. And it was the presidential administration itself that turned out to be the most active in drafting reform bills. Dmitri Kozak, deputy head of the presidential administration, created a working group in December 2000, which came up with several draft bills and finally had its reform proposal adopted by the State Duma in November 2001.

The Kozak Team's Reform Proposals

The Kozak team's draft bills were introduced to the public during a conference organized at the Institute of State and Law during the spring of 2001.[35] The "Kozak bills" were also discussed with court officials, law enforcement agencies, some governors and MPs in the State Duma. They are divided into four groups:

1. The first group of bills deals with financing and supplying the courts. The Kremlin plans to raise the notoriously low salaries of judges and carry out a major reconstruction of court buildings throughout the country. The estimated cost is 4 billion rubles (US$138,000,000).

2. The second category aims at maintaining the predominance of federal laws over regional ones. The Constitutional Court has traditionally had the power to decide whether a particular law, adopted at a regional level, violates the federal Constitution. However, local legislative bodies and governors have often ignored its judgments. According to Kozak's plan, from now on, the presidential administration, the federal government, as well as governors must obey the decisions of the Constitutional Court and prepare the neces-

sary draft bills not later than four months after the decision is made public. Regional parliaments (dumas) must adopt these bills in the shortest possible time. The Justice Ministry, together with presidential envoys to the regions, will oversee the efforts to bring regional legislation in line with federal laws.

3. The third list of Kozak's proposals concerns court proceedings. It has a twofold objective: to enlarge the rights of the defense during criminal trials, and to reduce the role of prosecutors in civil cases. One of the amendments of the Criminal Code is the introduction of jury trials, which will be mandatory as of January 1, 2003, in all regional courts for cases involving "dangerous" crimes, such as murder and rape. Defendants accused of crimes like theft (one of the most common charges among the country's nearly one million prisoners) would not be eligible for jury trials. According to Kozak's proposal, capital punishment, suspended in 1992 by the Constitutional Court, can eventually be reinstated. Under this provision, judges will be allowed to sign warrants.[36]

Kozak's proposal, adopted in third reading by the State Duma in November 2001, also expands the powers of defense lawyers. Under former Criminal Procedures Code, defense attorneys were not permitted to conduct their own investigation of their clients' cases. Only the Prosecutor General's Office and the Interior Ministry had the power to carry out such investigations. According to the new code, defense attorneys enjoy significantly wider powers, the defense being allowed to question private persons, to make inquiries with various organizations, and to invite independent experts to testify in court. At the same time, the new code curtails the powers of investigative authorities. Searches and warrants will have to be issued by a court, and not by a prosecutor as was traditionally the case. The new bill also provides for a so-called "adversary system," in which the defense and prosecution share equal rights in presenting their case to the court.[37]

4. The fourth and largest list of Kozak's proposals relates to the status of judges. From 2002 on, court chairmen will be appointed for a five- to ten-year period. The Qualification Collegiums that selects and dismisses judges is also to be restructured. Until 2001, it was comprised only of judges, but the Kozak team is willing to introduce representatives from the entire professional legal community. The purpose of this bill is to destroy the judges' lobby that was developing under the auspices of this institution. As a consequence of this reform, the Qualification Collegiums would no longer be able to prevent law enforcement bodies from accusing and prosecuting judges.

Kozak's package was examined and largely adopted by the State Duma in November 2001. One of the bills regulates measures under which judges may be charged with criminal deals. It says that such a decision may be taken by Russia's Prosecutor General, following a request by a collegium of three High Court judges. At the same time, while adopting Kozak's package, MPs tried to offer some immunity to judges: the bill also says judges, their offices, houses, private luggage, mail and telephone conversations should enjoy immunity from investigation.[38]

This reform plan faced strong opposition from the Prosecutor General and the Council of Judges. True, on the one hand, Kozak's package made it a clear priority to solve several economic issues of the judiciary and to correct some bureaucratic perversions of the Yeltsin reforms, such as appointing judges for life. But on the other hand, Kozak's approach to the judicial reform does follow up on Putin's main strategy to strengthen the top-down chain of order of the executive power, since the judiciary will eventually find itself under the direct influence of the federal government. Such influence will be exercised through three different leverages of control:

- Finances;
- Administration, including through the appointment of nonjudiciary members in the Qualification Collegiums, as well as through the appointment of court chairmen for short-term periods and their rotation;
- Politics, by placing elected governors under direct control of both the Justice Ministry and the president.

CONCLUSION: THE UNFORESEEN CONSEQUENCES OF ANTICORRUPTION CAMPAIGNS

This chapter argues that the Russian state, having transformed the struggle against corruption into a mere political tool, now faces a dual problem. The first lies in the numerous forms of political, bureaucratic, and economic corruption that is becoming endemic precisely because anticorruption campaigns are often used for short-term political reasons, and do not focus on structural causes. The second problem is the result of a lack of confidence among the Russian population vis-à-vis the state.

Repeated anticorruption campaigns have punctuated Russia's public life and exposed the political poverty of Yeltsin's regime. Because they were often ineffective, successive anticorruption campaigns were often seen as a sign of the state's weakness and the regime's inability to find another way out of political and financial crises. In addition, the gap between the political agenda of those who initiated anticorruption campaigns and the results was so deep that everyone who denounced corruption was soon perceived as fundamentally corrupt. To the public, the only reason for denouncing corruption of state officials was that it was a tool to help such people acquire power. The successive anticorruption campaigns that have already been launched by the Kremlin under Putin may well have the same negative effect.

Under Yeltsin, and during the first two years of Putin's presidency, the two first patterns of anticorruption campaigns described above (the power struggle and the search for legitimacy) were reproduced both at ministerial and regional levels. This led to further fragmentation of power. As examples, the Defense Ministry has seen several "anticorruption campaigns," each time following the appointment of a new minister. The same happened within the Interior Ministry after the appointment of Vladimir Rushailo at its head, and within the FSB, even when Vladimir Putin was in charge. Their usual way to rid themselves of competitors was, once again, to discredit them through accusations of corruption by launching "wars of *kompromat*"—by circulating compromising documents against their political and financial rivals.

The systematic distortion of the meaning of anticrime and anticorruption campaigns backfired. Already under Yeltsin, the rank-and-file had interpreted the Andropov-like campaigns merely as struggles for power directed exclusively against political rivals and they were ready to use this method to serve their own purposes. All the new power centers—the Prosecutor General's Office, the FSB, the Finance Ministry, and regional leaders—were now "struggling against crime and corruption" as a way to eliminate political and financial rivals and to support their own political and economic goals. The state was no longer able to implement an effective campaign at the federal level. Instead, it was confronted with multiple local campaigns, which often contradicted each other and were given different ideological meanings.

Under Putin's presidency, regional "wars of *kompromat*" not only still exist, but also proliferate with regional elections. All regional governors have resorted to rhetoric of struggle against corruption during electoral campaigns. This has undoubtedly tarnished the image of the state and undermined the authority of local governors. Facing such a situation, Putin will soon be forced to react. He will have to choose between two strategies, neither of which will be totally without political risk. One strategy will be to adopt more coercive measures, relying on law enforcement agencies including the FSB. Such a move would raise many critical comments both within the Russian Federation and abroad, a strategy that runs up against his effort to build rapprochement with the United States in the aftermath of the September 11 attacks on New York and Washington, D.C. Another strategy will be to reduce regional elections and eventually to appoint regional governors. This would allow Putin to implement the vertical executive power he has been referring to since the beginning of his presidential campaign. However, such a move would also force him to take entire responsibility for all economic, judicial, and political decisions at regional levels. This would include corruption cases and could eventually tarnish even more the image of the state. To strengthen the state's legitimacy, the Kremlin would then face the same dilemma: it would need to either adopt coercive measures or launch new anticorruption campaigns to build an image of incorruptibility. Neither of these measures would stop this vicious circle.

Analyzing the sequence of anticorruption campaigns, both under Yeltsin and Putin, shows that none of them fights the disease. Paradoxically enough, the more anticorruption campaigns the Kremlin launches, the more it needs to deal with unforeseen consequences of crucial importance: systematic delegitimization of the state at the regional and ministerial levels, and ongoing erosion of the Kremlin's authority.

PRESIDENTIAL DECREE

"On the guarantees to the President of the Russian Federation no longer in office, and to the members of his family."

December 31, 1999

For the purpose of providing legal, social and other guarantees to the President of the Russian Federation no longer in office, and to members of his family, and until the approval of an appropriate federal law, I decree:

1. To establish that the President of the Russian Federation no longer in office for the reason of expiration of his presidential term, resignation, or inability to perform his duties due to an illness ("The President of the Russian Federation no longer in office"), and members of his family, are entitled to the following legal, social and other guarantees:

   a. The President of the Russian Federation no longer in office has the right to 75 percent of a President's monthly salary regardless of age until he dies.

      If the President of the Russian Federation no longer in office is elected to a public post of the Russian Federation, a public post of a subject of the Russian Federation, or a public post in the state services, the salary mentioned above is terminated for the period of substituting one of the posts mentioned above.

   b. The President of the Russian Federation no longer in office is entitled to lifetime full state security services at permanent and temporary residence locations as provided by the federal law "On the State Security Services," including entitlement to special access and transport arrangements. His family is also protected by the state security services if traveling or residing with him.

   c. The President of the Russian Federation no longer in office and members of the family residing with him are guaranteed medical service as were granted while he was a President.

   d. Life and health of the President of the Russian Federation no longer in office are covered by the mandatory state insurance at the expense of the federal budget and in the amount equivalent to the annual salary of the President of the Russian Federation.

e. The President of the Russian Federation no longer in office enjoys full immunity from criminal and/or administrative prosecution. The President of the Russian Federation no longer in office cannot be detained, arrested, searched or questioned. The immunity extends to his living accommodations, offices, means of transport and communication, personal documents, belongings and mail.

f. The President of the Russian Federation no longer in office has the right to use one of the state dachas [summer houses] until he dies.

g. The President of the Russian Federation no longer in office has the right to use, free of charge, the chambers for officials and delegations at the airports, railway and riverside stations and seaports.

h. The President of the Russian Federation no longer in office has the right to use, free of charge, the government and other means of communication available to the offices of public service, offices of local governing authorities and organizations on the territory of the Russian Federation, and the right to use communication services out of turn. All types of mail and telegraph correspondence of the President of the Russian Federation no longer in office are to be forwarded, processed and delivered as a part of the official government mail.

i. The President of the Russian Federation no longer in office has the right to maintain, at the expense of the federal budget, a staff of assistants. The assistants to the President of the Russian Federation no longer in office are responsible only to him for the performance of their duties. The overall monthly fund for the salaries of the assistants to the President of the Russian Federation no longer in office is to be determined in the first thirty months after he stops performing his duties in the amount not exceeding twice the monthly salary of the President of the Russian Federation, and in the future—not exceeding one and a half of the salary of the President of the Russian Federation. The President of the Russian Federation no longer in office determines on his own and within the fund limits the amount of monthly salary for his assistants and the way in which they are to be rewarded. The President of the Russian Federation no longer in office is entitled to an office space housing the staff of assistants. The office is to be furnished and technologically equipped (including personal computers connected to the general network, all legal databases and government information systems, and copying machines and faxes), and to have the means of communication, including the government internal links.

j. After the death of the person who had acted as the President of the Russian Federation, each member of his family is entitled to a monthly subsidy in the amount of six times the minimum pension established by the federal law as of the day of the death. The list of family members entitled to the subsidy, as well as terms for the payments, are outlined in Articles 50 and 51 of the Law of the Russian Federation "On the state pensions in the Russian Federation."

k. Persons mentioned in j. have the right to use business auto transportation and retain medical services for the period of five years after the death of the person who had acted as the President of the Russian Federation.

2. To establish that the President of the Russian Federation no longer in office and members of his family may also be entitled to other guarantees provided for by the federal legislation.

3. To establish that the expenses designated in the present Decree are to be paid from the federal budget. Offices of public service, local governing authorities and organizations dealing with providing social guarantees to the President of the Russian Federation no longer in service are to be reimbursed for their expenses from the federal budget in terms established by the Government of the Russian Federation.

4. The Government of the Russian Federation to provide financial support in executing the present Decree in accordance with the federal budget fund for the Administration of the President of the Russian Federation.

NOTES

1. Konstantin M. Simis, *The Corrupt Society: The Secret World of Soviet Capitalism* (New York: Simon and Schuster, 1982); Dina Kaminskaya, *Zapiski advokata* (New York: Khronika Press, 1984); Ilya Zemtsov, *The Private Life of the Soviet Elite* (New York: Crane, Russak and Cie, 1985); Yevgenya Evelson, *Sudebnye protsessy po ekonom-icheskim dela v SSSR* (London: Overseas Publications Interchange, 1986); Fridrikh Neznansky, *Zapiski sledovatelya* (New York: Possev, 1989); Telman Gdlyan, Yevgueny Dodolev, *Mafiya vremen bezzakoniya* (Erevan, 1991).

2. Vladimir Putin, "Russia at the Turn of the Millennium," at www.ireland.com/newspaper/world/1999/1231/wor100.htm (last accessed December 31,1999).

3. Jeffrey Tayler, "The Unstoppable Descent of a Once-Great Power into Social Catastrophe and Strategic Irrelevance," *Atlantic Monthly* 5 (May 2001): 35.

4. Brian Whitmore and Bill Powell, "The Capital of Crime," *Newsweek International*, May 15, 2000, 28; "A Stain on Mr. Clean: How a Money-Laundering Indictment in Europe Could Haunt Putin, A Newsweek Investigation," *Newsweek*, September 3, 2001, 30.

5. Stephen Handelman, "Shadows on the Wall: Putin's Law-and-Order Dilemma," *East European Constitutional Review* at www.law.nyu.edu/eecr/vol9num_onehalf/feature/shadows.html.

6. The right expression in Russian is *brat' ne po chinu*.

7. Falsification of data was called *pripiska*.

8. Author's interviews with Soviet industrialists in her film "Red Mafia," June

1991, a seventy-five-minute documentary film on organized crime in the USSR broadcast on the French channels A2, FR3, as well as on BBC and NHK.

9. Gdlyan and Ivanov were initially considered to be part of Yeltsin's group while they were criticizing Party officials. It appeared later, during the legislative election, that they too were using the debate of the "struggle against corruption" for their own good. On the accusations against Ligachev, see *Radio Liberty, Russian Service*, September 15, 1989; on the Central Committee Plenum accusing Ligachev, see *TASS*, September 21, 1989; on the Gdlyan-Ivanov committee, see Julia Wishnevsky, *Radio Liberty Research Report* (*RL* 282/89); *Izvestiya*, May 13, 1989, and September 28, 1989. The first reports of the committee were also published in *TASS*, May 19, 1989. See also Yegor Ligachev, *Inside Gorbachev's Kremlin* (New York: Pantheon Books, 1993), 204–53. "Special Investigator" (*sledovatel' po osobo vazhnym delam*) was the highest rank among district attorneys.

10. This was notably the case in 1993, when Vice President Alexander Rutskoi threatened to disclose the compromising information he allegedly kept in eleven suitcases. A few months earlier, Rutskoi had chaired several meetings of the Security Council commission and given signs that he wanted to use it to supervise the so-called "power ministries" (interior, defense, and security and intelligence services), including the tax police, the customs committee, and the exchange control federal department. The Yeltsin administration and the power ministries became alarmed, considering Rutskoi's conservative political views and his rapprochement with the president's opponents in the Supreme Soviet, what was then the Russian parliament. See *Kommersant Daily*, October 23, 1992, 9.

11. The first example of such a counterattack came under Gorbachev when Prime Minister Valentin Pavlov created a so-called investigative think tank to elaborate measures against corruption. In 1990, Pavlov set up a group of investigators and prosecutors and asked them to gather evidence on the new methods used by organized crime to launder money. However, it is hard not to see this new structure as a move to neutralize Gorbachev's rival, Boris Yeltsin. Pavlov's think tank focused exclusively its attention on Yeltsin's team and their attempts to expose corruption within the Soviet leadership, not on criminal gangs.

12. The period 1992–93 witnessed a series of intricate scandals that opposed Rutskoi to Yeltsin, the Supreme Soviet to the Kremlin. Rutskoi launched a first attack that involved several high-ranking officials (Shumeiko, Burbulis, and Poltoranin). The executive branch counterattacked with a different scandal—Seabeco—involving Security Minister Viktor Barannikov and Deputy Interior Minister Andrei Dunyayev, who had sided with the parliament against the Yeltsin team.

13. On the Mabetex affair, see for example *Le Monde*, February 26, 1999; *Komsomolskaya Pravda*, March 18 and 23, 1999; and *Nezavisimaya gazeta*, September 21, 1999.

14. Mabetex was run by a man named Beghjet Pacalli.

15. Accusations of embezzlement were connected to Russian national air carrier Aeroflot, in which Berezovsky had a major stake. The company was run by Yeltsin's son-in-law, Valery Okulov.

16. Borodin was eventually given a position of responsibility within the new Russian-Belorusian Union. After having run for the presidential election, Skuratov was

eventually dismissed by the Russian Federation Council, the Upper Chamber of the Russian parliament. As of Primakov, he was dismissed by Yeltsin in the spring of 1999 and replaced by Sergei Stepashin.

17. Media-MOST Group then controlled the TV channel NTV, the radio station *Ekho Moskvy*, the daily *Segodnya*, and the weekly magazine *Itogi*. During the 1999 legislative campaign, the group stood on the side of Moscow Mayor Yuri Luzhkov and parliamentary leader Grigoriy Yavlinskiy, and strongly criticized the Kremlin policy.

18. See Paul Goble's analysis on this particular case, "Repression by Selective Prosecution," *RFE/RL Newsline* 4, no. 92, Part I (May 12, 2000).

19. In December 1999, economists and politicians, members of the Council for Foreign and Defense Policy, had prepared a joint appeal to the future president of Russia, in which they state that the executive branch needs to carry out a purge similar to that conducted in Italy in the Clean Hands operation. See NTV, program *Segodnya*, December 2, 1999, reprinted on Internet Securities at www.securities.com.

20. Stephen Hendelman, "Can Putin Strengthen the State While Attacking Corrupt Officials? Shadows on the Wall: Putin's Law-and-Order Dilemma," *East European Constitutional Review* 9, at www.law.nyu.edu/eecr/vol9num_onehalf/feature/shadows.html.

21. See the translation of the presidential decree in the appendix.

22. Lee S. Wolosky, "Putin's Plutocrat Problem," *Foreign Affairs* 79 (March/April 2000): 18; *New York Times*, July 15, 2000; *The Economist* (US), June 17, 2000, 49; *Nezavisimaya Gazeta*, June 15, 2000; Robert V. Daniels, "Putting Putin to Test," *The New Leader* 4, vol. 83 (September 2000): 11; Katrina Vandel Heuvel, "Putin's Choice," *The Nation*, July 24, 2000, 4; "Putin a la Pinochet?" *The Economist* (US), June 24, 2000, 21; "The Acid-Bath Solution: Want to Watch Some Billionaires Scream? Just Tune into Putin's Slow Roasting of Russia's Powerful Elite," *Time*, July 3, 2000, 41.

23. Congressmen called on Clinton to address this issue directly with Putin. "House Representatives to Target Russian Crackdown," *UPI*, June 20, 2000. See also "Russia's Oligarchs Cry Wolf," *Foreign Affairs*, Front Page Opinion www.freerepublic.com/forum/a3951045b2606.htm.

24. Sergei Stepashin, Chairman of the Anticorruption Commission of the State Duma, in a speech at Harvard University, March 14, 2000, at www.ksgnotes1.harvard.edu/BCSIA/Library.nsf/pubs/StepashinTrans.

25. See Stepashin's statement at www.gazeta.ru/lenta.shtml (last accessed August 24, 2000). Putin's meeting with representatives of Russia's big businessmen happened on July 28, 2000. See Donald Jensen, "Putin to Meet Oligarchs," *RFE/RL Newsline* 4, no. 144, Part 1, July 28, 2000.

26. *Kommersant-Daily*, July 28, 2000.

27. *Kommersant-Daily*, July 27, 2000.

28. *Izvestiya*, July 12, 2000.

29. Garfield Reynolds, "Putin Gives People Paternal Patriotism," *The Moscow Times*, December 30, 1999.

30. Capital punishment was officially abolished in December 1991.

31. In 1999, approximately 1.5 million people were deprived of freedom in Russia.

After the May 2000 amnesty (following Putin's presidential election), 970,000 prisoners remained in custody. It is worth noting, that, for the first time in Soviet and post-Soviet history, prisoners numbered less than a million. Judges examine 70,000 complaints on arrest per year and release one fifth of the defendants.

32. In 2000 judges considered approximately 900,000 criminal cases with 1.3 million defendants, more than 5 million civil cases, and 450,000 appeals. The burden of cases lying on judges became five times heavier than in 1991, when the judicial reform started.

33. Lev Ponomarev is executive director of the All-Russian movement "For Human Rights."

34. One repeated accusation concerns the record of hearings falsified by the judge: in 1999, twenty judges were dismissed for this offence.

35. See the presentation of Sergei Pashin, former Moscow city court judge, associate professor at the Institute of Youth, Moscow, at the Harvard Kennedy School of Government, June 1, 2001.

36. The main provisions of the new Criminal Procedure Code came into force on July 1, 2002, but certain clauses will come into force only in 2004. Not until 2004 will courts be able to issue arrest and search warrants. This delay in the implementation of the provision is reportedly due to a severe shortage of qualified judges and poor financing of courts.

37. German Prokhorov, Lisa Vronskaya, "Duma Approves Major Judicial Reform," *Gazeta.ru* at www.gazeta.ru/2001/11/23/DumaApproves.shtml (last accessed November 25, 2001).

38. See *ALLNEWS.RU* at www.allnews.ru/english/2001/11/22/reform/ (last accessed November 22, 2001) and *The Moscow Times*, November 23, 2001, 1.

Part Three

THE ECONOMY

Chapter Six

Putin and the Economy

James R. Millar

Esteemed members of the Federation Council and deputies of the State Duma, the last decade has been a turbulent and, one can say, without any exaggeration, a revolutionary one for Russia. Against that background, the year 2000 and the start of 2001 seem relatively calm. [P]ublic expectations and apprehensions [of possible structural and personnel changes] do not arise out of nowhere. They are based on the well-known logic that revolution is usually followed by counter-revolution, reforms by counter-reforms and then by the search for those guilty of revolutionary misdeeds and by punishment, all the more so since Russia's own historic experience is rich in such examples. But I think it is time to say firmly that this cycle has ended. There will be no revolution or counter-revolution. Firm and economically supported state stability is a good thing for Russia and its people and it is long since we learnt to live according to this normal human logic.

—President Vladimir Putin, Annual Address to the Federal Assembly, April 3, 2001, Russia TV, Moscow

The performance of the Russian economy in 2000 was the best since 1992 when radical reforms were introduced by Boris Yeltsin and Yegor Gaidar. GDP grew by more than 8 percent. Inflation was modest, about 20 percent, and official reserves of gold and hard currency increased from about $13 billion to $28 billion. The recovery from the financial crisis of 1998 is due largely to an increase in the price of oil exports, the favorable effect of the 1998 devaluation of the ruble on domestic industry, and the negative impact of higher prices on imports. The recovery continued in 2001, but at the lesser rate of 5 percent. Inflation remained at about 20 percent. Prospects for 2002 are for slower rather than faster growth. Real average wages, however, increased 7.8 percent in 2000 and another 25.9 percent in the first half of 2001. Real wages remain almost 20 percent below the level of 1998, and the benefits provided by the cheaper ruble continue to diminish over time. Moreover, another oil price boost is highly unlikely. Indeed, prices may decline. In fact, recently Russia has been increasing oil production and exports, thereby undercutting OPEC attempts to maintain the world market price of oil products.[1]

President Vladimir Putin can view economic developments with some satisfaction, but it must be tempered by the fact that the price of oil is not controlled by Russia and cannot be credited to his administration. Moreover, the devaluation of the ruble took place before Putin's watch. There is no assurance, therefore, that the relatively happy current state of the economy can be sustained for long, especially since economic issues have not been given high priority on Putin's action list. Yet, the promotion of domestic and foreign investment is critical if Russia is to sustain an acceptable rate of growth and modernization. Progress toward these goals is unlikely until reforms in corporate governance, secure legal protections of property rights, protection from economic corruption and predation, and rational land tenure systems are established. Admittedly, none of these ends will be easy to accomplish in Russia, but progress has been much slower than is necessary to avoid a decline in growth rates and stagnation in industrial modernization.

Putin's main efforts to date have been devoted to achieving political stability, maintaining the territorial and political integrity of Russia, the projection of Russia's influence into the former Soviet republics and allies, and the reestablishment of domestic *poryadok,* or order. Of these goals, the last appears to have had priority, as one might have expected of a former officer in the KGB. The vigorous pursuit of *poryadok* has led democratic forces in Russia and abroad to worry that Putin is seeking to undermine Russia's fragile democracy and establish an autocratic state. In his early tenure, Putin has focused more upon accumulating power than upon its exercise. This is a sign of insecurity in a leader who, above all else, intends to remain in power. Is there a real possibility that Putin could reestablish a variant of Stalinism and, with it, a return to central planning? Or will he press more firmly for the continuation of market reforms? The answer lies partly in an examination of the fundamental trends in Soviet-Russian history and partly in a resolution of the thus far ambiguous character of Putin himself.

THREE WHO UNMADE A REVOLUTION

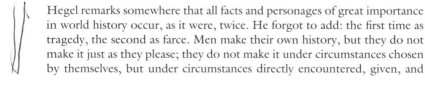

Hegel remarks somewhere that all facts and personages of great importance in world history occur, as it were, twice. He forgot to add: the first time as tragedy, the second as farce. Men make their own history, but they do not make it just as they please; they do not make it under circumstances chosen by themselves, but under circumstances directly encountered, given, and transmitted from the past. The tradition of all the dead generations weighs like a nightmare on the brain of the living.

—Karl Marx, "The Eighteenth Brumaire of Louis Bonaparte"[2]

Putin has inherited from Nikita Khrushchev, Mikhail Gorbachev, and Boris Yeltsin an intermittent but long and consistent policy of de-Stalinizing the Soviet social system. His actions and prospects for action are necessarily constrained by those prior efforts. A Putin seeking to be Stalin would be the farce to the Stalinist tragedy. It would be a mistake, therefore, to evaluate Putin's ambitions and prospects in the light of Yeltsin's heritage alone. The stage for de-Stalinization was set by Khrushchev. Gorbachev played Hamlet. And Yeltsin brought down the curtain. As the quote from Marx above suggests, these men made history, but they did "not make it just as they pleased." Things turned out quite differently than any of them expected. Let's examine what this tradition portends for Putin.

Nikita Khrushchev

After a brief struggle for power with Georgie Malenkov and a period of collective leadership, Khrushchev revealed himself as a determined reformer of the system he inherited from Stalin. Interestingly enough, the years of Khrushchev's rule (1958–64) were years of optimism and high confidence in the future of Soviet socialism. The Soviet consumer experienced a rising standard of living. The camps of the Gulag began to be emptied out, and, although the "fear" was not eliminated from private lives, it was diminished significantly, especially the fear of mass, widespread repression. Soviet industry was growing apace. The space program had great successes, and Soviet science prospered generally.[3]

Nikita Khrushchev was clearly a true believer in the promise of socialism and its ultimate victory on the world stage over capitalism. It was just a matter of time. However, all was not well. Stalin's legacy of repression threatened elite party members as well as the population at large. Khrushchev sought through his reforms to end the terror, to revitalize and purify the Communist Party, and to invigorate the economy. Khrushchev's expectations were dashed by reality. His economic reforms produced short-term gains, but failed in the long run to ensure sustained growth. There were numerous attempts to improve the incentive system for enterprise managers and workers. The so-called Kosygin reform of 1965 was, in fact, a carryover from Khrushchev's era. It was the end of Khrushchev's efforts, not the beginning, it turned out, of Brezhnev era reforms. Leonid Brezhnev lacked enthusiasm for fundamental economic reform and thus the Kosygin reform had no discernible long-term impact. As one astute observer noted, the effort to reform industrial management became merely a treadmill, continually repeating itself, going nowhere.[4]

Khrushchev's attempt to invigorate agricultural production was equally unsuccessful. A case study in the irrationality of Soviet economic thinking, the Virgin Lands program expanded cultivation, especially of grains, by one-third. The idea was to enhance the production of feed grains so that livestock herds and thus meat consumption could be greatly increased. Grain production did go up, but only in the short run. A large portion of the land brought under cultivation could not be maintained and had to be abandoned at great cost. One of Khrushchev's last acts was to authorize the import of grain from the United States and the West in order to continue to support the larger herds of beef animals. It would have been more rational for the USSR to import meat directly, because livestock in both the United States and Europe converted grain into meat much more efficiently than could poor quality Soviet livestock herds.

In any case, Nikita Khrushchev was removed from power in a palace coup in October 1964, and the impetus to reform diminished rapidly thereafter. His most lasting impact, however, was to initiate the process of de-Stalinization at the Twentieth Party Congress. He sought to undercut political opponents and disassociate the Communist Party of the Soviet Union (CPSU) from the worst of Stalin's crimes, but criticism of Stalin was limited to the years after 1934. Achievements such as collectivization and the rapid industrialization drive remained off limits to serious criticism until well into the 1980s. This was partly to protect himself and his colleagues from complicity in Stalin's crimes, but also to affirm the principal institutions of the Soviet system: central planning, emphasis upon heavy industry, collectivized agriculture, and comprehensive state ownership and management of productive assets. This was the core of Soviet socialism, and Khrushchev had no intention of undercutting it. He hoped instead to shift priorities toward the consumer and to attain a rate of growth of gross domestic product (GDP) that would catch up with the United States before the end of the twentieth century.

The embarrassing outcome of the Cuban Missile Crisis and the perception that Khrushchev was pursuing too many "harebrained" domestic reform projects and destabilizing the party bureaucracy led to a palace coup in 1964. His successors, Leonid Brezhnev and Alexei Kosygin, and then Brezhnev alone, did not continue the reform effort with the same vigor as Khrushchev. The CPSU and its leadership lapsed into a bureaucratic, self-satisfied, and self-rewarding pattern of behavior. The Brezhnev years have quite rightly been labeled the era of stagnation. The leadership grew long in the tooth, and the legitimacy of the party was badly eroded. Meanwhile, the economy suffered a loss of dynamism. In fact, our best measurements reveal that most economic indicators began to show declining rates of growth in about the middle of the 1970s. The downward trend continued into the 1980s and confronted Brezhnev's successors with stark alternatives. They could allow a very disappointing slow rate of economic growth to continue and abandon the goal that Khrushchev had set of "catching up with and surpassing" the United States in economic power and well-being, or they could carry out wide-ranging, deep economic reforms that would restore the rates of growth that the Soviet Union achieved in the 1950s and 1960s.

Mikhail Gorbachev

Mikhail Gorbachev and his political allies viewed themselves as "children of the Twentieth Party Congress." They were young men at the time of Khrushchev's anti-Stalin speech, and it left an indelible mark on their political consciousness. In this sense, Gorbachev's innovations of *perestroika* and *glasnost* were rooted in Khrushchev's reforms. In introducing these policies Gorbachev had no intention of undermining the planned economy or the CPSU. Instead, Gorbachev and his circle of advisors genuinely believed that an adjustment here and an improvement there and a limited opening to market forces and the world economy could provide a gradual improvement in economic performance and strengthen the party. It is true that Gorbachev used the word "revolution" early on in his speeches, but it is also perfectly clear that he did not have a real revolution in mind. However, as he ran into resistance and unanticipated fragmentation of the Soviet Empire, his reform efforts became more frantic and ambiguous. In the end, *"glasnost"* led to the repudiation of the party as the sole repository of political power; *"perestroika"* brought about the collapse of the system of central planning and a decline in economic performance; "democratization" fostered ethnic separatism; and the "new thinking" in foreign policy led to a rollback of communism in Eastern Europe. In each case, developments outdistanced the expectations of the reformers and careened out of central control.[5]

Gorbachev was more successful initially in controlling the transformation of the political process. No doubt this reflected his greater skill and interest in the art of political maneuver and the fact that political processes depend so largely upon personal relations and personality, at which Gorbachev excelled. Reforming the economy proved more intractable than political liberalization because the distribution of gains and losses that economic reform entailed were much more diffuse and uncertain than those associated with the redistribution of political power. Almost everyone had something to lose, whether it was privileged access to deficit commodities, or job security, or personal savings, while possible gains had to be viewed as highly uncertain and therefore highly discounted. It was naturally much more difficult to establish a consensus with the public much less with the elite, which was divided on ideological grounds as well. Ed Hewett wrote in November 1989, "Mikhail Gorbachev is writing a textbook on the political economy of transition—the first textbook of its kind."[6] Unfortunately for Gorbachev, his book had an unhappy ending.

The critical turning point for Gorbachev on economic reform came in mid-1990, when he rejected the radical S. S. Shatalin plan for conversion of the Soviet economy into a market-oriented economy in 500 days.[7] Although it was patently unrealistic, the Shatalin plan crystallized as no previous document had done the fundamental issues confronting economic reform. Gorbachev responded:

> They want to take a gamble. Let everything be thrown open tomorrow. Let market conditions be put in place everywhere. Let's have free enterprise and give the green light to all forms of ownership. Let everything be private. Let us sell the land, everything. I cannot support such ideas, no matter how decisive and revolutionary they might appear. These are irresponsible ideas, irresponsible![8]

The Shatalin plan assumed that political power would rest ultimately with the constituent republics of the USSR. All powers of the Kremlin would be derivative, and its economic base would depend upon the revenues and authority the republics would be prepared to cede to the central government. The Shatalin plan assumed that all forms of property would stand on a completely equal footing in the new economy. There would be no legal distinction made for socialist property. The plan also called for dismantling the institutions of central planning completely. Acceptance of the Shatalin plan, then, meant that Gorbachev would have to be prepared to accept the possible dissolution of the USSR and abandonment of belief in the superiority of socialist property and of socialism itself. This was more than he could stomach, and it was the end of Gorbachev the reformer. Reform was spinning out of control and threatening to become revolution. Henceforward, Gorbachev shunned all change, even in quite modest forms, and sought economic and political stability that would conserve the union against separatist ethnic forces. Gorbachev became the Hamlet of political and economic reform. As a child of the Twentieth Party Congress, he could not be Stalin. His few attempts at repression were too weak and failed. But he could not abandon Soviet socialism or the USSR either. Gorbachev's reform objective had been much more modest and conservative. It was best expressed by his first economics minister, Abel Aganbegyan: "*Perestroika* must carry Soviet society to a qualitatively new state, when thanks to the advantages of socialism we will surpass the capitalist countries in productivity, and other indicators of cost-effectiveness, in quality of production and the level of technology."[9]

Clearly Gorbachev had exactly the same goal as Khrushchev. When it could not be achieved without abandoning socialism, Gorbachev was stymied. Indecision led ultimately to the failed coup by party hard-liners in August 1991, and the rise to full power of Boris Yeltsin.

Gorbachev's place in history is secure, however, because he thoroughly de-Stalinized the USSR. He took Soviet society back as nearly as the arrow of time permits to the origins of the Stalinist system, back essentially to Vladimir Lenin's New Economic Policy of the 1920s. The year 1934 no longer remained as the limit for criticism of Soviet institutions. In criticizing and limiting the power of the central economic ministries, proposing substantial, if still restricted, private ownership of productive assets, retail outlets and dachas, he had traveled well beyond Khrushchev, if less far than his erstwhile radical economic advisors wanted. In this sense Gorbachev was a true heir of the Twentieth Party Congress.

Gorbachev took one enormous step that Khrushchev would not. Although Khrushchev was a reformer, he was not prepared to lose the post–World War II empire in East-Central Europe. Thus he put down the 1953 disturbance in East Germany, crushed the Hungarian revolution, and built the Berlin Wall. Gorbachev's "new thinking" in foreign policy allowed him to disassociate domestic reform and maintenance of Soviet power in Eastern Europe, a connection over which domestic reform had repeatedly stumbled. The Brezhnev doctrine was abandoned and the consequences accepted, even though they turned out much more definitive and anti-Soviet than Gorbachev and his ministers anticipated.

On August 19, 1991, Mikhail Gorbachev was made a prisoner in his villa in the Crimea, where he had gone for vacation. An eight-man "state emergency committee" had been formed of highly placed party and military men with the intention of carrying out a coup against the Gorbachev government. It sought to halt the reform process, to forestall opening the Soviet Union to the global economy, to restore to the Communist Party monopoly control of politics, and to preserve the command economy. Within forty-eight hours the coup had failed and the members of the committee were in disgrace. James Billington, the Librarian of Congress, was in Moscow on those days and present at the White House, where the decisive defeat of the coup took place. He recently reported: "It was unexpected, it really hasn't been adequately explained since. After all, most of the five and a half million people in uniform, the largest uniformed force at one command in the history of the world, was stared down by 150 armed people in the Russian White House."[10]

Boris Yeltsin

The coup elevated Boris Yeltsin, who had been elected president of the Russian Federation (RSFSR) the previous spring, to unanticipated political heights. The image of Yeltsin standing defiantly on a tank in front of the White House remains the prime emblem of the resistance. As president of the RSFSR, the largest and most important republic of the Soviet Union, Yeltsin was in a position to take political advantage of the failed coup. He was unique among experienced Soviet party officials in two respects. He had been a stout supporter of *perestroika* and *glasnost* as party chief for Moscow and as a member of the Politburo, but he had been alienated from Gorbachev and the Communist Party as a result of political differences. Dismissal from his positions of power and authority had led to a nervous breakdown and, in the end, repudiation of the Communist Party of the Soviet Union. As a result he had no brief for the party and was prepared to destroy it. Second, as president of the RSFSR he was willing to break up the USSR in league with other republic leaders and thereby unseat its president, Gorbachev. Yeltsin's own self-interest, then, was consistent with the final and complete destruction of the USSR and the Stalinist social system. The factors that caused Gorbachev to hesitate in the face of radical reform did not deter Yeltsin from bringing the curtain down once and for all on Soviet communism and the Soviet Union.

Yeltsin sought out a radical economist who would thoroughly undermine the command economy. It was teetering on the brink of collapse in any case. Inflation was soaring, the stores were empty and the federal budget was out of control. Under the influence of Yegor Gaidar and several Western economic advisors, he was persuaded to introduce what is known as "shock therapy" in January 1992.[11] His advisors assured him that the economy would decline sharply as prices were freed from controls and central planning abandoned, but an upturn could be expected in nine months. The close kinship of shock therapy with the Shatalin plan is obvious, but the latter was actually better reasoned and structured and more gradual as well. Yeltsin plunged where Gorbachev had hesitated—perhaps with good reason. It took almost nine years, not nine months, for the economy to turn up again. The economic depression of those years was deeper and more devastating than any in recorded peacetime period anywhere.[12] In the process the basic institutions of the Stalinist model of the Soviet economy, which were created in the crucible years of 1928–32, were completely abandoned. These institutions formed a true system in the sense that each component part depended upon all of the rest. They consisted of the five-year plan: centrally set, hyper-ambitious, physical-quantity monthly and annual targets; central supply allocation of priority commodities and services, the collective and state farms; strict controls over labor and residential mobility, heavy reliance upon welfare entitlements and subsidized consumption, egalitarianism in wage policy, and special incentives for members of the elite. Before 1992 was out these institutions had disappeared, and it is highly unlikely that such a combination could ever be restored in Russia. Yeltsin abolished the Communist Party too, and confiscated its assets. It reappeared subsequently only in much modified form as one party among many others.

The severely negative economic consequences of shock therapy for the majority of Russian citizens soured most on market reform and created political opposition to further reforms in the Duma and in the various republics of Russia. As a result, the process of creating new market institutions under Yeltsin was fraught with obstacles, and the process remained incomplete when he passed power to Vladimir Putin. Today many large-scale industries have been privatized, but many also remain either state owned or owned in part and dominated by the state. Privatization created a tiny class of very wealthy individuals, known as the oligarchs, and a large portion of the population became destitute. Market institutions are in place for the most part, but many need regulation or restructuring. The banking system remains weak and needs reform. Investment opportunities in Russia are so few and so risky that foreign capital fears to enter and domestic capital takes flight. However, the central bank and the state budget are now operating with greater sophistication than ever, and, as was mentioned earlier, export earnings, principally on oil, and the cheap ruble have stimulated the economy to its best performance in more than a decade. However, much remains to be done to turn the Russian economy into a market economy that can produce sustained growth and satisfactory performance.[13]

CONTINUITY AND CHANGE: PUTIN'S OPTIONS

The continuity of policy from Khrushchev through Gorbachev to Yeltsin, both in what they attempted and what they tried to avoid, is clear. It is also obvious that together they unmade the Bolshevik Revolution. Like Humpty-Dumpty, the Soviet Union as it existed cannot be put back together again by Putin or anyone else. The evidence is that Putin can be taken at his word when he states that he seeks, "Firm and economically supported state stability." That does not, of course, rule out autocracy, but it does imply a conservative approach to further economic reform—that those efforts will be incremental and based on consensus. It is also consistent with stagnation as a reaction to the hectic series of changes and mistakes that have characterized the last decade or so, just as Brezhnev sought stability and found stagnation following Khrushchev's riot of reforms.

During the difficult early days of shock therapy a Russian babushka was interviewed on TV. She was asked what she hoped would happen. "All we want," she said, "is to live in a normal economy like everyone else in the world." What did she mean by a "normal economy?" It can be defined in the first instance as an economy in which the everyday citizen can form reasonably assured expectations of the future. That means an economy where personal savings decisions can be made with confidence that they will not be confiscated by inflation or by the state, one in which daily necessities can be expected to be available in stores all day every day, employment will not fluctuate wildly, and plans can be made for the more distant future, such as for education for one's children, or for retirement, with reasonable certitude. A normal economy is one in which citizens may gauge the degree of risk associated with various economic options with some accuracy and therefore choose the risk profile he or she prefers. In this sense, the Russian economy today approximates the "normal economy" the babushka wished for, but it remains highly sensitive to volatile global raw material prices, especially for oil, and it is not attracting the volume of domestic and international capital investment required to ensure sustained economic growth. To achieve these ends additional reforms are necessary, but they need not be made in a radical fashion. The greater danger is that in the quest for political stability and continuation in office Putin will fail to achieve the reforms necessary to sustain a normal level of economic performance.

An examination of economic reform efforts of the twenty-five independent countries that emerged from the collapse of the Soviet Empire indicates that success or failure has been determined by three major factors. First, and perhaps most important, has been a strong, unambiguous commitment to economic reform. The most successful states have been those that wanted desperately to escape Soviet power. They have sought successfully to link their fortunes to Europe, especially the European Union (EU). Second, the more successful reformers are those that had experienced a period of independent existence as states before falling under Soviet influence. A complementary interpretation would be that these states practiced the Soviet economic model for a shorter period of time and could draw upon past experience with market institutions. Third, progress in economic reform, as measured by the European Bank for Reconstruction and Development (EBRD), and in democratization, as measured by Freedom House, are highly correlated. The Pinochet model, in which political authoritarianism is used to force market reform, has not offered any promise in Central and Eastern Europe or in the former Soviet states. Alternation of power between different political parties and shared political power between the executive and the legislature appear to have produced the best economic results.[14]

As has been the case for the leaders of the other former republics of the USSR, except in the Baltic states, Yeltsin's commitment to economic reform was never constant, and it diminished over the years of his erratic and increasingly autocratic rule. Sixty years of central planning would be difficult to overcome with the greatest determination and consistency, so it is not surprising that Russia remains stuck halfway to market reform, a stark example of the failure of Pinochetism in this region. Vladimir Putin remains something of a mystery. Is he a cautious but ultimately determined reformer seeking step-by-step change based on consensus with the Duma and the population at large? His statement on Russia Day 2001, a celebration of ten years as a republic, might be interpreted in this way: "Everything we endured over the past decade, all our experiences, successes and failures, shows one thing—any reform only makes sense when it serves the people."

Or is Putin primarily concerned with maximizing political power in order to maintain his position? Putin has talked like a true reformer, but his actions have been more ambiguous. His presidency has benefited from two windfalls: a rising and relatively high price of oil and the devaluation of the ruble in the financial crisis of 1998. Unfortunately, he has not used this breathing space to push economic reform vigorously. He has been more concerned with hushing up critics, burnishing his image, and seeking to project Russian influence in the former republics of the USSR, among old Soviet allies in the Middle East and East Asia, and on the world scene. With a few exceptions the oligarchs remain in place, economic and bureaucratic corruption and crime remain almost untouched, and capital flight continues unabated.[15]

At the outset of his presidency, Putin indicated that he planned to reduce the political and economic power of the wealthy individuals known as oligarchs, who had benefited so greatly from the highly inequitable privatization of Soviet industry and natural resources. Thus far two of the most prominent and vocal oligarchs, Boris Berezovsky and Vladimir Gusinsky, have been thoroughly undermined. Gusinsky has lost his media empire, and Berezovsky has gone from kingmaker (for both Yeltsin and Putin) to political outcast. Putin's motive, however, appears to have had less to do with economic power than with the desire to quiet criticism of his policies by their media enterprises. Subsequently, Putin engineered the removal of Rem Vyakhirev, who had been CEO of the giant natural gas monopoly Gazprom since 1992, and replaced him with a longtime Putin loyalist, Aleksei Miller. Vyakhirev was a variant type of oligarch, one appointed essentially by the central government to manage the huge, partly private, partly state enterprise. In replacing Vyakhirev, Putin strengthened his hand in many respects because Gazprom is such an important cash cow for the budget. This change will represent a major economic advance, if indeed Miller manages Gazprom more efficiently and does not use access to its great wealth mainly to enrich himself, which remains to be seen. The remaining oligarchs, with one exception, are lying low and staying out of visible politics. The exception is Anatoly Chubais, who has metamorphosed from radical reformer to oligarch and now runs the national electric monopoly. Putin's policy toward the oligarchs has, therefore, been inconsistent.

Privatization of land remains highly controversial. Putin has urged the regional governors to support "coherent land legislation" and a federal land code. German Gref, Mikhail Kasyanov, and Andrei Illarionov all agree on the economic benefits that private land tenure would bring about. Legislation passed in the Duma in October 2001 declared that urban land, which comprises less than 5 percent of all land area in Russia, is now open to private, and perhaps even foreign private, ownership. But the opponents of privatization of rural land in the Duma have managed to stall legislation on ideological and historical grounds. Agricultural land has been treated as commons or as communal property in Russia for as long as anyone can remember, and most peasants want it to stay that way. Urban land has been controlled by mayors and regional leaders for local ends and personal profit, and they may still find ways to frustrate private ownership. Until both urban and rural land become clearly subject to private tenure and may be traded on markets like other commodities, both domestic investment in agriculture and foreign direct investment in Russia in general will be inhibited.[16]

More problematic, there is no single systematic economic program in place. In fact, two quite distinct initiatives have been circulating at the highest levels of the Russian government. Thus far, apparently, Putin has not decided which to adopt, if either. The plan that has received the most attention was prepared under the auspices of Minister of Economic Development and Trade German Gref. It was reportedly adopted by Prime Minister Mikhail Kasyanov in June 2000, but it still has not been made. The Gref plan attempts to prescribe developments through the year 2010. The plan has undergone countless revisions and amendments at various levels and departments of the government. Curiously in this respect, it has certain earmarks of Soviet-era Five-Year Plans, and it may meet the same fate—to be announced with great fanfare and then forgotten. One of Putin's other prominent economic advisors, Andrei Illarionov, has criticized it harshly as insufficiently reformist (read liberal) and unrealistic. Perhaps the Gref plan is being used as a general guideline for economic policy, but the public cacophony of voices from a variety of economic advisors and policy makers, including Gref, Illarionov, Kasyanov, and Anatoly Chubais, makes that doubtful. Economic policy seems to be made on an ad hoc basis when it is made consciously at all. One thing is clear, despite Putin's carefully projected image in other arenas, economic policies have not been bold, coherent, or decisive.

The other plan, also prepared at Putin's instance, has yet to be published officially. It was drawn up under the auspices of Viktor Ishayev, governor of Khabarovsk, by a group of "leading economists," or so it was reported. Entitled "Strategy for Development of the State to the Year 2010," it was presented to the Russian State Council in November 2000.[17] Although billed as a "supplement" to the Gref plan, reports indicate that the two are fundamentally different and impossible to reconcile. According to Jonathan Tennenbaum of the Executive Intelligence Review, the document is based upon the reviews of the nineteenth-century German economist Friedrich List and Russia's own nineteenth-century economist and prime minister, Sergei Witte. That may be the case in a general sense, but what it recalls more vividly is the Soviet practice of resource mobilization. This approach requires a strong state and a leading role for the state in the mobilization process. This is necessary, the report claims, because the middle class in Russia is not large enough to generate the savings required for significant breakthrough to high rates of growth. Without high rates of growth, the standard of living of the great mass of the population cannot be elevated sufficiently.

> Reaching the proposed level of consumption dictates the need for high rates of growth of the real productive sector of the economy, which in turn depends on achieving a 'break-out' in terms of investment. This means a "forced increase in capital investment" on the order of 8–9 percent growth per year, as well as state support for key sectors, including agriculture and infrastructure areas such as electricity, which are not able to generate the required rates of investment themselves.

The document goes on to give the state primary responsibility for the direction of investment. It is to judge investment opportunities not on the basis of profitability but in terms of the benefit of the industry and its products to the economy as a whole, whatever that means.

The Ishayev plan naturally brings to mind Stalin's program of forced industrialization in the 1930s. In fact, it can be read as calling for the creation of "capitalism in one country," that is attempting to build modern economy using entirely or mainly only internal sources. It is not a plan that relies on market institutions, and it appears to shun foreign investment. The changes it calls for in the way of the banking system, investment policy, wage policy, and so forth represent an implicit restoration of the institutions of Soviet central planning. If attempted, the outcome would be either a tragedy or a farce.

According to reports, President Putin has asked to have the Gref and Ishayev plans integrated (harmonized), an impossible task because they rest on different and irreconcilable foundations. Once again, Putin may be simply postponing a decision on differing courses of action. Or, perhaps he simply does not understand economics and the different ramifications of the two plans. In this case, he would be avoiding a decision because he cannot be confident of the outcome, and, if so, he resembles Gorbachev in the last years of his reign, where, like Hamlet, he could neither move back to Stalinist methods nor forward to the possible abandonment of socialism. Of course Putin, in this instance, may simply be acting as a typical bureaucrat in the absence of decisive instructions from above. If so, this is not a promising outlook for successful economic reform in Russia under his presidency. There is no one to give them.

In foreign policy Putin has sought to restore economic and political relations with the Soviet Union's old allies: Iran, Iraq, Cuba, and North Korea. He has also strengthened relations with China. Foreign Minister Ivanov has stated that the "near abroad," Russia's term for the former republics of the USSR, falls within Russia's sphere of influence. The implication is clear: Putin has been seeking to reestablish Russia's dominant position in the region and, to the extent possible, restore the Soviet empire through energy dependency, aggressive military exercises, showing the flag, and minatory behavior in the Caspian region. With the exception of China, the countries that Putin has been reaching out to are either global outcasts or economic basket cases. It appears to be an alliance of losers. This policy, if continued, could be a costly one internationally and economically. The attempt to attain hegemony over the former Soviet republics represents a serious drain on Russia's military and economic resources. So is the interminable war in Chechnya. What the new conflict between the United States and Afghanistan portends for Russian foreign policy is not yet clear, but it has all the makings of a quagmire Russia might not be able to avoid.

Putin's positive response to the terrorist attack on the United States and to President Bush's declaration of war on international terrorism appears to contradict his attempt to create an alliance to counterweight America as the sole remaining superpower in the world. Not only has he moved sharply back toward the Western camp, he has acceded to U.S. action in Afghanistan and, more surprisingly, to the placement of U.S. troops and other military assets in Uzbekistan and perhaps elsewhere in Central Asia. Putin will ultimately have to choose between attempting to create a "multipolar" strategy and becoming a junior partner in the international alliance against terrorism. This is a real contradiction, one that Putin cannot hope to waffle on very long.

CONCLUSION

Viewed in historical perspective, Putin appears to have more in common with Brezhnev than with his more decisive, risk-taking predecessors. Khrushchev, Gorbachev, and Yeltsin risked their positions in attempts to de-Stalinize the Soviet Union. Putin cannot reverse that long historical process. It would take an ideology, a mass party and a fearless sense of purpose, none of which exist today. The long process of bringing the Soviet Union, and then Russia, back into the world economy has featured radical changes and long pauses with some backtracking. Putin's rule seems to be more pause than reform to date, and that is, incidentally, what the public wants, too.

The outlook for economic reform and continued economic growth over the next several years is positive, but only marginally so. Gorbachev sought to reform the Soviet socialist economy, to make it more humane and more responsive to the popular will by introducing certain elements of democracy and of a market economy. His efforts failed. Yeltsin led a revolution that destroyed the coordinates of the Soviet planned economy and attempted to replace it quickly with the most liberal of market institutions. The revolution achieved partial success. The planned economy was totally destroyed, but the revolution had disastrous consequences for the population at large as it was captured by the *nomenklatura* and ground to a halt halfway to workable markets. Putin is now leading a partial restoration of Russia, a pause in the radical changes that have been taking place since *perestroika* and *glasnost* were introduced in the 1980s. In this sense the transition is over, but, of course, a good deal remains to be done to complete market institutions.

The state committees, such as the Gosplan, and the other institutions of central planning have disappeared, but public surveys both before and since the collapse of the Soviet economy reveal that very substantial majorities expect the government to provide price stability, job security, free medical care, free public education through college, subsidized housing, and cheap transportation. Similarly, the majority has repeatedly indicated a strong preference for public ownership of railroads, airlines, heavy industry, communications, banks, and other large-scale enterprises such as defense industries. Moreover, many enterprises, both private and public, still operate like company towns and have yet to rationalize employment practices.[18] The Russian economist Nikolay Shmelev aptly pointed out that it had taken "three generations" to build the "insane asylum" that was the Soviet economy and that it would take at last three more to escape from it. To escape fully will require changes in both the thinking and the behavior of citizens and leaders alike.[19]

Although Russia is not now a candidate for accession to the EU, its institutional structure can be expected to shape Russian economic and legal institutions to a substantial degree in the future. In fact, the EU is much more likely to influence economic reform and development in Russia from here on out than are the International Monetary Fund (IMF) or the World Bank, both of which have been associated with major policy failures in Russia and other transition economies. The EU is an important trading partner and likely to become increasingly important over time, if only because Russia is such a critical source of energy supplies to Europe. Russia also trades with East-Central Europe, and many of these countries are either on the path to accession in the EU or hope to be in the near future. The EU has spelled out in chapter and verse just what a country needs to do to harmonize its institutions with those of Europe. Russia is certain to be influenced both directly and indirectly to do the same. This is the most optimistic outlook for the future of capitalism in Russia in the next decade regardless of who is president.[20]

As many observers have noted, the criteria for accession to the EU are essentially the same as the requirements for a successful transition to a market economy. Accession indicators that are used to determine eligibility for membership include measures of the extent of large-scale and small-scale privatization, of success in restructuring enterprises to harden budget constraints, rationalize production and employment, and improve corporate governance. The indicators also seek to measure the degree to which markets are competitive, prices have been liberalized, and import and export restrictions have been eliminated. In addition, banking and other financial institutions are evaluated against international standards of regulation and performance. Basically, the accession process involves modeling the aspiring economy upon the most successful members of the EU and moving toward the model in stepwise fashion.

Countries are scored on each of the eight principal indicators on a scale ranging from one for little progress to four + for achieving standards and performance typical for advanced industrial countries. According to my own rough estimate, Russia's scores today range from a two, for example, on large-scale privatization and corporate governance, to a three + on price liberalization and foreign trade and exchange system policies, for an overall score of three or three −. These scores would not be sufficient to earn Russia membership in the EU, but they are indicative of the progress that has been made in market reform since 1991. The long-run outlook for Russia is therefore positive if the Putin and subsequent governments continue to press consistently for gradual reform and avoid foreign policy adventures and domestic distortions caused by corruption and an ambiguous commitment to joining the global economy.

It does not necessarily follow that the market economy that is developing in Russia will be any more successful than many other late-developing market economies, such as Brazil, Mexico, or Argentina. Stop-go economic policies have been endemic in much of Latin America and elsewhere because economic reform runs into resistance from the public and also from the elite members of society. The adverse consequences of stopping reform eventually generate another round of reform, which, in turn, generates public resistance. Escaping from this circular process of reform and reaction is Russia's challenge in the long run. Catching up with the developed economies, or even catching up with the more successful economies of East-Central Europe, is not likely in the foreseeable future. Instability of the global economy may pose problems also. As Marie Lavigne concludes: "The countries in transition do know where they want to go. We are all on the same boat; we know how to make it float but we don't know how to steer it."[21]

Russia has yet to decide definitively where it wants to go, but it has little choice in the long run to do other than to join the world economy in the "boat." The alternative, autarky, failed miserably. The sooner the leadership commits to joining the global economy as a fully fledged market economy, the better off Russia will be.

NOTES

1. Secretariat of the Economic Commission for Europe, *Economic Survey of Europe 2001*, no.1 (New York and Geneva: United Nations, 2001), 109–20; WEFA Group, Emerging Europe Economic Outlook, Second Quarter 2001 (Eddystone,

Pa.: DRI-WEFA, 2001), 3.3–3.15; *World Economic Outlook* 2, first quarter 2002 (Eddystone, Pa.: DRI-WEFA, 2002), 9.3–9.4.

2. Lewis Feuer, ed., *Marx & Engels* (Garden City, N.Y.: Anchor Books, 1959), 320.

3. Gertrude E. Schroeder, "Post-Soviet Economic Reforms in Perspective," in *The Former Soviet Union in Transition*, ed. Richard F. Kaufman and John P. Hardt for the Joint Economic Committee, Congress of the United States (Armonk, N.Y.: M.E. Sharpe, 1993), 65.

4. James R. Millar, *The ABCs of Soviet Socialism* (Urbana: University of Illinois Press, 1981).

5. James R. Millar, "Perestroika and Glasnost: Gorbachev's Gamble on Youth and Truth," in *The Soviet Economic Experiment*, ed. Susan Linz (Urbana: University of Illinois Press, 1990), 269–88.

6. Ed A. Hewett, *Is Soviet Socialism Reformable?* The Ernest Sturc Memorial Lecture, November 8, 1989 (Washington, D.C.: SAIS, Johns Hopkins University, 1989), 1–16.

7. S. S. Shatalin et al., *Transition to the Market, Parts I and II* (Moscow: Cultural Initiatives Foundation, 1990).

8. James R. Millar, "Prospects for Reform: Is (Was) Gorbachev Really Necessary?" in *Europe in Transition: Political, Economic, and Security Prospects for the 1990s*, ed. J. J. Lee and Walter Korter (Austin, Tex.: Lyndon B. Johnson School of Public Affairs, 1991), 76.

9. Abel Aganbegyan, *The Economic Challenge of Perestroika* (Bloomington: Indiana University Press, 1988), 226 (italics added).

10. *Johnson's List*, #5403, August 21, 2001.

11. Yegor Gaidar, *Days of Defeat and Victory* (Seattle: University of Washington Press, 1999).

12. James R. Millar, "The De-development of Russia," *Current History: A Journal of Contemporary World Affairs* 98, no. 630 (October 1999): 322–27.

13. James R. Millar, "Can Putin Jump-Start Russia's Stalled Economy?" *Current History: A Journal of Contemporary World Affairs* 99, no. 639 (October 2000): 329–33.

14. James R. Millar, "The Post–Cold War Settlement and the End of the Transition," Presidential Address, *NewsNet, The Newsletter of the AAASS* 41, no. 1 (January 2001): 1–5.

15. James R. Millar, "The Russian Economy: Putin's Pause," *Current History: A Journal of Contemporary World Affairs* 100, no. 648 (October 2001): 336–42.

16. Sophie Lambroschini, "The Government's Uncertain Role in Land Privatization, Part 1," *RFE/RFL Daily Report*, February 9, 2001.

17. Jonathan Tennenbaum, "The Ishayev Report: An Economic Mobilization Plan for Russia," *Executive Intelligence Review* 28, no. 9 (March 2, 2001).

18. James R. Millar, "Empire Envy and Other Obstacles to Economic Reform in Russia," *Problems of Post-Communism* 45, no. 3 (May/June 1998): 58–64.

19. James R. Millar, "The Economics of the CIS: Reformation, Revolution or Restoration?" in *The Former Soviet Union in Transition*, ed. Richard F. Kaufman and

John P. Hardt for the Joint Economic Committee, Congress of the United States (Armonk, N.Y.: M. E. Sharpe, 1993), 34–56.

20. James R. Millar, "The Post–Cold War Settlement."

21. Marie Lavigne, *The Economics of Transition: From Socialist Economy to Market Economy*, 2d ed. (New York: St. Martin's Press, 1999), 280.

Patriarch Alexy II of Moscow and All Russia presents a jubilee book to former Prime Minister Yevgeny Primakov. January 30, 2000. Photo ITAR-IASS.

Boris Yeltsin leaves the Kremlim after transferring power to Vladimir Putin. December 31, 2000. Photo ITAR-TASS.

Putin meets with Prime Minister Mikhail Kasyanov at a meeting of the State Council. January 25, 2001. Photo ITAR-TASS.

Putin meets with new members of the Federation Council. January 31, 2001. Photo ITAR-TASS.

Funeral procession for a Russian general who died in Chechnya. September 21, 2001. Photo ITAR-TASS.

Putin addresses the German Bundestag. September 25, 2001. Photo ITAR-TASS.

Putin and President George W. Bush field questions at a press conference in Crawford, Texas. November 15, 2001. Photo ITAR-TASS.

Putin and his wife, Lyudmila, are shown the site of the September 11, 2001, attack on the World Trade Center towers in New York, by former Mayor Rudolph Giuliani. November 16, 2001. Photo ITAR-TASS.

Chief of the General Staff, Army General Anatoly Kvashnin (back center) and Duma Deputy Yegor Gaidar prepare for a meeting on military reform. December 7, 2001. Photo ITAR-TASS.

Defense Minister Sergei Ivanov and Colonel Gennady Trosheve, Commander of Federal Armed Forces in the North Caucasus District. December 11, 2001. Photo ITAR-TASS.

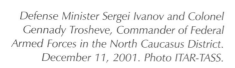

Boris Yeltsin and Vladimir Putin at a ceremony honoring Constitution Day. December 12, 2001. Photo ITAR-TASS.

Vladimir Putin meets with Justice Minister Yuri Chaika at the Kremlin. January 29, 2002. Photo ITAR-TASS.

Putin in Ulyanovsk. July 8, 2000. Photo ITAR-TASS.

Chapter Seven

Putin and the Oligarchs

Peter Rutland

Politics, like nature, abhors a vacuum. With the collapse of the USSR, a huge void of political and economic power opened up in the post–Soviet Union. Key institutional structures such as the Communist Party and the central planning system were dismantled, and the new entities that emerged in their wake (the presidential administration, the State Committee for the Administration of State Property, regional governors) were hard-pressed to expand their effective zone of control.

In the chaos of transition, power shifted from formal political institutions to informal networks of influence among individuals who had political connections or economic resources at their disposal. While market forces penetrated large sections of economic activity, the Russian economy was only partially marketized by the liberalization reforms. A whole parallel barter economy sprang up, accounting for perhaps half of all business-to-business transactions.[1] The interface between polity and economy was mediated by corruption and mutual favors, instead of political orders as under the old regime.

The rise of the oligarchs was unexpected and unpredicted. Nobody watching the tentative *glasnost* reforms of 1986 would have predicted that ten years later thirty-something billionaires would be bankrolling a presidential election campaign with rock concerts, direct mailings, and pop jingles. As the economic controls were gradually loosened under Gorbachev, journalists noted the appearance of bright young entrepreneurs, making money by importing personal computers or selling phone directories. But no one would have imagined that these people would become owners of large swathes of Soviet manufacturing industry, or would push up the price of villas on the Spanish Riviera. Rather, they were portrayed as heroic but somewhat comic figures out of an Ilf and Petrov novel of the roaring 1920s; part of Russia's rich history of eccentrics.[2]

There were bigger stories to pursue in 1989–92: the fall of the Berlin Wall; the titanic duel between Gorbachev and Yeltsin that led to the collapse of the Soviet Union; and the dramatic decision to free prices in January 1992. The reformers hoped that the lifting of economic controls would lead to a surge of entrepreneurship, while the privatization program, involving the distribution of vouchers to all citizens, would produce a "popular capitalism" with ownership distribution among the general population. However, the voucher privatization was hijacked by incumbent directors, who used it to turn their de facto control over their enterprises into de jure ownership, while the expected surge of entrepreneurship in the newly freed private sector failed to materialize. Although about one million small businesses were registered, their development was choked off by bureaucratic regulation on one side and mafia extortion on the other.

Russia's raw capitalism threw up a new class, not of small entrepreneurs, but of powerful oligarchs. The first important signal that the Russian transition had gone badly off track came, curiously enough, in a short newspaper article by an American diplomat in November 1995.[3] Thomas Graham argued that Russia was in fact ruled by a small number of individuals, loosely allied into rival "clans" that were jostling for the ear of the all-powerful president. Yeltsin's crushing of the Congress of People's Deputies in October 1993 had removed the last major challenge to presidential rule. But Yeltsin lacked the power, and the inclination, to rule as a dictator. Instead he was pulled this way and that by cliques of influential advisers—the security apparatus, represented by head bodyguard Aleksandr Korzhakov; the economic reformers, led by Anatoly Chubais; the gas lobby, represented by Victor Chernomyrdin; the military-industry complex, whose advocate was Oleg Soskovets. Real power lay with these individuals, and not with the formal democratic institutions—parliament, the courts, political parties. Russia had dismantled an autocracy, but instead of rule by the many (democracy) it had arrived at rule by the few (oligarchy).

The "clan" metaphor did not quite catch on. It sounded a little archaic and mysterious; and it overstated the extent to which the individuals involved had a group loyalty and identity. People seemed more comfortable with the idea that power was being wielded by clearly identifiable individuals. Hence, by 1996 the favored term was "oligarchs." The word was first used by Aleksandr Privalov of *Ekspert* magazine, who started a regular poll of elites, publishing rankings of who were seen as the most influential political and business figures.[4]

The oligarchs fell into two overlapping groups.[5] One contingent included officials formerly in the middle or upper reaches of the Soviet *nomenklatura*, who managed to negotiate the transition to capitalism and stayed in charge of organizations which were no longer in state ownership, or at least no longer under effective state control.[6] Examples include the natural gas giant

Gazprom, the electricity monopoly Unified Energy Systems or EES, the railways ministry, and the coal conglomerate Rosugol. Even the Central Bank itself can be seen as an autonomous player, since it pursued a fairly independent monetary policy, indulged in all sorts of dubious accounting practices, and rewarded its top officials with lavish salaries.

The second, and more visible, group were young businessmen who had grown rich during the process of market reform.[7] Some of them came from academia, some from the criminal world. Most of them made their initial capital in business start-ups in the late 1980s, mainly through trade or banking operations spun off from state-owned enterprises. Alfa Group, Inkombank, Rosprom, SBS-Agro, and Rossiiskii Kredit all had their origins in enterprises formed under the auspices of the Communist Party of the Soviet Union (CPSU) or its youth branch, the Komsomol. Vladimir Potanin's Oneksimbank came out of the foreign trade ministry, but grew into the most extensive and diversified of the oligarchic holdings.[8] Only Vladimir Gusinsky's Most and Boris Berezovsky's Logovaz can be regarded as relatively independent start-up operations. The oligarchs expanded their scope by gaining control of companies during the voucher privatization launched in 1992.[9] A few years later, a small group of favored insiders bought lucrative state assets such as Norilsk Nickel or the Tyumen Oil Company at giveaway prices during the notoriously corrupt loans-for-shares auctions of 1995.

The leading oligarchs united in their efforts to ensure the re-election of Boris Yeltsin in 1996, after which several of them directly joined the government. The oligarchs had much to offer the Yeltsin administration: energy, leadership, organizational skills, Western contacts, and above all lots of cash. Their most important political asset was control over the main media: print, radio, and television. Most of these media outlets were making huge losses, but they enabled the oligarchs to convert money into political power. The media gave them the power to mould public opinion, to make or break reputations, and to shape elite perceptions and policy debates. The path was blazed by entrepreneurs such as Vladimir Gusinsky and Boris Berezovsky, but they were followed by mainstream oil companies and banks. Gusinsky's Most Bank founded NTV television and the newspaper *Segodnya* in 1993, by 1996 Berezovsky had control over the TV stations ORT and TV-6 and papers *Nezavisimaya gazeta* and *Novye izvestiia*. Potanin's Oneksimbank controlled the papers *Komsomol'skaia pravda*, *Izvestiya*, *Russkii telegraf*, and *Ekspert*.[10] Another political asset was the private security services that each magnate assembled. Apart from providing physical protection, such services gathered intelligence (*kompromat*) which could be used to discredit rival oligarchs or uncooperative politicians. In return the oligarchs grew fat from government favors: export and import licenses, soft loans, the right to handle government accounts ("authorized banks"), government contracts, lax taxation, and first claim on assets to be privatized.

In the spring of 1997, the liberal wing of the government tried to launch a second wave of reforms, raising utility prices and cracking down on corruption. Deputy Prime Minister Boris Nemtsov started attacking the oligarchs in the name of "popular capitalism." But the reforms were blocked by an unholy alliance of business interests, regional governors, and the communist opposition. There was no constituency in favor of raising utility prices, and cheap energy seemed vital for domestic political tranquillity. Subsidized fuel suited some oligarchs very well (especially the metals producers), and those whom it harmed (the oil and gas companies) were compensated through tax breaks and permission to pocket the lion's share of their export earnings. In the summer of 1997, the oligarchs started feuding over how to divide the spoils in the next wave of privatization—most notably, the telecommunications monopoly and the remaining state-owned oil companies. By September the fighting—in the form of personal attacks and corruption allegations in rival newspapers—was so intense that Yeltsin called the six leading bankers to a meeting and persuaded them to declare a truce.[11]

Crony capitalism, it seemed, was here to stay. The reform process was stalled in midstream.[12] Powerful leaders had a vested interest in preserving the status quo, and there was no significant coalition of groups with a stake in further reform. Ordinary citizens were dissatisfied but felt powerless. The economy had been sufficiently liberalized to enable the oligarchs to enrich themselves, but not so much as to expose them to effective competition (from foreign companies, for example). They showed little interest in the creation of effective legal and regulatory institutions, which could threaten their power and independence. The downside of this partial reform was that economic output fell for seven years in a row, while investment declined even more precipitately. One reason for the slump in investment was that the property rights of the new owners were precarious, and could be challenged by a rival clan, or by the state, at any time.

The rise of the oligarchs was a striking and unexpected development in post-Soviet Russia, but the fact that business elites exercise political power is hardly unusual in a global and historical perspective. In that broader comparative context, what is striking about contemporary Russia is how important a role is still played by the state, and in particular by the presidential apparatus. Russia is still quite a way from a Latin American model, with "all power to the oligarchs."

THE AUGUST CRISIS

The key turning point in Russia's economic evolution in the 1990s was the August 1998 financial crash. The crisis was caused by two erroneous policies. First, the government borrowed money to defend the ruble at an exchange rate that was overvalued against the dollar, and second, it issued $40 billion of short-term debt to cover its yawning budget deficit instead of trying to cut government spending. Russia was also struggling to meet payments on $150 billion of foreign debt and was kept afloat only by $80 billion in annual earnings from oil, gas, and metals exports. The 1997 Asian financial crisis caused a slump in commodity prices; Russia's trade surplus eroded; and international investors panicked. In August 1998 the Russian government defaulted on its debts, the ruble lost 75 percent of its value, and most private banks collapsed, wiping out much of the savings of Russia's nascent middle class. The oligarchs were seriously weakened by the August 1998 financial crisis. Many went bankrupt, and the survivors were even more dependent on financial assistance and other favors from the state. A few banks survived the crisis and were able to strengthen their position as a result (such as Alfa Bank and SBS-Agro). The oil, gas, and metals producers were generally unaffected.

At the insistence of the State Duma, in September the conservative Yevgeny Primakov was appointed prime minister, and he launched anticorruption probes against some of the oligarchs, notably Boris Berezovsky. Berezovsky's holdings included Aeroflot, the auto company Logovaz, and oil interests. He also had effective control over Russian Public Television (ORT). Berezovsky was close to Yeltsin's daughter Tatiana Diachenko: his network of contacts in the Kremlin was known as "the Family."

Primakov's anticorruption campaign led to his own dismissal by Yeltsin in March 1999. He subsequently joined forces with regional leaders, Moscow Mayor Yuri Luzhkov and Tatarstan President Mintimer Shaimiev, to mount the most serious political challenge yet to the Yeltsin establishment—the Fatherland/All Russia (OVR) alliance. To meet this threat Yeltsin installed Vladimir Putin, the head of the Federal Security Service (FSB), as prime minister in August 1999. From his new position, Putin oversaw the launch of the second Chechen war, in retaliation for terrorist bombings and raids on Dagestan. The war drew broad public support, and Putin showed himself to be a competent and effective leader.

Kremlin aides launched the Unity party to challenge OVR in the December 1999 State Duma election. Berezovsky's media rallied to the Kremlin cause, with the ORT channel launching blistering attacks on Luzhkov and Primakov. The campaign worked. Unity finished second with 23 percent of the vote, only just behind the Communists, and Fatherland/All Russia was placed third with 13 percent.

On December 31, 1999, the eve of the new millennium, Yeltsin resigned and appointed Putin acting president. Putin then set about preparing himself for the March 2000 presidential election. The main challenger, as in 1996, would be the anemic and uncharismatic Communist stalwart, Gennadiy Zyuganov. Key figures from Berezovsky's clique stayed on in the Kremlin. The only leading figure to be let go was Yeltsin's daughter, Tatiana Diachenko.

Most notably, Putin reappointed Aleksandr Voloshin, the éminence grise of the Berezovsky clan, as chief of staff of the presidential administration, a pivotal position controlling access to the president. Allegations repeatedly surfaced over the next two years about Voloshin's financial machinations at Sibneft and the AVVA auto concern back in 1994–95, but Putin has kept him on.[13] The financial linchpin of the Family, Pavel Borodin, was appointed to head the Russia–Belarus Union. This post granted him diplomatic immunity, which was useful given that on January 26, 2000, he was indicted by Swiss prosecutors for money laundering during his time as Kremlin property chief.[14]

Already by February 2000 it was clear that Putin was headed to certain electoral victory, so Russia's political and economic elite was lining up to support him. Berezovsky gave out the impression that he personally had been the architect of Putin's rise to power.[15] This seemed to be confirmed by a February government decision to allow the Berezovsky-allied Sibneft oil company to merge with Oleg Deripaska's Sibal to form a company that would control 70 percent of Russian aluminum production. However, one week before the election Putin sent a warning signal. Speaking to Radio Mayak on March 18, he attacked the oligarchs who have been "merging power with capital" and declared, "Such a class of oligarchs will cease to exist." With state and private media rallying to his cause, Putin's approval ratings continued to rise, carrying him to a first-round victory over Zyuganov.[16]

PUTIN IN CHARGE

At the time of his election, Putin was widely regarded as a tool of the Family with no independent standing or room for maneuver. These skeptics underestimated Putin's ability to use the authority vested in him as acting—and then elected—president to chart his own course.

Yeltsin's penchant for political reshuffles and aversion to the routine tasks of government had produced administrative chaos. Putin wanted to restore a stable chain of command, but it was not clear whether he had the administrative experience or the team of loyal cadres to pull this off.

The officials in the government and presidential apparatus were divided into three rival groupings in the spring of 2000:

1. "The Family"—Chief of Staff Aleksandr Voloshin, Prime Minister Mikhail Kasianov, Railways Minister Nikolai Aksenenko, Procurator-General Vladimir Ustinov, Energy Minister Viktor Kaliuzhnyi, Atomic Energy Minister Yevgenii Adamov, Science Minister Valerii Kirpichni-

kov; plus other figures outside government such as former Yeltsin aide Valentin Yumashev and MDM-Bank head Aleksandr Mamut.

2. "The Petersburg Liberals"—Economics Minister German Gref; Deputy Prime Ministers Aleksei Kudrin and Viktor Khristenko; Dmitrii Kozak, deputy head of the presidential administration in charge of legal reform; Antimonopoly Minister Ilya Yuzhanov; and presidential economics advisor Andrei Illarionov.[17]

3. "The Security Men"—Security Council Secretary Sergei Ivanov, FSB head Nikolai Patrushev, Viktor Cherkessov (deputy head of FSB), Defense Minister Igor Sergeev, Deputy Prime Minister and defense industry chief Ilya Klebanov, Interior Minister Vladimir Rushailo, Igor Sechin, the head of the presidential chancellery; Viktor Ivanov, the deputy head of the presidential administration; Viktor Zolotov, the head of the Presidential Security Service.

A significant proportion of both the liberals and security men (*siloviki*) were acquainted with Putin from St. Petersburg, where he had spent most of his career. His four years in Moscow also enabled him to forge some links with the Kremlin apparatus and with the FSB and other security ministries.[18] But generally it was thought that the St. Petersburg team (both its liberal and security wings) were not sufficiently experienced and influential to really pose a threat to the political and economic establishment that had emerged in Moscow under Yeltsin's rule. The continuation in office of staff chief Voloshin and Premier Kasianov signaled to many that the Family was still calling the shots.

Putin apparently had good working relations with all three groups in his administration, and wanted to delineate duties more clearly in order to stamp out factional conflicts—something that Yeltsin had actually encouraged as part of his "checks and balances" style of rule. There was no immediate purge of ministers after Putin took over. Kaliuzhnyi was dropped as energy minister, but even he was kept on in the government as special representative for development of the Caspian basin. It was widely reported that the Family had dissuaded Putin from appointing his first choice for procurator general, Dmitrii Kozak, in favor of Vladimir Ustinov. But the expected open warfare between rival clans fighting for the spoils of the new administration failed to materialize. Instead, Putin initially turned his attention to reining in the power of the regional bosses who, like the oligarchs, had grown fat during the Yeltsin era.

THE MEDIA CRACKDOWN

One oligarch who remained outside the broad tent that Putin had erected was Vladimir Gusinsky, whose media outlets had backed the wrong horse (the OVR alliance of Primakov and Luzhkov) in the 1999 Duma election. Gusinsky's television channel, NTV, ran into financial problems after the August 1998 crash, and the government refused to help out. NTV ended up borrowing $400 million from the Gazprom corporation (still 40 percent state-owned and closely tied to the Kremlin). Putin grew increasingly displeased with NTV's objective coverage of the war in Chechnya. Another bone of contention was NTV's puppet satire show *Kukly*, which portrayed Putin in a variety of unflattering scenes. (At the end of May 2000 *Kukly* agreed to drop the Putin puppet.)

These tensions boiled over in the aftermath of the presidential election. Masked tax and security police staged a dramatic raid on Gusinsky's Media-MOST offices in downtown Moscow on May 11. Media-MOST was not only a media company, it also ran an extensive private security service that snooped on business and political rivals to gather *kompromat*. On June 13, Gusinsky himself was arrested and locked in the infamous Butyrka prison, on vague charges dating back to 1998 involving the privatization of a small Petersburg company called Russkoe Video. He was released three days later, after an international outcry. Putin was on a state visit to Spain and Germany at the time, and he neither endorsed nor condemned the arrest. Gusinsky, who was also the president of the World Jewish Congress, was a highly visible international figure. During his visit to Moscow just a week earlier, on June 4–5, President Bill Clinton had done a phone-in on Gusinsky's radio station *Ekho Moskvy*. Gusinsky's respected *Itogi* news magazine, which was forced to close, had been a joint venture with *Newsweek*.

In July Gusinsky made a secret deal with Press Minister Mikhail Lesin and the head of Gazprom-Media, Alfred Kokh, under which he agreed to cede control over NTV in return for the cancellation of its debts to Gazprom and the dropping of criminal charges. Gusinsky was allowed to leave the country, and in September, from the safety of Gibraltar, he publicly denounced the deal. Lesin was reprimanded by Prime Minister Kasianov for making the obviously illegal deal, but was not fired. In November Gusinsky reluctantly agreed to allow Gazprom-Media to take a 46 percent stake in NTV with an additional 19 percent as collateral.

During the summer months a number of other oligarchs also felt the hand of the state on their shoulder. Vladimir Potanin's Interros, Anatoly Chubais's electricity monopoly EES, and the Tyumen Oil Company were all accused of irregularities during their privatization, while LUKoil, auto giant AvtoVAZ, Gazprom, and Roman Abramovich's Sibneft were all subject to tax inspections. None of these probes led to any actual arrests or legal actions, but they served their purpose of warning the oligarchs. Polls suggested that the Russian public were either indifferent to these struggles or sympathetic with Putin: 44 percent expressed approval, and only 6 percent expressed concern about his moves against the oligarchs.[19] In a bid to calm the waters and consolidate his position, on July 28, 2000, Putin met with twenty-one leading businessmen in the Kremlin.[20] In contrast to previous meetings between Yeltsin and select oligarchs, this time it seemed to be the president laying down terms to the oligarchs, rather than the reverse. Also noteworthy was the absence of some key figures from the meeting. Gusinsky, Berezovsky, and Sibneft's Abramovich were not invited, and Chubais declined to attend. The outcome of the meeting was a bland statement that the state would cooperate with businesses "whose actions function in the state's interests." Putin was signaling that the age of the oligarchs was over, but in reality it was business as usual for those who were willing to avoid mounting a political challenge to Putin. Putin made no serious effort to reverse the corrupt privatizations of previous years, nor to overhaul the sweetheart deals under which the oligarchs reaped rich dividends from exporting Russia's natural resources.

The oligarchs seemed content with or perhaps resigned to the new order, at least once Gusinsky had been released from jail. After the June meeting with Putin, most of the top oligarchs decided to join the Russian Union of Industrialists and Entrepreneurs (RSPP), a rather staid organization representing traditional state-owned factories headed by a Gorbachev-era functionary, Arkadii Volskii.[21]

Apart from Gusinsky, the other oligarch in Putin's sights was Berezovsky. On May 31, 2000, Berezovsky published an open letter denouncing Putin's plans to revise Russia's federal structure and weaken the power of regional leaders. In June, under pressure to repay a $100 million loan from state-owned Vneshekonombank, Berezovsky announced that he was ready to transfer his 49 percent stake in the television company ORT back to the state. On July 14, procurators interviewed Berezovsky in connection with Aeroflot's foreign currency accounts. In a curious move, Berezovsky gave up his seat in the State Duma on July 19 (a post which gave him immunity from prosecution) and tried to create a political movement in opposition to Putin. He recruited a handful of intellectuals and movie stars to sign his manifesto, "Russia at the Crossroads," which was published on August 9, but there was no public response. In October, Berezovsky was again questioned over the Aeroflot case, and he was forced to vacate the state-owned villa near Moscow that he was renting for $300,000 a year. In November he went into exile. In an interview with NTV on November 16, Berezovsky claimed that money from Aeroflot had been channeled into the Unity and Putin election campaigns. However, exile was not necessarily a safe haven for the oppositional oligarchs. On December 12, 2000, Spanish police arrested Gusinsky, acting on an Interpol warrant filed by Russian prosecutors. Gusinsky was released on bail, and on December 26 a Moscow court dismissed the fraud case against him.

In the midst of the NTV crisis, leading businessmen from the RSPP issued a statement disowning Berezovsky, stating, "We view the attempt of big business to monopolize control over the country as the worst mistake of the past decade. The same goes for the attempt to force its will on the government through the use of controlled media."[22] On January 24, 2001, Putin held a second meeting with the oligarchs. Those present included Mikhail Fridman (Alfa Bank), Mikhail Khodorkovsky (Yukos oil company), Yevgennii Shvidler (Sibneft), Vladimir Bogdanov (Surgutneftegaz oil), Anatoly Chubais (EES), Rem Viakhirev (Gazprom), and a couple of new faces: Vladimir Kogan, chairman of Promstroibank–St. Petersburg, and Oleg Deripaska, head of Russian Aluminum. Deripaska had just (November 2000) managed to acquire, in a hostile takeover, 25 percent of the auto giant Gorkii AZ in Nizhniy Novgorod.

Interestingly, the same month Deripaska was uninvited from the Davos World Economic Forum, following the filing of a suit by three Western companies accusing him of making death threats.[23] Later in 2001, Deripaska married the daughter of Valentin Yumashev, Yeltsin's ghostwriter and former head of the presidential administration. Yumashev in his turn married Yeltsin's daughter, Tatiana Diachenko.

Although some saw Putin's summer offensive against the media barons as signaling the end of the oligarchs, Putin's crackdown was limited to those who mounted an open political challenge to his rule. Critics saw Putin's moves against Berezovsky and Gusinsky as targeting not so much those individuals themselves, but the relatively critical and independent media that they controlled. They viewed it as part of a systematic campaign to limit free speech and reassert state control over the media. Indeed it is clear that the main targets of Putin's campaign were those oligarchs who had used their wealth to create media empires. Putin's defenders argued that it was appropriate for Putin to end the manipulation of the media by the oligarchs, and that it did not necessarily mean that he was an enemy of democracy.

THE RETURN OF THE CLAN WARS

Putin kept the Family appointees in place during his first year in office, but in March 2001 he dismissed most of the top security officials he had inherited from Yeltsin and replaced them with his own people, many drawn from the "Petersburg Chekists."[24] Defense Minister Igor Sergeev was replaced with Sergei Ivanov, a former KGB official and close Putin ally. Vladimir Rushailo, a Family appointee, replaced Ivanov as head of the Security Council, and Petersburg politician turned Unity party leader Boris Gryzlov took over from Rushailo as interior minister. Among those who left were Minister of Natural Resources Boris Yatskevich and Nuclear Energy Minister Yevgenii Adamov. Adamov was reportedly implicated in shady business around a $12 billion project to import and process spent nuclear fuel.

However, this shuffling of the security apparatus did not touch the Family. Through the rest of 2001, observers argued that the various Kremlin factions were waging a bitter, but hidden, struggle for power. It was assumed that a victory for the Chekists over the Family could pose a serious threat for the oligarchs as a whole.[25] Presidential economic adviser Andrei Illarionov openly stated in December 2001 that the power struggles under Putin "are no less vicious than they were under President Yeltsin."[26] Valerii Yakov argued that there was "a constant battle for access to the president's ear."[27] These battles within the administration did not directly involve the oligarchs, however. As one editorial cynically observed: "No one is competing with the president for power; all are competing for a place under his right heel."[28] Yet Natalia Astrakhanova argues that "the president doesn't hold the controlling interest in Russia Inc. There are many shareholders in this corporation; making decisions acceptable to everyone is difficult, and making decisions fast is altogether impossible."[29] Inessa Slavutinskaia argued that "the people from St. Petersburg want the financial channels of the Railroads Ministry, Alrosa and the State Customs Committee, which are all still controlled by the Family."[30]

A new wave of anticorruption investigations was launched in 2001 by the procurator's office and the Duma's Audit Chamber—but behind them observers saw the hand of the "Petersburg Chekists." However, Svetlana Babaeva warns against oversimplifying and polarizing the Kremlin intrigues. "The concepts of 'St. Petersburg team' and 'family' are flexible, because too many changes have taken place in Russia. It is not a geographic location, it is rather a way of thinking. It is a system of recognition, of telling 'us' from 'them.'"[31]

Putin did recruit some loyal executives from St. Petersburg and placed them in key national companies.[32] Most notably, on May 30, 2001, he ousted the long-standing head of Gazprom, Rem Viakhirev, and replaced him with a young economist from Petersburg, Aleksei Miller, who had spent six months as deputy energy minister. Gazprom's $15 billion exports make it Russia's largest cash earner and the second largest company after Unified Electricity Systems (EES). It has more than its share of scandal, with new revelations surfacing in 2001 about its Enron-like transactions with subsidiary Itera.[33] Similarly, Sergei Zivenko was parachuted into the alcohol manufacturer Rosspirtprom and Valerii Yashin into the telecom holding company Svyazinvest. Putin even brought in people he had known in East Germany (Andrei Belianinov and Sergei Chemezov) to head the newly merged arms export companies.[34]

In the absence of major reform initiatives from the Kremlin, business elites had little to complain about. At their third meeting with Putin on May 31, 2001, the assembled businessmen raised few complaints: the main grouse seemed to be the continuing requirement that 75 percent of dollar earnings be exchanged into rubles.[35] Of the twenty-two men at the meeting, nine came from the oil and gas sector, six from metals and engineering, six from banking, and only one from a high-tech company. The most sensitive political decision was the setting of export duties on oil and natural gas.[36] Finance Minister Kudrin and Central Bank chief Gerashchenko argued for higher rates to enable Russia to meet its foreign debt repayments, while the energy bosses pleaded for more profits to finance investment.[37] A new unified tariff body, the Federal Energy Commission, was created to fix prices in all the natural monopolies. Its head, Grigorii Kutovoi, was seen as a member of the Family, hostile to Chubais's pleas to raise electricity prices, but approving higher rates for Gazprom.[38] Chubais devised an ambitious program to split EES into twenty regional divisions and divide its generation and transmission businesses, in a bid to separate out the profitable sides of the operation. This plan was attacked by regional elites fearful of losing their cheap power, and even by foreign owners of EES shares, who feared being cheated. Despite these attacks from all sides, Chubais has managed to hold onto his position as head of EES.[39] It helps that he has long-standing ties with Gref and Kudrin, Putin's leading economic officials.

Meanwhile, it was largely business as usual for the oligarchs. In the course of 2001 there were ownership conflicts over major regional companies such as Rospan, Ust-Ilim combine, Karabash, and Kuzbassugol. Ironically, the new 1998 bankruptcy law opened up new opportunities for rivals to tie up the assets of companies they coveted, by filing suit for bankruptcy often in corruption-prone provincial courts. Major companies such as Severstal, Gazprom, Mosenergo, LUKoil, and Transenergo found themselves entangled in such proceedings in 2001.[40] Vladimir Potanin's Interros group bought a 34 percent stake in Novolipetsk Metal Combine, the third largest steelmaker, but was not able to win full control. He did however manage to block George Soros's efforts to restructure Svyazinvest.[41] In general, an OECD study concluded, "There is no unified economic space, or level playing field in Russia" for foreign investors.[42] Projects were undermined, for example, by the sudden withdrawal of phone frequencies or changes in rail tariffs, plus many "unforeseen hurdles" such as negotiable regional taxes.

Ekspert magazine continued to track the rise and fall of various oligarchs. The end of 2001 saw the decline of Sibneft's Abramovich (who had retreated to the post of governor of distant Chukotka) to be replaced at the head of the list by Victor Gerashchenko, the head of the Central Bank (a post he had held in the Soviet Union). The rising figures on the list are not independent players, but those with close ties to the Kremlin: Sergei Pugachev (Mezhprombank), Leonid Reiman, Vladimir Kogan.[43] Inessa Slavutinskaia still sees the key oligarchs as those from the Family stable: Deripaska, Abramovich, Chubais, and Mamut.[44] In December 2000, Mamut's MDM Bank managed to recruit some top officials from rival Alfa-Bank, and Mamut headed the commission of the Russian Union of Industrialists and Entrepreneurs (RSPP), which prepared the first draft of the anemic bank reform in fall of 2001.

MEDIA WAR, PART TWO

The struggle against the independent media of Gusinsky/Berezovsky continued in 2001.[45] Although Gusinsky, living abroad, was beyond the Kremlin's reach, Media-MOST's chief financial officer Anton Titov was arrested in January on embezzlement charges. Efforts by Gusinsky to transfer ownership of his assets such as *Ekho Moskvy* radio station to the journalists who worked there were blocked by Gazprom-media. In April 2001, Gazprom-media took over NTV, and looked around for new owners.[46] Moves by foreigners such as Ted Turner to bail out the station were rebuffed, and in mid-May 2001, Yevgenii Kisilev and his team of talented journalists quit NTV and moved to TV-6, taking with them key commentary programs like *Itogi* and *Glas naroda*. Boris Jordan, an American banker and associate of Chubais, became the new chief of NTV, and the channel has managed to retain a degree of its professional integrity.

Attention then shifted to the Moscow-based TV-6 channel. Berezovsky owned 37 percent of MNVK, which operates TV-6, and in 1999 the station head Eduard Sagalaev sold him another 37 percent. LUKoil-garant, the oil giant's pension fund, owned 15 percent. The arrival of the Kisilev team at TV-6 prompted LUKoil-garant to sue, presumably at the Kremlin's instigation, although claiming that as the company was making losses and not paying dividends it should be liquidated. In November the Moscow Arbitration Court threw out the LUKoil-garant case, but this decision was reversed on appeal to the federal arbitration court on December 29. TV-6 was ordered closed on January 11, 2002, shutting down the last non-state-controlled TV station in Russia.[47] TV-6 had reached 80 million viewers through 156 regional affiliates, so the impact of the closure would be felt beyond Moscow.[48] Meanwhile, in October 2001, a new arrest warrant had been issued for Berezovsky, currently living in London, in the case of diversion of revenues from Aeroflot that had been originally investigated (and dropped) in 1999. The case was revived and four top Aeroflot officials were indicted in July 2001.

HUNTING SEASON

One utility that had ridden the storms of transition fairly successful was the railways ministry, MPS. Trains somehow managed to run on time, and more or less made a profit, using revenues from freight customers to subsidize passenger travel. MPS head Nikolai Aksenenko was widely tipped as a possible successor to Prime Minister Kasianov. However, on October 22, 2001, criminal charges were filed against Aksenenko, charging him with illegally spending $2.3 million on apartments for his deputy ministers.[49] The charge stemmed from an investigation by the parliament's Audit Chamber, headed by ex-premier Sergei Stepashin. The MPS was also under investigation for hiding $1.9 billion revenue in off-budget funds, and failing to pay $370 million in federal taxes. Aksenenko was replaced by Gennadii Fadeev, who had previously served as railroads minister from 1992 until 1996.

In December 2001, prosecutors arrested the director of Gazprom subsidiary SIBUR, Yakov Goldovskii, and two assistants and charged them with embezzling 2.6 billion rubles (US$90 million). The arrests sent shock waves through the business community: a delegation from the Russian Union of Industrialists and Entrepreneurs spent two hours with Procurator-General Vladimir Ustinov, seeking assurances that a witch-hunt of businessmen was not in the offing.[50] They were probably not reassured by Putin's comments in a January 14 interview in France, where he said, "It so happens in Russia that a man who drinks too much vodka and beats up his neighbor is jailed as a hooligan, and man who stole a sackful of potatoes is jailed as a thief. On the other hand, the men who embezzled capital running into tens or hundreds of millions are viewed as politicians."[51]

THE OLIGARCHS IN THE REGIONS

During the Yeltsin years, attention was riveted on the clashes between oligarchs struggling for the commanding heights of the national economy, in major privatization deals that were decided in Moscow. Under Putin, attention has shifted to the role of oligarchs at the regional level. From the beginning, of course, oligarchs had a strong presence in the regions, since that was where their mines and oil fields, their smelters and steel mills were located. In most cases, it was mutually beneficial for business leaders and regional governors to work in tandem. The former would finance the governor's election campaigns, would pay local taxes, and would invite the governor and/or his cronies into lucrative business ventures. In return, the governor would provide a political "roof" (*krysha*) for the entrepreneur. The governor could use his influence over the regional police and courts to protect businessmen from challenges to their property rights (such as creditors seeking payment) or from worker unrest. In 1996, Gazprom was the only major corporation to run its own candidates in gubernatorial elections in ten regions—winning only in Yamal-Nenets Autonomous Okrug. More typical was for a corporation to "domesticate" the governor—witness Siberian Aluminum and Aleksei Lebed in Khakassiia or Severstal and Viacheslav Pozgalev in Vologda.[52]

Corporations also had some interest in placing their people in local legislatures.

In some cases there was more than one important business located in a region, which could lead to fierce battles between rival elites. For example, in the oil-rich Nenets Autonomous Okrug in 2001, Severnaia neft backed the incumbent governor Vladimir Butov, beating off a challenge from a LUKoil-sponsored candidate. In Murmansk, Norilsk Nickel, the MDM bank, Severstal, and Menatep-Yukos began competing for influence. Some governors, most notably Yurii Luzhkov in Moscow, have managed to forge corporate structures of their own which can stand up against outside rivals. The controversial Governor Yevgennii Nazdratenko had created such a power base in Primorskii krai, in Russia's Far East. Once Putin had engineered his removal in 2001 (he was "promoted" to minister of fisheries), Severstal and Evrazkholding moved in, buying shares in the province's major ports.

Robert Orttung notes that "Russia's richest businessmen are much more powerful than its governors, so the appearance of these big businesses in the regions puts severe constraints on what the governors can do in their own region."[53] Increasingly, as the decade wore on one saw businessmen looking to move directly into political office, sponsoring their own candidates or even running for governor themselves. This is not a favored option for most business leaders, however. It distracts them from their moneymaking activities and lays them open to the vagaries of political competition. Still, the year 2000 provided some striking examples. Roman Abramovich, the head of Sibneft and Siberian Aluminum, got himself elected governor of the impoverished province of Chukotka, on the shores of the Bering Sea.[54] This baffling move was driven by a sudden attack of altruism, and/or a desire to take time out from the snake pits of Moscow. Abramovich was not alone, however. Norilsk Nickel director Aleksandr Khloponin was elected head of the equally remote Taimyr republic; Yukos director Boris Zolotarev became head of Evenkiia; and in January 2002 the head of the diamond monopoly Alrosa, Viacheslav Shtyrov, was elected president of Sakha.[55] Putin's reform stripping governors of their seats in the Federation Council created a new opportunity for businessmen to seek appointment as senators. Some see the potential for a powerful coalition of regional leaders and business magnates lining up to constrain Putin's authority.[56]

Another interesting development in recent years has been the emergence of new regionally based conglomerates as successful metals producers plough back their profits into buying upstream manufacturing plants—unlike the financial-industrial groups of the mid-1990s, which were typically put together by Moscow-based banks. Hence 2001 saw Aleksei Mordashov, director of the Severstal steel mill in Cherepovets, acquiring the Ulianovsk and Zavolzhskii auto plants, the UGMK (Magnitka) metals combine, and

Kuzbasugol coal mine.[57] Similarly Deripaska's Rusal bought Nizhniy Novgorod's Gorki AZ auto plant, Avtobank and insurer Ingosstrakh.

CONCLUSION

Putin's crackdown against the media barons in the summer of 2000 did little to alter the structure of oligarchic capitalism in Russia. Contrary to the hopes of the communists, there was no mass reversal of privatization, no top-level convictions for theft and corruption during the loans-for-shares and other scandals. Despite his background as a seventeen-year KGB veteran, Putin was apparently comfortable with the idea of an economy based on private ownership and market pricing. He was even, apparently, comfortable with the type of crony capitalism that had emerged in Russia. Aleksandr Tsipko argues that "[j]ust as under Yeltsin, Russia is still ruled by a group of oligarchs via their protégés in the president's administration, the government and the security services."[58]

Putin's outlook on life had been transformed during the years 1989–95. In Dresden he witnessed firsthand the irrelevance of the security state, when he saw crowds of unarmed demonstrators topple the East German regime. Then, as head of the department working with foreign investors in the administration of the reformist mayor of St. Petersburg, Anatoly Sobchak, Putin learned the ropes of doing business in the new Russia. He was a pragmatist, not a zealot: neither a zealot for anticorruption, nor a zealot for market reform. He had no desire to roll back the market reforms that had been put in place under Yeltsin, but nor did he have any desire to disrupt the status quo with further change. Rather, the direction of Putin's reforms would be to streamline procedures and regularize the legal–administrative framework: to routinize what had previously been managed by informal norms and relationships.[59] The new philosophy was summed up by Gleb Pavlovskii, the architect of Putin's election campaign, who related how Putin told a private meeting with businessmen that "[t]hey could keep what they had already stolen, but now they had to play clean, pay taxes, make investments and stay out of politics."[60]

However, it is not clear that the political economy that Putin inherited from Yeltsin is either stable or capable of generating economic recovery. Commentators began talking about the onset of a "new stagnation" era, with a moribund economy kept afloat by oil earnings.[61] Liberals were convinced that business as usual would not suffice and that another round of reforms was necessary.[62] Putin even appointed such a radical thinker, Andrei Illarionov, as his official economic advisor.

Whatever Putin's real views on this issue, in his first years in office he did not develop a serious plan for dismantling the power of the oligarchs as a class. Reform efforts were concentrated on controlling the regional leaders, and plugging some of the legal and administrative gaps in the architecture of the new state (tax law, land code, labor code, judicial reform, etc.) Measures that aroused public anxiety, such as reform of the financially strapped pension fund and public utilities, were postponed. Likewise steps that would seriously threaten the politics of backroom favors, such as banking reform, made glacial progress. It's not clear whether the slow pace of change is because Putin does not understand the need for reform, or because he still lacks the political authority to carry it out.

NOTES

1. Alena V. Ledeneva, *Russia's Economy of Favours: Blat, Networking and Informal Exchanges* (Cambridge: Cambridge University Press 1998), David Woodruff, *Money Unmade: Barter and the Fate of Russian Capitalism* (Ithaca, N.Y.: Cornell University Press, 1999).

2. For an amusing account, see Craig Copetas, *Bear Hunting with the Politburo* (New York: Simon and Schuster, 1991).

3. Thomas Graham, "The New Russian Regime," *Nezavisimaya gazeta*, November 23, 1995.

4. Olga Romanova, "News," *Vedomosti*, January 29, 2002.

5. Sergei Peregudov, "Corporate Capital in Russian Politics," *Polis* 6, no. 4 (2000).

6. David M. Kotz and Fred Weir, *Revolution from Above: The Demise of the Soviet System* (New York: Routledge, 1997); David Lane and Cameron Ross, *The Transition from Communism to Capitalism: Ruling Elites from Gorbachev to Yeltsin* (New York: St. Martin's, 1999).

7. For journalists' accounts of life among the oligarchs, see Rose Brady, *Kapitalizm: Russia's Struggle to Free Its Economy* (New Haven, Conn.: Yale University Press, 1999); Chrystia Freeland, *Sale of the Century: Russia's Wild Ride from Communism to Capitalism* (New York: Crown Business, 2000); Paul Klebnikov, *Godfather of the Kremlin: Boris Berezovsky and the Looting of Russia* (New York: Harcourt, 2000); Matthew Brzezinski, *Casino Moscow: A Tale of Greed and Adventure on Capitalism's Wildest Frontier* (New York: Free Press, 2001).

8. Tatiana Lysova, "Reform of the Oligarchs," *Ekspert*, March 18, 1998.

9. Interview with Uralmash head Kakha Bendukidze, "Russian Business: What Kind of Life," *Ekspert*, January 21, 2002.

10. Laura Belin, Floriana Fossato, and Anna Kachkaeva, "The Distorted Media Market," in *Business and the State in Contemporary Russia*, ed. Peter Rutland (Boulder, Colo.: Westview Press, 2001); Yelena Rykovtseva, "No Unity within Russia's Matryoshka Media," *Russian Journal*, August 10, 2001.

11. Dmitrii Pinsker, "Anti-Davos in Moscow," *Itogi*, September 23, 1997.

12. Joel Hellman, "Winners Take All: The Politics of Partial Reform in Post-Communist Transitions," *World Politics*, no. 50 (January 1998): 203–34.

13. "Informed sources say that leaving Voloshin alone for at least a year was one

of the agreements between Yeltsin and Putin when the matter of succession was discussed." Inessa Slavutinskaia, "Aleksandr the First," *Profil*, no. 21 (May 5–11, 2000).

14. Andrew Higgins, "Swiss Money-Laundering Probe Finds a Kremlin Link," *Wall Street Journal*, July 23, 2001.

15. One specific indicator of their familiarity was that Putin, then head of the FSB, attended Berezovksy's wife's birthday party in February 1999, a time when he was facing corruption charges.

16. Peter Rutland, "Putin's Path to Power," *Post-Soviet Affairs* 16, no. 4 (December 2000): 313–54.

17. Thanks to Oleg Kharkhordin for clarification on the composition of this team.

18. Ivan Trefilov, "Muscovites Swell the Ranks of the People from St. Petersburg," *Vedomosti*, no. 45 (July 2–4, 2001).

19. VTsIOM poll, July 20–25, 2000.

20. Inessa Slvutinskaia, "Liberalissimo," *Profil*, August 7, 2000.

21. They included Kakha Bendukidze, Oleg Deripaska, Aleksander Mamut, Vladimir Potanin, Mikhail Fridman, Mikhail Khodorkovsky, and Anatoly Chubais. Aleksei Germanovich, "Tycoons Will Repent," *Vedomosti*, February 14, 2001.

22. Aleksei Germanovich, "Submission," *Vedomosti*, February 15, 2001.

23. Jamestown *Monitor*, January 25, 2001.

24. The Cheka was Lenin's secret police. This group is also known as the "ghosts" and "oligarchs in uniform." Konstantin Smirnov, Andrei Bagrov, "Putin's Warriors," *Kommersant-Vlast*, no. 45 (November 2001); Konstantin Smirnov, "Winter Hunt," *Kommersant-Vlast*, no. 48 (December 2001).

25. Kirill Rogov, "Snake Eating Its Own Tail," at www.polit.ru (last accessed December 7, 2001); Boris Vishnevsky et al., "Equidistance in Different Directions," *Obshchaia gazeta*, June 7–13, 2001.

26. Yelena Tregubova, "Things Will Get Worse," *Kommersant*, December 21, 2001.

27. *Novaia gazeta*, November 6, 2001.

28. *Novaia gazeta*, December 25, 2001.

29. Natalia Astrakhanova, "Natural Clan Selection," *Ekspert*, no. 46, December 2001.

30. Inessa Slavutinskaia, "It Takes a Clan to Expel a Clan," *Profil*, no. 46 (December 2001).

31. Svetlana Babaeva, "Relatives versus the St. Petersburg Team," *Izvestiya*, November 29, 2001.

32. Yulia Latynina, "A Muzzle for the Oligarchs," *Novaia gazeta*, no. 93, (December 2001).

33. Anna Raff, "Gazprom Takes PwC Audit to Heart," *Moscow Times*, August 1, 2001. After Gazprom in export revenues in 2000 came oil companies LUKoil ($5.7 bn), Yukos ($5.2 bn), Tyumen NK ($3.5 bn) and Tatneft ($2.6 bn), followed by Rusal ($2.2 bn) and Norilsk Nickel ($2.2 bn). Alla Startseva, "Ten Firms Have 40% of Exports," *Moscow Times*, July 19, 2001.

34. Ol'ga Gladkova, "Putin's Obscure Followers," *Argumenty i fakty*, no. 47 (November 2001); Viktor Litovkin, "Jammed Weaponry," *Obshchaia gazeta*, June 7–13, 2001.

35. Almira Kozhakhmetova, "Obedient Oligarchs Go to the Kremlin," *Novye izvestiia*, June 1, 2001; Boris Kagarlitsky, "No Magnate Storms in Sight," *Novaia gazeta*, June 7–14, 2001; Denis Prokopenko, "Putin Promises Oligarchs to Liberalize Hard Currency Legislation," *Nezavisimaia gazeta*, June 1, 2001.

36. Aleksandr Tsipko, "Putin's Power Hierarchy Sinks into the Sand," *Prism 7*, no. 3 (March 2001).

37. Stanislav Menshikov, "Budget Battles to Start," *Moscow Tribune*, June 1, 2001.

38. Vladimir Ustinov, "Tariff Increase Unavoidable," *Vedomosti*, January 28, 2002.

39. See the Chubais interview "Happy New RAO EES," *Profil*, no. 44 (November 2001).

40. Bulat Stolyarov, "Oligarchs Are Judged," *Vedomosti*, October 4, 2001.

41. Yurii Granovskii, "Potanin ubil Mustcom," *Vedomosti*, June 20, 2001.

42. *Investment Environment in the Russian Federation*, May 2001 at www.oecd.org/daf/investment/fdi/russia.pdf.

43. Andrei Grigoriev, "Twelve and a Half," *Kompaniia*, no. 1 (January 2002). On Pugachev, see Oleg Lurie, "Putin Likes Skiing," *Novaia gazeta*, November 26–28, 2001.

44. Inessa Slavutinskaia, "The Battle of Vladimir," *Profil*, no. 13 (April 2001)

45. Christian Caryl, "Twilight of the Oligarchs," *Newsweek International*, February 5, 2001.

46. Denis Shevchenko, "The Kremlin and the Opposition," *Rossiia*, July 10, 2001; Andrei Zolotov, "Six Months On, NTV Still up in the Air," *Moscow Times*, October 15, 2001.

47. "Economic Swan Lake," *Ekspert*, January 28, 2002.

48. Floriana Fossato and Anna Kachkaeva, "Russian Provincial Broadcasters to Suffer Most in Moscow TV Battles," *New York Times*, January 24, 2002.

49. Bulat Stoliarov, "Aksenenko Retreats," *Vedomosti*, October 23, 2001; Andrei Savitskii, "Kremlin Ghosts," *Nezavisimaia gazeta*, November 29, 2001.

50. Mikhail Kozyrev, "Imprison and Defend," *Vedomosti*, January 29, 2002.

51. Cited in *Kommersant*, January 17, 2002.

52. Nataliya Zubarevich, "Russia's Big Businesses in Regional Elections," *Russian Regional Report 7*, no. 4 (January 30, 2002).

53. Robert Orttung, "Money and Power in Putin's Russia," *Russian Regional Report 7*, no. 2 (January 16, 2002).

54. Elena Dikun, "Abramovich's Golden Hills in Chukotka," *Prism 7*, no. 9 (September 30, 2001).

55. Pavel Isaev, "Fusion of Oligarchs and Governors," *Russian Regional Report 7*, no. 2 (January 16, 2002).

56. Valerii Fedorov, Vladislav Sakharchuk, "Horn of Plenty for Regional Leaders," *Vek*, no. 24 (June 22, 2001).

57. Yuliia Bushueva, "Unfortunately, I Am from Petersburg," *Vedomosti*, October 4, 2001.

58. Aleksandr Tsipko, "The Family Takes Control of Domestic Politics," *Prism 7*, no. 9 (September 30, 2001).

59. A. Nikolskii, "State Regulation of the Economy," at www.polit.ru (last accessed September 5, 2001).

60. Frederick Kempe, "On the Russian Front, President Putin Advances," *Wall Street Journal Europe*, March 21, 2001.

61. Otto Latsis, "Breakthrough to Stagnation," *Novye izvestiia*, June 9, 2001.

62. Aleksei Makarkin, "What Awaits Putin on the Road of Liberal Reforms," *Ekspert*, no. 30 (August 2001).

Part Four

MILITARY AND SECURITY

Chapter Eight

Putin and the Armed Forces

Dale R. Herspring

The Russian armed forces were in a disastrous state when Putin took over as president. Morale was at rock bottom, planes were crashing, troops were deserting, draftees were doing everything possible to avoid military service, junior officers were leaving in droves, the quality of both cadre and equipment was falling drastically, crime was on the rise, Chechnya was a millstone around the army's neck, and the idea of military reform had been a joke. To his credit, Putin has begun to take some modest steps in the direction of reforming the armed forces, but the magnitude of the job ahead is so great that it will take years, if not decades, before the Russian Army will be able to return to anything even resembling the Soviet armed forces that preceded it.

CREATING THE RUSSIAN ARMY

The chaotic situation facing the military when Putin took over was years in the making. When Russia was created as an independent state in 1992, the vast majority of the military's best-equipped and best-trained troops were outside the country's borders. Its first-line troops were stationed in Eastern Europe, especially in the former East Germany. Many of its second-line troops were in what we now know as Ukraine or Belarus. To make matters worse, its air defense system was located on the periphery of the USSR—an action that made sense since the purpose was to protect the country from external threats. However, with the breakup of the Soviet Union, almost all of the country's air defense assets—and especially its radars, were lost. They were now located in newly independent—and sovereign—countries. To quote former President Boris Yeltsin, "We have almost no combined combat units in the west and south, so it turned out." To give the reader a picture of just how bad things were—40 percent of repair facilities (80 percent for tanks) were now outside of Russia![1]

Furthermore, when the USSR broke up, these newly independent states seized whatever conventional Soviet equipment was stationed in their territory. Soldiers were permitted to return to Russia if they chose, but their equipment formed the basis for the creation of new military forces—the Kazak Army, the Uzbek Army, and so forth. Chaos reigned for troops stationed in Eastern Europe, and they were withdrawn to Russia proper only to find themselves pariahs in their own country.

If the military's problems were bad, the situation facing the military–industrial complex was even worse. During the Soviet era, the Kremlin spread weapons production factories (as well as component-producing units) all over the country. By dispersing these facilities, Moscow not only made them harder to destroy in the event of a war, it made efforts to undercover their existence more problematic—often their location was secret. In practice, this meant that one tank factory might be located in Siberia, while others were in Ukraine, Central Asia, or the Baltics. Furthermore, the factory in Siberia might be dependent on parts produced in Central Asia. As a result, the rationality of the military–industrial production process was undermined. Furthermore, factories that had previously been assured of a steady—and predictable—stream of orders often found a bankrupt army unable to pay for needed weapons, which forced many to either go out of business or shift to producing civilian goods.

Thus in a short period of time, both the structure of the Soviet military and its production process were ripped apart. Moscow made a vigorous effort to keep the military together in the form of the Commonwealth of Independent States (CIS), but to no avail. Memories of Soviet troops putting down civil demonstrations in Georgia, Azerbaijan, and the Baltics led the leaders of the former Soviet republics to fear that the Kremlin might again try to use the military to reassert its control over these regions—especially given Russian President Boris Yeltin's "Russia first" approach in dealing with them.

By the beginning of 1992 it was becoming increasingly clear that if Russia was to have a military, it would have to create its own. Consequently, on April 4, 1992, Yeltsin signed an instruction creating a state committee to consider the establishment of a new Russian armed forces. A month later, the Russian Army was formally established and General Pavel Grachev, who had supported Yeltsin during the aborted coup attempt a year earlier, was appointed defense minister.

Where to begin? How to put Humpty-Dumpty back together again after he had fallen into hundreds, if not thousands, of pieces? This was the problem facing Grachev. And in spite of the best efforts of a number of senior military (and political) officials, the situation would only worsen over the years. It is to a discussion of the decay—if not disintegration—of the Russian armed forces prior to Putin that we now turn.

THE BUDGET

Central to the decline of the Russian armed forces has been the commensurate decline in the military budget. Without a predictable and meaningful budget, there is little senior military officers in any country can do to field an efficient, competent military. Indeed, the one word that constantly runs through Russian military thinking and policymaking is *predviedenie*, or predictability. Everything the Russian military does is based on its ability to predict accurately the resources it will have to carry out the tasks assigned to it. Unfortunately, under Yeltsin the Russian military's budget was neither predictable nor meaningful.

Even under the Soviets, the generals themselves did not know their budget. When Marshall Sergei Akhromeyev told Admiral William Crowe that he did not know his overall budget, he was not obfuscating. The military component was hidden in hundreds of different parts of the budget, and the kind of pricing or accounting system that we utilize in the West was lacking. Besides, the generals generally got whatever they asked for—so why worry about it? Individuals like Grachev came to the job without the kind of fiscal expectations that American flag officers face—with a watchful Congress or White House looking over their shoulders for spending on everything from toilet seats to missiles—or a budgetary system that requires the military to pay real money for its orders. Dealing with a transparent or a competitive budget was particularly difficult for Russian officers. As the late General Dmitri Volkogonov told me in 1990, "[T]ransparency is a new idea for us. Five years ago, no one outside the military would have even dared ask a question about the budget; it was top secret."

The Russian defense budget decreased steadily as a percentage of the national budget from 1994 until 2000. While exact figures are not available—the Russians themselves often are unsure of how much money was being allocated to defense because of a continued lack of transparency and problems in converting the ruble—Moscow's generals and admirals make it very clear that they were forced to live on an ever-decreasing starvation budget prior to Putin.

The official budget was bad enough, but the reality of what was received and what the military had to cover with their limited means made the situation even worse. In 1993 the shortfall was 1 billion rubles, in 1994 it was 12.2 billion, and in 1997 it was 34.4 billion. The military was also heavily in debt to a variety of civilian creditors. By 1995 the figure stood at more than 9 billion rubles.[2]

Not only did the military face budgetary restrictions and shortfalls—it also was forced to spend money on items outside critical areas such as arms acquisition, training, and maneuvers. Consider Grachev's comment: "Our budget for 1994 was corrected in an attempt to tackle, first, the social problems of 120,000 homeless officers, thousands of people without jobs. This will consume 50 percent of our resources."[3] The situation only grew worse over the years. Indeed, there is not a single area of military activity that has not been adversely affected. Let us take a look at some of the more critical ones.

Weapons

Buying New Weapons

Russian arms procurement fell by more than 80 percent between 1991 and 1994. Because of cutbacks in weapons purchases (only two combat aircraft were purchased in 1995 compared to 585 in 1991), by 1998 only 30 percent of all weapons in the Russian inventory were modern—while in NATO countries the number stood at 60–80 percent. If these conditions continued, by 2005 only 5 to 7 percent of weapons would be new. As one Russian officer put it, "Gradually, we will slide toward the category of armies of third world countries"—albeit one with nuclear weapons.[4]

During the first four years of its existence, the Russian military tried to compensate for these financial shortfalls by relying on reserves. However, by 1996 senior officers complained that there were almost no reserves left. The only way the Russian air force could fight in Chechnya was by cannibalizing its existing aircraft. Similarly, as another source noted in 1996, "the army has not received the nine million uniforms it ordered and . . . soldiers stationed in Chechnya have been forced to wear sneakers and winter hats donated by Menatep bank."[5] By August of that year, General Rodionov, the new defense minister, was complaining that "70 percent of armed forces personnel do not have regulation clothing and related gear."[6]

The year before Putin took over was even more dismal. The country's defense minister himself lamented that Russia's dreadful economic situation was so bad that the country would not be able to increase military spending to the level needed to reequip the army until 2006.[7]

Maintaining Equipment

Moscow's problems went far beyond the need to replace aging weapons systems. Existing equipment was also in bad need of repair. Indeed, the lack of serviceable equipment had a major impact on Russia's two wars in Chechnya—and especially the second one. During both conflicts it was necessary to take money out of the military budget and to rely on weapons and ammunition from as far back as World War II.

What is most surprising is that Russian military officers have made no secret of just how bad the situation had become—in contrast to the days of the Soviet military when such problems were covered up. Take, for example, the following interview with Sergeyev in December 1998:

> About one third of the armed forces' military hardware is not combat ready and some 60 percent of the country's strategic missile systems have been in service for twice their service life. Some 70 percent of the ships in Russia's Navy require repair, he continued, while in the air force about two-thirds of all aircraft are incapable of flying. So far this year, Sergeyev said, the armed forces have not received a "single nuclear submarine, tank combat plane, helicopter, or piece of artillery."[8]

The lack of new equipment and aviation fuel was so extreme that young men who had been through four years of training to become air force pilots were sent "to the infantry, the armored troops, artillery and communications."[9]

Personnel Problems

Junior Officers

Who could have foreseen that the highly prestigious occupation of a military officer during Soviet times would have sunk to the point where highly qualified specialists were leaving faster than the country's academies could produce them? For example, competition among candidates for officers' schools, once intense, dropped sharply. In addition, there was a hemorrhage of junior officers from the military. By 1996 more than 50 percent of all junior officers had left the military as soon as their obligation was finished in order to enter the business world. Many were moonlighting during duty hours in order to feed their families, and nearly half of all new lieutenants wanted to resign as soon as they graduated from an officer school.

It is difficult enough to attract and train young men (and some women) to serve as officers in the Russian military, but then they leave at the first opportunity. Yet why should they stay? Forty-five percent of young officers were living below the poverty level, paid between $50 and $100 per month to do a job that requires heavy physical work and has all of the discomforts that go with it. Poor salaries, an insecure future, inadequate family quarters and supporting institutions, prestige at an all-time low, and the reality of service in Chechnyna all took their toll.

Conscripts

The situation among enlisted personnel was even worse. The draft in Russia was a joke. Not only had draft avoidance become a national sport, the quality of those who ended up in the military had reached rock bottom. During the 1992 spring induction period the rate of fulfillment in Moscow was only 7 percent.[10] In fact, the situation was so bad in the Moscow Military District that "officers and warrant officers are forced to pull guard duty on military installations in order to relieve the extreme loads on extended service personnel."[11] By 1996, the Russian Army was understaffed by 380,000 noncommissioned officers and enlisted personnel.[12]

As General Grachev put it: "Last year 34,000 conscripts had a criminal record. As a result, there has been a 25 percent increase in the numbers of serious crimes. They are becoming increasingly audacious and aggressive, and are frequently linked to physical abuse."[13] By 1998 it was being reported that 40 percent of new recruits had not attended school or held a job in the two years prior to their military service. One in twenty had a police record, and others were "drug addicts, toxic substance abusers, mentally disabled and syphilitics." Some 71,000 of those drafted had committed crimes, while 20,000 who had been given suspended sentences were drafted anyway.[14]

Dedovshchina

Not surprisingly, these problems are carried over into military life. To begin with there is the age-old problem of hazing (*dedovshchina*), a direct result of the failure of the Russian Army (or the Soviet one before it) to create a noncommissioned officer (NCO) corps. NCOs are the heart of Western militaries. Indeed, I would argue that Western militaries would collapse overnight without these senior enlisted men and women. They are experts at their jobs and more important, they are given considerable authority and expected to lead, supervise, and care for those who serve under them.

The Russian system is quite different. The Russian military refuses to delegate authority to subordinates. I can cite cases where one petty officer in the U.S. Navy did the job of two officers in the Soviet/Russian Navy. In the mid-1960s, the Soviet military created warrant officers, but in contrast to their Western equivalents, who often serve as division officers and key leaders, these individuals were technical specialists. Thus the question: How can enlisted personnel be controlled without an NCO corps?

The answer was *dedovshchina*. The Russian military has traditionally relied upon two call-ups per year with everyone serving two years, and four groups serving at any one time. The first two groups are the rookies. The third group, comprising *deds* or grandfathers, is in charge. The fourth group is focused simply on getting out. It is a brutal life. There are many stories of beatings, rapes, and outright inhuman treatment of junior soldiers or sailors. I have personally witnessed the use of physical force against sailors. More-senior soldiers steal their possessions, and in some cases have even killed them. Not surprisingly, this system of iron discipline has led a number of young men to desert.

Suicides

Suicide has become a major problem for the army. During 1997, 487 soldiers committed suicide, an increase of 57 over the previous year.[15] Another source reported that between January and April 1998 another 132 committed suicide.[16] In addition to *dedovshchina*, the poor working and living conditions, as well as the lack of food, also played important roles.

Suicides have also been prevalent among officers. Sixty percent of all suicides were by officers. In October 1998, for example, a major and a lieutenant colonel killed themselves in Moscow. An investigation revealed that their families were starving, and both officers knew that if they committed suicide their monthly pensions would be paid to their families when it was due—in contrast to the paycheck delays of weeks and months faced by their colleagues on active duty.

Desertion

Given the problems noted earlier, it should come as no surprise that desertion—at one time almost unheard of in the Soviet Army—was an increasingly serious problem. Indeed, the number of those who deserted was so large that "often their commanders don't even look for them." Eighty-six percent of the deserters were new recruits who had been in the army less than a year—a clear sign of the impact of the *dedovshchina* phenomena.[17]

Substance Abuse and AIDS

Meanwhile, the Russian Army was learning that it was not immune from problems like alcoholism, drugs, and AIDS.

Alcoholism has long been a problem in Russia in general—and the military has not been exempt. What was new, however, was the increasingly frequent use of drugs. In 1996 there were only 256 drug offenses in the Russian armed forces. In 1998 there were 605, and the vast majority of those who took drugs *began* their habit while serving in the armed forces! Even more worrisome was the 2.4 percent increase in drug-related incidents in the Strategic Rocket Forces—the troops who have charge of the country's nuclear weapons.[18]

AIDS cases too have been on the rise. In 1999, the prosecutor for the Moscow Military District claimed that there were 128 cases of HIV, up from 32 for the entire period from 1993 to 1996.[19]

Discipline

One of the most serious and seemingly intractable problems that faced the Russian armed forces was the collapse of discipline and resulting problems with crime and operational readiness. Under Yeltsin, discipline deteriorated to the point where the prosecutor's office had a full-time job pursuing those guilty of the most serious crimes; for example, murder. In this regard, the chief military prosecutor noted in 1997 that some fifty soldiers were gunned down by their fellow servicemen. And this was just the number of individuals on guard duty who shot each other! He further reported that by March 1998 another ten had died in the same way. And the problem continued to grow. In the Far Eastern Military District in May 1998, four soldiers reportedly shot and killed their commanding officer. Even more alarming was the spate of shootings at nuclear weapons facilities. The situation became so serious that on October 20, 1998, Yeltsin ordered an inspection of troops at a nuclear weapons facility.[20]

The prosecutor's office noted on December 1, 1998, that 10,500 crimes and criminal incidents had been reported that year in comparison with 10,000 the previous year—and this in a downsized military.[21] Bribery too was a major concern. According to Russian sources, such actions had risen 80 percent, accompanied by a 44 percent increase in cases of physical violence.[22]

Corruption

Corruption was rampant throughout all parts of Russian society, and the military was no exception. In 1992, Grachev openly admitted that officers were engaged in the illegal sale of Russian military assets. Russia's chief military prosecutor complained in late 1996 that "crime is growing among Russian military officers and 100 officers of the rank of colonel and above—including fifteen admirals and generals—are among those being investigated."[23] According to General Lev Rokhlin, speaking in 1996, "[o]ver 28,300 crimes have been committed by troops since 1992. The number of serious crimes totals 11,000. One in six is a group crime. The number of crimes committed under the influence of drugs has doubled."[24]

Abolishing Conscription?

During his 1996 presidential campaign, Boris Yeltsin promised to end conscription by the year 2000. However, as was often the case, Yeltsin had not taken the hard economic facts into consideration. According to senior officers, a professional army is 300 percent more expensive than a conscript one. To quote Colonel General Vladislav Putilin, "A conscript costs us 17,900 rubles a year, while a professional soldier costs 32,000 rubles. A professional army would require the corresponding infrastructure, which would also cost a lot. It's not realistic now."[25]

Contract System

Faced with the many problems outlined here, the military turned to the contract system in the hope that these individuals, who would be paid better than conscripts and offered specialized training, would not only be better trained, but better disciplined as well. After all, they presumably would be in the army because they wanted to be soldiers.

The process began on December 1, 1992, and targeted soldiers with certain specialties who were offered two- and three-year contracts. The program was gradually expanded until on April 11, 1996, the chief of the Russian Defense Ministry's Planning and Mobilization Directorate estimated that there were 270,000 contract soldiers in the military.[26]

Unfortunately, contract soldiers were not the answer. From 1993 to 1995 some 50,000 resigned, mainly for financial reasons. The average wage in Russia in September 1995 was about 550,000 rubles, including supplements. The subsistence minimum per person in Russia was 300,000 rubles, and in some regions it was two or three times that.[27] Contract soldiers made even less.

More than half of the 15 percent of contract soldiers in the army were women (i.e., about 8 percent of all soldiers), generally the wives of officers who joined the army as a way of supplementing their husbands' meager incomes. While the performance of the women was very good—in many cases better than the men they served with (they were sober and more accurate in administrative positions), the army wanted men for combat units. Unfortunately, many of those who did not quit were later fired for poor performance.

The chief of recruitment, GLT Vladislav Putilin, probably said it best when he observed that given the dangerous conditions and low pay faced by many contract soldiers, a person who volunteered for such service "would either be one of the long-term unemployed or someone who has already poisoned his mind with alcohol."[28]

Operational Problems

Budgetary shortfalls had a major impact on the operational readiness of the Russian armed forces under Yeltsin. Indeed, the financial situation was so severe that on several occasions civilian power stations cut off electricity to military installations. At least one of these blackouts threatened the Strategic

Rocket Forces, while another created a major threat to the Navy's nuclear missiles. In the latter instance, the Navy sent in sailors to force the installation to restore power. Incidents of this type led Prime Minister Viktor Chernomyrdin to sign a resolution on September 23, 1995, banning civilian plants from turning off power to military facilities, regardless of unpaid bills.

Training

Training was one of the areas that was hardest hit given the budgetary—not to mention morale and equipment—problems described earlier. As in other areas, the situation was nothing short of catastrophic.

> Pilots are now doing one-tenth of the statutory flying hours. You do not have the full complement of air defense fighters on alert duty. Aviation school students cannot go into the forces, because they cannot fly. Some 80 percent of airfields lack fuel stocks for current needs. The army is doing practically no combat training and exercises are performed entirely on maps.[29]

The difficulties were not limited to the air force. During 1994, 70 percent of all military exercises and maneuvers were cancelled because of a lack of fuel. Of the 190 "exercises" that took place, 60 percent were command-post exercises without forces in the field. Because of budgetary limitations, the Russian army had not conducted a single division-level ground-force exercise since 1992.[30]

Given how important nuclear weapons have been to a military that has increasingly lost its conventional clout, it is particularly worrisome when the lack of training hits in those areas as well:

> The actual situation is as follows: the troops are manned by 45 to 50 percent; troops material provision has been cut by 60 percent, as a result of which approximately 70 percent of games and maneuvers had to be scrapped; combat flying practice has been reduced sharply; from 100–120 hours to 30–35 hours a year; and only one to two divisions are deemed fully combat-ready in each military district, and one to two ships in each fleet.[31]

Moscow made much of the West-99 joint military exercise, and it evoked considerable interest on the part of some in the West, especially when Russian bombers flew close to the Norwegian coastline. In fact, it was primarily a command and staff exercise. While better than nothing—it involved a number of ships, planes, and troops—it fell far short of the kind of exercises the Soviet Army carried out.

The outlook for the future was bleak. Speaking in 1998, Marshal Sergeyev stated that "80 percent or more is spent on maintaining the armed forces, while combat training is funded from what we have left—whatever can be scraped together, is allocated for combat training, and that is obviously insufficient for maintaining combat readiness."[32]

The military was even having trouble feeding its troops. The inevitable was temporarily delayed by distributing emergency food reserves. But by the beginning of 1996 the military had used up 90 percent of its emergency food rations, and each soldier was on half-rations. "The soldier does not have enough to eat. He is hungry. And it is painful to see young guys in uniform begging in the streets."[33] Commanders often told troops to pick mushrooms or to work part-time on farms as a way to supplement their diet. To quote Pavel Felgenhauer, "Today, Russian soldiers are surviving mostly on bread and stocks of vegetables. Each fall, military units traditionally enter into Russian-style production sharing agreements with farmers. Army divisions provide free conscript labor to harvest cabbages and potatoes; in return the soldiers are allowed to take some back to the barracks."[34] Noting the irony of the current situation, Felgenhauer observed that it was food from the U.S. Defense Department that was keeping Russian soldiers alive. And unpaid bills were another major problem.

Perusing official military reports, one could easily have gained the impression that the reform process within the Russian military was well advanced under Yeltsin. If fact, if the reader were to count the number of times the phrase "military reform" had been mentioned in Russian military circles under Yeltsin, I suspect he or she would have discovered that it was discussed literally thousands of times—perhaps the most frequently mentioned term of its kind in Russian military journals, speeches, and newspapers. Unfortunately, little of substance moved beyond the printed page.

PUTIN TAKES OVER

As we have seen, the military problems facing Putin when he became president were daunting, and most have continued to worsen. For example, Aleksei Arbatov, Deputy Chairman of the Duma's Defense Committee, noted in 2001 that no more than 20 percent of the weapons in the Russian army were modern.[35] Furthermore, during the same year, Russia's defense minister announced that given the country's economic situation, Russia would not be able to increase spending to the level needed to reequip until 2008–2010.[36]

If nothing else, the tragic loss of the giant nuclear submarine *Kursk* in the Barents Sea in August 2000 highlighted just how serious the problems facing the military had become. This, after all, was one of the Northern Fleet's most modern and threatening boats—a submarine that was taken very seriously by Western navies. Yet it sank, and the Russian Navy did almost nothing to help. The major reason was financial. For example, the Northern Fleet's only submarine rescue vehicle was unavailable. Why? Simple: a lack of funds had forced the navy to use her for spare parts.

Indeed, it was becoming increasingly clear that the navy and the air force were in particularly dire straits. According to one source:

> The fleet has shrunk dramatically since the Soviet Union's dissolution in 1991, with the number of surface vessels and submarines having fallen by more than one-half. . . . In 1991, for example, the Soviet navy is believed to have had about 400 nuclear and diesel submarines and 700 surface vessels. According to a recent report published by *Izvestiya*, the naval command now fields a total of about 100 submarines and a little over 300 surface ships. And these numbers continue to fall.[37]

In May 2001, the commander in chief of the air force flatly stated that 100 percent of all helicopters and planes needed modernization. Furthermore, "military transport pilots are getting 50–60 hours of flight time, while fighter pilots are getting only 20–25—instead of the recommended 120–180 hours." The accident rate in the air force also remains high. "It now amounts to 8.3 based on 100,000 flight hours, whereas in the beginning of the 1990s it was at the 3–3.5 level. (In comparison, the accident rate in the American Air Force reached a low last year . . . 1.04 per 100,000 flight hours)."[38]

Indeed, the head of the air force carried on a lobbying campaign throughout most of 2001, stressing that a mere 5 percent of the overall number of aircraft were modern. While he made it clear that the air force was willing to modernize existing aircraft, there was no doubt that he preferred some of the new, fifth generation (or four + as it is often referred to the Russian press) aircraft for the Russian Air Force.[39]

Neither is the problem with conscripts improving. For example, by the end of 2000, there were reports that the army was rounding up young men on the streets "in a desperate attempt to fulfill its quotas for its conscript forces."[40] And the quality of recruits also has continued to decline.

> Some 54 percent of men in active service have health restrictions. . . . As recently as 1989 only 4 percent of draftees were regarded as fit for military service with reservations. According to the General Staff's statistics, one-third of young people waiting for the draft did not work or study; many of them had encounters with drugs and alcohol. The number of young people with expunged or erased criminal records is unprecedentedly high. The hopes pinned on contract service did not prove their worth.[41]

From all appearances, the pool of conscripts will not improve any time soon. "According to one estimate, by the year 2005 the state will experience great problems manning its security agencies; the demographic slump of the late 1980s will take its toll." The population of Russia is falling—leaving a smaller and smaller group for conscription, and current statistics suggest that only one Russian high school senior in twenty is healthy enough to serve in the armed forces.[42]

The officer corps is also worsening. According to one source, 100,000 officers have "left the armed forces over the past three years and the army now faces significant shortages of junior officers." In fact, another source claims that "senior officers now outnumber junior officers in the Russian armed forces and there is now one officer for every two soldiers—an astonishing ratio." Discipline also continues to be a factor—even in some of the better units. For example, when Putin assumed the post of acting president, top military officers were complaining about the quality of soldiers being sent to Kosovo because of their alcohol and drug problems as well as their criminal pasts—and these forces were supposed to be among the best in the Russian army! To quote one source:

> An inquiry has been conducted that discovered a number of cases where servicemen with low moral and work ethics, inadequate professional training, alcohol or drug problems or criminal pasts were deployed with the Russian army contingent, military sources have told *Interfax*. As a result, 286 servicemen—184 airborne, 77 Moscow district, and 25 Volga district troops—have been sent back to Russia.[43]

Corruption has also continued to grow, as even admirals and generals have come under investigation.

Desertion remains a major problem as well. According to one source, there are currently some 40,000 deserters in Russia, and there are signs that these individuals are a major source of crime in the country. There are hints that the suicide rate may be increasing. One report contends that more than one-third of the sailors who died in the Baltic Fleet during the first half of 2001 committed suicide.[44]

Harassment of soldiers has continued unabated since Putin took office. In September 2001, the Russian Committee of Soldiers' Mothers claimed that 30,000 soldiers "experience beatings and harassment on the part of their fellow servicemen and commanders each year."[45] And another Russian source reported that seventy-two Russian servicemen left their base because they were being harassed by other soldiers from the Caucasus. They were apprehended, but not disciplined, because "the unit command shares the blame too."[46]

Accidents as a result of a lack of discipline continue to plague the Russian military. In February 2000, some 6,000 23-millimeter aircraft cannon shells exploded during a fire on an air force base, while in Volgograd at the same time, some 2,000 tank shells exploded. Then in June, at least two dozen soldiers were killed at an ammunition depot near Sverdlovsk. In all of these cases, negligence was listed as the cause.

Military exercises—so critical for combat readiness—has far to go, though some improvements can be seen. For example, the armed forces carried out an exercise in June 2001 in the Leningrad Military District. Involving 7,000 troops, including 2,000 reservists, it was the first exercise of this magnitude in twelve years and at least demonstrated that the high command is making an attempt.

PUTIN, CHECHNYA, AND THE ARMY

While space prohibits a lengthy discussion, Chechnya is too important for Putin and the military not to mention here. Almost every Russian army or naval infantry officer above the grade of captain has spent time in Chechnya. During a recent visit to Russia I did not encounter a single colonel or warrant officer, including Naval Infantry (Marine) officers, who had not done at least one tour in that beleaguered land. It appears to have become a necessity for those who hope to be promoted to senior ranks, suggesting that someday we may have a group of officers—the "Chechens"—much like the "Afghans" who now occupy senior positions in the military. As a consequence, the war will continue to have an impact on the army for many years.

It is impossible to overemphasize just how serious the Chechen wars have been for the Russian military. As Pavel Felgenhauer reported:

> Russia has been fighting an intermittent war in Chechnya without any serious procurement of heavy equipment or munitions. Instead, the Defense Ministry has each time dipped deeper and deeper into Soviet Cold War stocks. . . . The troops in Chechnya have made extensive use of heavy artillery, and this has severely depleted munitions stockpiles, as there has been no serial production of heavy shells in Russia for a decade. During the 1994–1996 Chechen war, offices complained that they were using shells produced in the 1980s. In the present conflict, shells produced in the 1970s and even the 1960s have been supplied to the front. It has been reported that in December 1999 the government released 8 billion rubles ($285 million) for the purchase of new heavy shells, but the defense ministry apparently has not yet managed to resume serial production. Reports from Chechnya say that Russian troops are running out of ammunition for the most-used heavy gun—the 122mm D-30 howitzer. One of the remedies being considered by the General Staff is to bring the pre-World War II M-30 122mm howitzer out of strategic storage. Millions of rounds of shells for this weapon have been kept in storage since the 1940s.[47]

One can only wonder how the Russian Army was functioning at all in Chechnya given the lack of modern equipment, not to mention the many personnel problems it has experienced. For the Russian military, the Chechen war may (I repeat, *may*) have taught it a number of lessons. First, some wars simply cannot be won. This was the lesson of Afghanistan, and it may well be the lesson of Chechnya. When during my visit to Russia in the summer of 2001 I asked the question "Do you think you can win?" the almost universal answer I received was that "it can only be decided politically." Or as one colonel put it to me, "The longer we keep fighting, the more Chechens and Russian soldiers will be killed. Either we talk with them or we wipe them out. Those are the alternatives!" My point is simple. Russian officers have been confronted with a second "unwinnable war." Having dealt with Soviet and Russian officers for many years, I can confidently say that the idea that a war cannot be "won" is one they are having a difficult time getting used to—first Afghanistan, and now Chechnya. If this concept is taken seriously, it could have a major impact on Russian military doctrine and the military's relationship with Putin. If the latter should decide at some future point to negotiate a settlement with the Chechens, he may find the military supportive.

Second, in addition to showing how far the Russian army has slipped from its combat readiness in 1992, the Chechen war has also exposed the brutal way Russians fight wars to public scrutiny on an unprecedented scale. There are daily reports out of Chechnya charging the Russian military with one atrocity after another. Most of the complaints appear to be legitimate (although that does not excuse the Chechens, who are fighting an equally brutal and dirty war). What is new about Chechnya—in comparison to Afghanistan, for example—is that the army has been held accountable for its sins. For example, in July 2001, the Russian army carried out a retaliatory sweep through the villages of Assinovskaya and Sernovodsk. The wanton killing of innocent civilians was so appalling that the commander of Russian forces in Chechnya, General Lieutenant Vladimir Moltenskoy, condemned them publicly. He admitted that his troops had committed "widespread crimes" during the two-day action. In addition, President Putin blasted the military in a speech to senior officers on July 23 arguing that "every military operation must take place exclusively within the framework of existing legislation, and . . . every citizen must be aware of that fact."[48] While it would be naive to think that this one incident will change the way the Russian army fights a war, it does suggest that the high command will have to be more aware of the importance of public opinion and the media in the future.

The third lesson the military has learned is that when sent to war, unlike during the Soviet period, the army cannot count on the civilian leadership to provide it with the money it needs to carry out the job. The war in Chechnya has been a constant drain on the Russian economy, as well as the army's budget. For example Pavel Felgenhauer estimated that in the year 2000, the military spent 60 billion rubles ($2.2 billion) on the war. Looking at the war from the perspective of 2001, Felgenhauer stated that "the war in Chechnya is in its third fiscal year with total costs fast approaching $4 billion. In fact, Felgenhauer argued, the real cost (when corrected dollar equivalents are utilized) could be at least $10 billion, "a cost that Russia can hardly afford."[49] While there is nothing to suggest that the army will not fight whatever wars the Kremlin orders in the future, it may be more aggressive behind the scenes in pushing for financial guarantees before sending troops to carry out the required actions.

PUTIN AND MILITARY REFORM

Putin is well aware of the problems facing the armed forces, as he signaled by appointing Sergei Ivanov, arguably the second most influential politician in Russia, to be defense minister. And some limited steps have been taken under Ivanov's direction. First, the air force and the air defense forces have been combined in order to avoid personnel redundancy, and the country appears to be headed toward a three-service military: navy, army, and air force. Furthermore, in September 2001 a new military district was created—one that combined Privolzhskiy and Uralskiy Military Districts. Third, the size of the Russian military is being reduced from a total of 1.2 million in 2001 to between 800,000 and 850,000 by 2005. In 2002 alone, 250 generals have retired.

In addition, Ivanov has made it clear that the military educational system will be reformed. According to *Interfax*, Ivanov described the purpose of the reforms "to bring military education as close as possible to real life and the needs of the armed forces and other security and law enforcement structure." Ivanov went on to argue that the value of some of the military colleges is "open to question."[50] Changes are clearly underway.

Of all of Putin's actions since becoming president, none has been more important than his decision to increase the military budget significantly as noted in this table:

Year	1999	2000	2001	2002
Rubles (in billions)	109.0	111.0	218.9	284.1

The new budget includes R10.3bn for the acquisition of new weapons and R16.5bn that will be used for military reform. As anyone working with Russian budgetary figures knows, these numbers are at best estimates.

Finally, in accordance with a suggestion by Putin, General Vladislaw Putilin announced that in 2005 Russia will begin a gradual transition to manning the armed forces primarily with professionals, signaling an end of conscription. The military has been ordered to have a plan in place by the end of 2004. Meanwhile, Putilin noted that only 12 percent of those eligible for the draft in spring 2001 are likely to be conscripted—a figure that is down from 24 percent in 2000 and 13 percent in 1999.[51] According to General Staff representatives, Moscow expects to be able to field a fully professional army by 2010.[52]

PUTIN AND FOREIGN POLICY

Putin's decision to support the United States as a result of the events of September 11 has alienated many of Russia's senior officers, who fear that this will lead to permanent U.S. bases in Central Asia, or at a minimum undercut Russian influence in the region. The same could be said of his decision to close down Russian bases at Lourdes, Cuba, and Cam Rahn Bay, Vietnam. Russian military officers do not like to see Moscow pulling back, but at the same time, they realize that money is at a premium and that the $4 million rent Moscow was paying to Cuba as well as the equal sum that Vietnam would request could be better spent elsewhere.

One of the two most difficult security issues in U.S.–Russian relations has been the question of NATO expansion. From the Russian standpoint—and especially that of the country's conservative generals—this appears to be an effort by the West to build up an even stronger alliance against Russia. For most of the Kremlin's generals, the idea that NATO could become a positive factor in East–West relations is heresy. NATO was created to counter the USSR, and the situation has not changed. If it is not aimed at Moscow, why does it continue to exist?

The second policy that has bedeviled East–West relations (and especially U.S.–Russian relations) has been Washington's desire to build a theater missile defense system. Such a development would immediately violate the 1972 Anti-Ballistic Missiles Treaty (ABM). The latter specifically outlaws defensive weapons, leaving each side with only offensive weapons. If the United States were to develop defensive weapons, it would put the Russians at a serious disadvantage.

Putin seized on the events of September 11 to hammer home the message that the Cold War is over and that both the United States and Russia now face a common enemy, regardless of what the generals may think. This became especially clear on September 24, when Putin made it very clear to his generals and admirals that as far as he was concerned, it was time for a major change in U.S.–Russian relations. Terrorism was now the primary enemy of both countries. As a result, the Russians began an unprecedented policy of sharing highly sensitive intelligence with the United States on Afghanistan (and the United States reciprocated). Putin also convinced Bush to agree to make a unilateral cut in U.S. strategic weapons—a step he announced at the summit in Texas in November 2001 that Russia would emulate. Then in May 2002 it was announced that Russia and the United

States had reached agreement on a treaty to limit nuclear weapons to be signed at the summit scheduled for later that month.

In another collaborative step, in November 2001, Lord Robertson invited Moscow to intensify its relations with the Western alliance. The Kremlin is a part of the permanent joint council, but unlike NATO's other nineteen members does not have voting rights. In May 2002 it was announced that NATO had decided to accept Russia as a full discussion partner in all areas except those issues involving military questions. Putin has told his generals that he expects them to work more closely with NATO regardless of how they feel about that organization.

This new approach for dealing with the West has been unpopular with Russia's generals. Just how deep such opposition runs within the high command is unclear at present. The Russian Army does not have a tradition of getting involved in politics, and usually follows whatever orders it receives from its political masters.

PUTIN AND THE MILITARY–INDUSTRIAL COMPLEX

In the meantime, Putin is placing major emphasis on reforming the country's military–industrial complex. In October 2001 he addressed a joint meeting of the presidium of the State Council and the Russian Security Council at which he said that the country's military–industrial complex is "archaic and does not correspond to contemporary military–political tasks." He went on to note that only 20 percent of the plants are functioning and that Russia must adopt modern management techniques if it hopes to meet world standards in this critical area.[53] Even those that are functioning would be considered bankrupt by U.S. standards. Putin is pushing these firms to consolidate, to become more competitive, while at the same time encouraging them to sell their wares overseas. At present, the primary focus is on China, India, and Iran.

As far as the future is concerned, Putin reportedly had a "stormy" meeting with his generals on October 17, 2001, on the question of military reform. He told them that they should do three things: prioritize matters while focusing only on the most important issues; eliminate "parallel structures"; and spend money on the "most important of the country's defense agencies, such as the Russian space forces."[54] There has even been speculation that he may be "using changes in the international environment brought on by the September 11 attacks in the United States not only to recast Moscow's relations with Washington and the West, but also to drive an intensified reshaping of his own country's defense development plans."[55]

CONCLUSION

While the enormity of the problems facing Putin and Sergei Ivanov as they attempt to restructure the Russian military and at the same time keep it from collapsing appear almost overwhelming, we must remember that for the first time since the collapse of the Soviet Union, a serious effort is being made to address the military's problems. Its budget has been significantly increased, a new defense minister—with the president's ear—has been appointed, a serious effort is underway to reform the country's military–industrial complex, Moscow is out to increase its weapons sales abroad as a way of paying for the modernization of the country's military, and some of the personnel problems are beginning to be addressed.

It is easy to be cynical about the future of the Russian military. Indeed, Pavel Felgenhauer, one of the best observers of the Russian military anywhere, was right when he observed, "Ivanov has consolidated his control of the Defense Ministry. But his reforms have up to now been, in essence, personnel changes. Generals replace other generals, but the system that leads the Russian armed forces to decay and misery is still in place."[56] Or as Christopher Donnelly noted, "the fundamental problems of reform have not been faced."[57] Yet for the first time in many years it is possible to argue that a serious effort may be underway to rebuild a shattered, dispirited, corrupt, and incompetent army. It will, however, be a lengthy, and difficult process.

NOTES

1. "Predsezdovskie khlopoty vlastey," *Nezavisimaya gazeta* (November 25, 1992), in *FBIS*, November 25, 1992.

2. "The Sword of Crisis Over the Military Budget," *Oriyentir*, no. 2 (February 1999), in *Military Affairs* (February 1, 1998) and "Conversations without Middlemen," Moscow Television, September 14, 1995, in *FBIS:CE*, September 18, 1995, 19.

3. "Armiya vypolnaet svoi zadachi, nesmotrya na vse slozhnosti i problemy," *Krasnaya zvezda*, March 17, 1994.

4. "Conversations without Middlemen," 20.

5. Jamestown Foundation *Monitor*, February 27, 1992.

6. *Krasnaya zvezda*, August 1, 1996.

7. "Russian Armed Forces Equipment at 100%, *ITAR-TASS*, September 28, 1999.

8. "Russian Army's Woes Outlined," Jamestown Foundation *Monitor*, December 14, 1998.

9. "March of 'Dropped' Lieutenants; Airmen Will Be Retrained as Infantrymen," *Moskovskii Komsomolets*, March 3, 1999, in *WNC Military Affairs*, March 3, 1999.

10. Stephen Foye, "Rebuilding the Russian Military: Some Problems and Prospects," *RFE/RL Research Report*, November 6, 1992, 53.

11. "Lyubit Rossiyo i v nepogodu," *Krasnaya zvezda*, December 10, 1992.

12. "Armed Forces Manpower Shortage Threatens Country's Security: Politicians May Come to Understand This Too Late," *Nezaivisimoe voennoe obozrenie* (February 1996), in *FBIS:SOV*, April 9, 1993, 42.

13. "Grachev Tells Duma: 'I Am Clean Before the Army,'" Moscow Mayak RadioNetwork, November 18, in *FBIS:CE*, November 21, 1994.

14. "The Russian Army, Reeling from the War in Chechnya and Facing Brutality within Its Ranks, Has Found a New Enemy; Itself." *Transactions* (November 1998).

15. "Suicide Rate in the Military Remains High," *RFE/RL Daily Report*, June 23, 1998.

16. "Duma Says over 2,500 Soldiers Died in Russia in 28 Months," *ITAR-TASS*, June 10, 1998.

17. "5,000 Soldiers Desert Each Year," *RFE/RL Daily Report*, July 18, 2000.

18. "A Stoned Army: The Spread of Drug Addiction in the Military Is Threatening the Defensive Capabilities of the Nation," *Nezavisimoe Voennoe Obozrenie*, June 4, 1999, in *Military Affairs*, June 24, 1990.

19. "Rising Drug Rate in the Russian Armed Forces," Jamestown Foundation *Monitor*, July 20, 1999.

20. "Yeltsin Orders Probe of Security for Nukes," *Washington Times*, October 21, 1998.

21. "Armed Forces Crime Figures for 1998 Announced," *Interfax*, December 1, 1999.

22. "But Armed Forces Still Wracked by Social Ills," Jamestown Foundation *Monitor*, July 19, 1999.

23. Jamestown Foundation *Monitor*, October 17, 1996.

24. *Rabotchaya tribuna*, July 9, 1996, in *FBIS:SOV*, July 10, 1996, 8.

25. "Russia's Army Still Mired in Conscript Crisis," *The Russia Journal*, April 24–30, 2000, in *Johnson's List*, April 27, 2000.

26. "Staffing Levels in the Russian Military," Jamestown Foundation *Monitor*, April 11, 1996.

27. "Conversations Without Middlemen," 2; *Krasnaya zvezda*, September 12, 1995.

28. "Russian Army Struggles with Contract Military Service," Jamestown Foundation *Monitor*, October 15, 1997.

29. *Trud*, November 5, 1995, in *FBIS:SOV*, November 7, 1995, 26.

30. *Nezaivisimoe voennoe obozrenie*, February 1996, in *FBIS:SOV*, March 13, 1996, 1.

31. Viktor Yershov, "The Defense Minister Has It in for Everyone," *Novaya Yezhednevaya gazeta*, December 9, 1994, 33.

32. "Russia's Sergeyev on Military Reform," Moscow Mayak Radio Network, February 23, 1998, in *WNC Military Affairs*, February 28, 1998.

33. *Rabochaya tribuna*, March 23, 1996, in *FBIS:SOV*, April 3, 1996, 23.

34. "US Gunning for Red Army," *Moscow Times*, December 17, 1998.

35. "Only 20 Percent of Russian Arms Are Modern," *RFE/RL Daily Report*, May 21, 2001.

36. "Russian Military to Begin Major Arms Purchases in 2008–2010," *Interfax*, January 16, 2001, in *WNC Military Affairs*, January 18, 2001.

37. "Keeping Russia's Navy Afloat," Jamestown Foundation *Monitor*, August 3, 2001.

38. "Russian Commander Says All Russian Military Aircraft Need Modernization," *WNC Military Affairs*; "Air Force Accident Rate Remains High: Modernization Programs to Go Forward," *Moscow Vremya*, in *WNC Military Affairs*, August 24, 2001.

39. "Air Strike on Budget, "*Obshchaya gazeta*, 23 August 2001, in *WNC Military Affairs*, October 3, 2001.

40. "Russian Soldiers Recruited on Streets," *Moscow Times*, December 26, 2000.

41. "Russian Armed Forces Fall Draft Viewed, Problems of Dodgers Noted," *Rossiyskaya gazeta*, October 3, 2001, in *WNC Military Affairs*, October 5, 2001.

42. "Only One Russian High School Senior in 20 Is Healthy," *RFE/RL Daily Report*, June 4, 2001.

43. "Kosovo: Top Russian Military Unhappy with Servicemen," *Interfax*, January 3, 2000.

44. "40,000 Deserters Said a Major Source of Crime," *RFE/RL Daily Report*, October 31, 2001.

45. "Watchdog Committee Reports Army Beatings, Harassment," *Interfax*, September 10, 2001, in *WNC Military Affairs*, September 12, 2001

46. "Russian Soldiers Flee . . . Their Comrades in Arms," *Kommersant*, August 24, 2001.

47. "Paying for the War in Chechnya," *Moscow Times*, April 26, 2001, in *Johnson's List*, April 29, 2001.

48. "Putin Says Soldiers Must Act Within the Law," *RFE/RL Daily Report*, July 24, 2001.

49. "Paying for the War in Chechnya," *Moscow Times*, April 26, 2001, in *Johnson's List*, April 29, 2001.

50. "Russian Defense Minister Wants to Bring Military Education Closer to Real Life," *Interfax*, in *WNC Military Affairs*, September 4, 2001.

51. "Russia to Begin Transition to Professional Army in 2005," Jamestown Foundation *Monitor*, November 26, 2001.

52. This assumes the Russian military will get the money it needs to pay for a much more expensive professional army. It also assumes that the quality of those who become professional soldiers will improve significantly. According to one source, 80 percent of the 150,000 contract soldiers currently serving in the Russian Army "were fired before their contracts ended because their professional training and moral qualities were sharply unsatisfactory." See "Russia to Begin Transition to Professional Army in 2005."

53. "Putin Says Military–Industrial Complex 'Archaic,'" *RFE-RL Daily Report*, October 31, 2000.

54. "Assessing Putin's Meeting with Military Command," Jamestown Foundation *Monitor*, October 29, 2001.

55. "Assessing Putin's Meeting with Military Command."

56. "Making Sense of Manilov," *Moscow Times*, July 5, 2001.

57. "The Pattern of Military Transformation in Central and Eastern Europe," *Defense Diplomacy in Central and Eastern Europe: Challenges to Comparative Public Policy* (February 2000): 11.

Chapter Nine

Putin and Russia's Wars in Chechnya

Jacob W. Kipp

Over the past decade Chechnya has become the great defining issue of Russian statehood and the test of Russian military power. Conflict there did much to undermine the tenure of one president and became the distinguishing element in another president's march to office. At present, President Vladimir Putin has linked the end game of the conflict in Chechnya with Russian participation in a broad, antiterrorist coalition. In the wake of the events of September 11, Putin has chosen to redefine the former conflict to fit within the latter. This was not a particularly onerous task because Putin had long been describing the war in Chechnya as a campaign against bandits and terrorists. As early as March 2001, the Russian government sent to the UN Security Council a memo making an explicit linkage between elements of the Chechen resistance and Osama bin Laden's Al Qaeda organization in Afghanistan, and describing a network of camps that included at least 2,560 Chechens serving or training with the bin Laden organization.[1]

In a September 24, 2001, address to the Russian people, Putin announced his support for the war against terrorism. Labeling the attacks barbaric, Putin offered Russian support for the antiterrorist struggle.[2] He noted that Russia had long called for a unified effort against international terrorism, had been battling it in Chechnya and Central Asia, and was now ready to take an active part in a multilateral coalition against it. "Russia has not changed its stance. Surely, we are willing now, too, to contribute to the antiterror cause. As we see it, attention must turn primarily to enhancing the role of international institutions established to promote international security—the United Nations and its Security Council."[3] On specific cooperation in the Afghan theater of military operations, Putin pledged Russia in five areas: intelligence sharing between security services, air passage over Russian territory for "humanitarian cargo" in support of antiterror operations, use of Moscow's good offices to secure access to the airfields of its Central Asian allies, engage-

ment of Russian forces and facilities in international search and rescue operations, and closer relations and greater assistance to the Rabbani government
and Northern Alliance forces. Putin put Minister of Defense Sergei Ivanov in
charge of coordinating the intelligence sharing and practical cooperation
with the antiterrorist coalition.[4]

As he pledged support for the antiterrorism coalition, Putin also addressed
Chechnya in a manner that tied the two topics directly to one another. "As
we see it, Chechen developments ought not to be regarded outside the context of efforts against international terrorism." This was clearly a marker on
the table. Putin noted the historical peculiarities of the Chechen conflict that
made it a distinct part of the struggle against terrorism and then appealed for
the misguided and/or misinformed to lay down their arms.

> That is why I call all paramilitaries and self-styled political activists urgently to
> sever whatever contacts with international terrorists and their organizations; and
> to contact official spokesmen of federal ruling bodies within 72 hours to debate
> the following: the disarmament procedure of the paramilitary groups and forma-
> tions, and arrangements to involve them in peacetime developments in Chech-
> nya. On behalf of federal authority, Victor Kazantsev, envoy plenipotentiary of
> the President of the Russian Federation to federal district South, which incorpo-
> rates Chechnya, has been authorized to affect such contacts.[5]

Putin's challenge was to make peace with those Chechens who were willing
to seek a political arrangement within the Russian Federation as opposed to
the creation of an Islamic state or a Jihad against Russia. Since then, while
the fighting has continued, the Putin administration has entered into negotiations with President Aslan Maskhadov's rebel government. These talks will
not be easy and carry grave risks for both governments after many years of
war and chaos in the region.

A nation in a region of many nationalities, the Chechens have emerged as
the most formidable challenge to the sovereignty and territorial integrity of
the Russian Federation. Moscow came to view a Chechen victory as a geopolitical "domino" that would subject the Russian Federation to the same
forces of disintegration that had torn apart the Soviet Union. The Chechens'
struggle, which has combined a call for national self-determination and a
revival of Islam, pitted a small but proud and warlike nation against a state
struggling to redefine itself after seven decades of communism. At the heart
of the conflict remains the question of Russia's relations with those nations
brought into the tsarist empire by force of arms and subjected to repression
by the most ruthless totalitarian methods.

The Yeltsin administration, having invoked Russian nationalism to bring
about the end of the Soviet Union, found its sovereignty challenged by a

nation of less than a million people and sought to thwart Chechen self-determination by force in 1994. After a year and a half of inconclusive warfare and fragile cease-fires, the Yeltsin government waited until after the second round of the presidential election to renew fighting, only to be embarrassed by the Chechens' recapture of Grozny on the same day as Yeltsin's inauguration. An infirm president was forced to accept a cease-fire and the withdrawal of Russian forces from Chechnya in August 1996.[6] With an armistice and a five-year period to negotiate a political settlement, both sides watched law and order deteriorate in the region and began preparing for renewed hostilities. Chechen rebels with a radical Islamic ideology took to exporting their insurgency beyond Chechnya into multiethnic Dagestan on the southern border of the Russian Federation and Azerbaijan.

In September 1999, in response to Chechen armed incursions into Dagestan, Moscow renewed hostilities. Under the leadership of a new prime minister, Vladimir Putin, it embarked upon the systematic pacification of Chechnya by brutal military assault and mass repression. Putin staked his own rise to power on military success in Chechnya, and between his appointment as acting president and his election, Russian forces captured as the flattened Chechen capital, Grozny. The uneven struggle, however, continues, pitting regular Russian troops and paramilitary formations against Chechen Mujahadeen. The Chechens cannot expel the Russians and the Russians cannot prevent Chechen raids and terrorist actions. This struggle is a manifestation of what Samuel Huntington has described as a "clash of civilizations." Like other such conflicts, it has its roots in the history of the interactions between the protagonists, Russians and Chechens, and how they define themselves and the "other."[7] Many Chechen fighters have embraced an Islamic revival to foster internal solidarity and to mobilize a broader struggle across the region. It is the region itself that defines the clash.

Since the border conflicts of the nineteenth century, the Islamic peoples of the Caucasus have posed a stark challenge to Russian state builders. Russian writers—Pushkin, Lermantov, and Tolstoy—understood that the mountain warrior was different. A challenge to Russia's imperial pretensions, he was the Other who could be admired for his bravery and ferocity but never tamed. The cleavages—cultural, religious, geographic, political—run deep.

By the time Vladimir Putin took charge of the Russo–Chechen War there was a long legacy that shaped the parameters of the conflict. Putin would have to operate within a well-delineated context that would dictate his course of action. Insofar as he defined his own political future and Russia's national recovery in terms of a strong, stable, centralized state, Chechen independence could not be accepted, only imposed, and certainly not by the Chechen resistance alone.

THE CHECHEN THEATER
OF MILITARY OPERATIONS

Geography

Chechnya is a small, landlocked, autonomous republic within the Russian Federation. Covering an area of 6,000 square miles, an area slightly smaller than the state of New Jersey, and with a population of about one million before the present round of fighting, Chechnya has been an area of confrontation between Imperial Russia/Soviet Union and the Chechen nation for several centuries. It is surrounded on three sides by Russian territory—on the north by Stavropol' Krai, on the west by Ingushetiya, and on the east and south by Dagestan.

Chechnya has one international frontier—to the south with Georgia. Two-thirds of the country north of the Terek River is open steppe; the land south of the Terek is dominated by the foothills of the Caucasus Mountains that stretch east to west across the region. Chechnya has limited oil production, but part of the pipeline system to carry oil from Baku, Azerbaijan, to the Russian Black Sea port of Novorossiysk is located in Chechnya, giving the region a role in the politics of the emerging Great Game of Caucasian, Caspian, and Central Asian oil, gas, and pipelines.

History: The Chechens and Islam[8]

Steppe and mountain, Cossack and mountaineer, Christian and Muslim, soldier and warrior, oppressor and bandit—these dichotomies describe the conflict between Russians and Chechens. Chechen President Aslan Maskhadov, a colonel who served in the Soviet Army, described the current war as the continuation of a four-century struggle: "Here, the Chechen people are fighting Russia. Russia does not want to clarify its relations with Chechnya. For this reason, the war has been continuing for more than 400 years."[9] This is no exaggeration since the struggle between Russians and Muslims of the Caucasus began in the seventeenth century. That unequal and bitter struggle has defined their mutual relations and the Chechens' sense of their place in the world. The protracted and episodic nature of the contest has had a profound impact on the character of the Chechen nation, its social organization, and self-perceptions. For the Chechen, clan loyalty and personal freedom gave meaning to a warrior culture that sets the nation apart from the Cossack settlers north of the Terek River. South of the Terek is the hill country that rises steadily to the peaks of the Caucasus. These mountains stretch 650 miles from the Caspian to the Black Sea and form a natural rampart separating Europe from Asia. The Arabic language and Islamic faith gave Chechens access to a literate world that linked Chechen culture to a greater identity.

Chechens embraced the religion brought by Muslim missionaries and made it their own. By the eighteenth century most of the peoples of the Caucasus, with the exception of the Georgians and Armenians, were Muslims. Islam provided the basis for alliances with the many other Islamic peoples of the region in their struggle with Orthodox Russia.

Clan life in a Chechen mountain village (*aoul*) revolved around raising sheep and raiding. The fortified stone villages were located on high peaks. The clans practiced the blood-vendetta (the *kanli*) where no offensive against clan honor could go unpunished, and feuds could go on for generations. Only the strong survived. Chechens continue to identify their nation with the wolf, the embodiment of elemental freedom. To supplement their meager existence, Chechen warriors frequently raided north of the Terek, carrying off goods, animals, and slaves from Cossack settlements. Horsemanship, marksmanship, and personal bravery defined a warrior's place in the clan. As the Russian frontier leaped across the steppe and toward the Terek, the imperial government in St. Petersburg turned its attention to the intractable mountain people.

Tsarist Intervention and Chechen Resistance

Under Catherine II, Russia defeated the Crimean Tartars, vassals of the Ottoman Empire, and began to push Russian settlements into the North Caucasus, extending serfdom into the new lands. The vehicle of that control was the Russian Imperial Army, setting in motion a conflict between soldiers of the regular army and Chechen warriors. Catherine II deployed Russian troops to revenge the defeat of a Russian column south of the Terek and made war against a coalition of mountain Islamic peoples, including Chechens, led by Sheikh Mansur Ushurma. The Russian advance culminated with the capture of the Black Sea Ottoman fortress of Anapa and the Sheikh himself in 1791.

After the Napoleonic Wars, Russia renewed its advance south. The Russians established fortress settlements at Grozny, Khasav-Yurt, and Mozdok to provide bases of operations. General Aleksei Yermolov, the first Russian commander in the protracted war that ensued, set the tone for an uncompromising and unforgiving struggle of extermination. Confronted by a barren and dry steppe north of the Terek River, Russian forces set their operational line east-west and set about building up a chain of fortress settlements on the Terek that would block raids from south and provide the foundation for campaigns against the mountain villages to the south. That conflict defined the myth of Chechen nationhood by linking the protracted struggle to a charismatic leader, Shamil, and to national and religious self-determination.

In the 1820s a profound spiritual movement swept the Chechens and other Islamic peoples of the North Caucasus, led by Mullah Muhammad Yaraghi, a scholar and Sufi, who set out to establish a Koran-based social order which embraced the "*Naqshbandi* Way." Those who accepted the mystical path of enlightenment known as Sufism, became the disciples, *murids*, of the mullah. He called for the suppression of customary law and the blood feud and the establishment of the *Shari'ah*, or Islamic law. In keeping with Islamic tradition, he preached temperance. His followers included Qazi Mullah, an Avar from Dagestan. In 1829 Qazi Mullah preached a *jihad* (holy war) against the Russians as the final stage of the revival. He warned: "Your marriages are unlawful, your children bastards, while there is one Russian left in your lands!"[10] The Islamic scholars of Dagestan gathered at Ghimri, and, acclaiming him imam, pledged their support.

The Russians responded to this threat by co-opting some clans with concessions and using military power against the resistance. Like the Yeltsin government a century and a half later, Nicholas I's agents had only limited success in this policy of divide and rule. Ultimately, the Russian military faced two wars in the North Caucasus: in the west against the Cherkess people and in the east against the peoples of Dagestan, Chechnya, and Ingushetia.[11] The eastern struggle produced a Dagestani warrior and imam who would embody the Chechen myth of resistance.

Shamil Imam (1796–1871), an Adar noble of Dagestan, joined the resistance led by Qazi Mullah. Shamil fought heroically in the defense of Ghimri in 1831. Wounded in the fighting, Shamil escaped capture, as he would on many later occasions. Proclaimed imam in 1834, he rallied the peoples of the east Caucasus to resist the Russian advance. Supported by the *murids*, Shamil checked Russian power for almost three decades and built an Islamic state to prosecute a guerilla war, relying upon the impenetrability of the forests and mountains of the Caucasus to protect his force.[12] Undeterred, the Russians made war on the Chechen population, striking at the *aouls*. While they could not level the mountains, the Russians could and did cut back the forests to allow their columns to move against the fortress settlements. For a brief moment during the Crimean War it appeared that Shamil might get Western support for his struggle, but following the war, Shamil was isolated from outside support and forced to surrender to General Alexander Bariatinsky in 1859. The war ended in 1864 with a Russian victory.[13]

From the beginning, Russian rule in the North Caucasus had been imposed by force and was thus maintained. When war broke out with Turkey in 1877, Chechens joined an armed uprising, which was suppressed by the tsarist authorities. In the early twentieth century some of Chechnya's leading families emigrated to Turkey and thereby created a Chechen diaspora. In the chaos that overtook Russia after 1914, the empire collapsed, with much of the non-Russian periphery seeking self-determination. On May 11, 1918, the North Caucasus peoples declared the formation of the Republic of the North Caucasus Federation under the sponsorship of the Central Powers. Germany's defeat and the outbreak of civil war in southern Russia turned the North Caucasus into a battleground for Reds and Whites. The Reds supported the independence of the region as part of their struggle with the Whites and in the hope of using Islam against the imperial powers. The Whites found support among the Russian Cossack populations living on the steppe and resistance among the Chechen mountaineers. In Bolshevik propaganda Shamil became a revolutionary and symbol of resistance to imperial rule. However, after the civil war the Bolsheviks sent the Red Army into the region, overthrew the existing order, and annexed it in 1922.

Stalinism and Chechnya

Joseph Stalin, the Bolshevik commissar of nationalities and a Georgian, adapted the class struggle to the traditional policy of divide and rule. Soviet federalism provided a national veneer to a centralized state controlled by the Communist Party that sent Russians to staff the key party posts within the various republics.[14] However, the Chechens again proved a difficult people to subdue. In 1929 they revolted against collectivization, and for a decade Chechnya was rife with revolt and repression. Soviet propaganda now cast Shamil as a class enemy. Soviet interest in Chechnya grew with the development of its oil fields and the arrival of Russians to manage the oil industry.

During World War II, when the German Army advanced into the Caucasus, there were more signs of Chechen unrest and collaboration with the enemy. In late February 1944, Lavrenti Beria's NKVD carried out Stalin's "solution" to the Chechen Question—mass deportation of Chechens to Central Asia. Over 70,000 of the 450,000 Chechens expelled died during transit or upon arrival. Chechnya ceased to exist. The exile became the defining event for succeeding generations of Chechens.[15] In 1957 Nikita Khrushchev decreed that the Chechens could return to their ancestral homelands. Chechnya and Ingushetia were joined administratively into the Chechen-Ingush Autonomous Republic. This arrangement joined the rebellious Chechens with the traditionally loyal Ingush in a clear continuation of Moscow's policy of divide and rule. Inside Chechnya, Soviet officials made their own arrangements with local clans while keeping an uneasy eye open for signs of resistance to Communist rule.

THE FIRST CHECHEN WAR OF THE RUSSIAN FEDERATION, 1994–96

Road to War

When Mikhail Gorbachev embarked on his ill-fated attempt to save the Soviet system via *glasnost* and *perestroika*, Chechen nationalists saw an opportunity to attain national self-determination. Then in the chaos and collapse of the Soviet Union, Boris Yeltsin led a resurgent Russian Federation and championed greater self-rule within the Union republics. In his political struggle for control of Russia, Yeltsin encouraged the national republics within Russia to seek greater autonomy. The Chechens exploited this opportunity. In late November 1990, a national Chechen conference, including delegates representing all ethnic groups in Chechnya, convened in Grozny. The conference declared the independence and sovereignty of Chechnya and its secession from the Soviet Union. On November 27, 1990, the soviet of the Chechen-Ingush Republic unanimously dissolved the union of Chechnya and Ingushetia and declared their independence and sovereignty.

General Major Dzhokar Dudaev quickly emerged as the leader of the self-proclaimed Chechen government. Dudaev, the first Chechen officer to reach the rank of general, had served in Afghanistan and commanded a strategic bomber unit in the Baltic. In June 1991, Chechen and Russian nationalism moved in lockstep against Soviet power as Yeltsin won 80 percent of the vote in the Chechen-Ingush returns from the Russian presidential elections. In the aftermath of the August coup of 1991 and the collapse of efforts to reform the Union, Chechens voted for independence and elected General Dudaev as president by an overwhelming majority. The Yeltsin government proved quite ineffective in countering these moves, and their ham-handed tactics again convinced most Chechens that whoever was in power in Moscow was an enemy of self-determination. In December 1991, the Soviet Union collapsed when the presidents of Russia, Ukraine, and Belarus voted to abolish the Union. Now Chechnya was a matter to be resolved by the Yeltsin government in Moscow and Dudaev's government in Grozny.

At this juncture as the struggle for Chechen independence began, Moscow was weak, and Grozny drifted into chaos as crime and corruption grew at a staggering pace. Yeltsin viewed Chechen independence as a threat to Russia's territorial integrity and sovereignty and a magnet for other disgruntled Caucasian peoples chafing under Russian rule. Initially, the Yeltsin government paid little attention to the Chechen problem. Dissolving the Soviet system, trying to create a viable Russian government, and transforming the economy through privatization and marketization were given top priority. The Chechens, thanks to corrupt and incompetent Russian officials, seized large quantities of Soviet arms left in Chechnya. Dudaev distributed the arms but did not create an effective regular military.

The Yeltsin administration, having invoked Russian nationalism to bring about the end of the Union, watched Chechen separatism under General Dudaev become an effective challenge to Moscow's rule. While the Dudaev government managed to gain control of most of the Soviet weapons left in Grozny, it did not create an orderly or stable government. Chechnya sank into a morass of crime and terrorism that adversely affected Russian economic and political interests. The Russian population of the republic began to leave. At first, the government tried to build an alliance with disgruntled Chechens, who opposed Dudaev's increasingly arbitrary and corrupt government. However, in 1994, fearing that Yeltsin's rival and former speaker of the overthrown Russian parliament, Ruslan Khasbulatov, would emerge as leader of that opposition, the Yeltsin government attempted to overthrow Dudaev's regime by covert action, with disguised Russian military personnel spearheading the attack on Grozny. When this attempt failed, the government resorted to force of arms in December 1994. While invoking the threat of instability in Chechnya to justify intervention, the Yeltsin government sought to present military intervention as something less than a war. The intervention was to involve a peacemaking mission (*mirotvorchestvo*) that would restore "constitutional order" and require that the Russian forces deploy to separate the warring "factions" and de facto reestablish Russian sovereignty in Chechnya. Yeltsin and his advisors wanted to use military power to awe the Chechens but not to fight a protracted partisan war. The problem was that once the black operation had failed, they had no plausible explanation for their "peacekeeping intervention."

That plan began to unravel in late November 1994 when Russia-sponsored, anti-Dudaev Chechens mounted an assault on Grozny and were badly defeated. In spite of the qualitative and quantitative decline in Russian conventional military power and the defeat of their covert attempt to overthrow Dudaev, the Yeltsin government did not anticipate serious or effective military resistance from the Chechens, either Dudaev's troops or a popular insurrection. Competent military professionals did warn the government regarding the condition of Russian forces and the danger of underestimating Chechen resistance. General Edvard Vorob'ev turned down the position of theater commander when Minister of Defense Pavel Grachev refused his request for additional time to prepare Russian forces for the operation. Grachev, an airborne commander with experience in Afghanistan, dismissed these concerns and did not provide sufficient or timely leadership in the preparation of the forces for combat, which he treated as another contingency operation, like those that Soviet and Russian forces had been engaging in since 1989. Indeed, speaking of a *coup de main* to take out Dudaev's government, Grachev had estimated one airborne brigade and two hours to finish the task. Russia's military leadership gravely underestimated the risks of a popular uprising in support of Chechen independence. The Yeltsin government made the common mistake of reinforcing failure with tragic consequences. Rather than redrafting their plans with the failure of the anti-Dudaev opposition to take the city, they stuck with their peacekeeping operation and went into combat in the dead of winter with forces unprepared for combat.

Confronted with a failed covert operation, Yeltsin's government sought to use force to recover from the disaster. The political leadership, while eager for a military solution, was unable to provide a plausible explanation for the use of force in Chechnya and was still suffering from a serious challenge to its credibility after its ill-judged support of a Russia-sponsored faction in Chechnya. Denials of Russian involvement gave way to admission of "volunteers" and then to reports of active recruiting of military personnel by the Federal Counter-Intelligence Service (FSK) for the opposing force's unsuccessful assault on Grozny. When the Security Council voted to overtly deploy Russian forces to Chechnya, Boris Yeltsin absented himself from the public eye, leaving it to others to explain his administration's course of action and rationale. The First Chechen War never invoked broad public support, and the Russian media, with few exceptions, critically questioned the government's account of the campaign.

The Assault on Grozny

In early December 1994, three Russian columns—made up of composite units and numbering at most 23,000—began their advance on Grozny from three directions: northeast, west, and east. The slow pace and uncoordinated nature of the Russian advance allowed the Chechens to organize their defense. Ad hoc detachments defended the presidential palace and took on the advancing Russian columns in a series of ambushes. With the Russian advance stalled, the Chechen defenders organized strong points, which over time became three concentric defensive belts around the presidential palace.

The total number of defenders, regular Chechen troops, volunteer detachments, and foreign mercenaries numbered between nine and ten thousand under Colonel Aslan Maskhadov, Dudaev's chief of staff. By the last day of December, Russian forces were in position to begin their occupation of Grozny, advancing as though Grozny was a Russian city. In fact, many Russian residents of the capital had already fled and others were already fearful because of Russian air attacks upon the city. The Chechen population was united in the struggle against the Russian assault. In the course of their advance into the city, the Russian columns were ambushed by Chechen fighters. The Chechens operated in small ten to twelve-man mobile groups fighting from building to building and making good use of off-the-shelf commercial communication equipment. Unprepared for the demands of urban combat and suffering from poor coordination and intelligence, the Russian attackers had 1,500 casualties on the streets of Grozny during the New Year's Day battle. Of 120 BMPs (armored personnel carriers) that advanced into the city, over 100 were destroyed by enemy action. The attacking forces lost twenty of twenty-six tanks in the initial assault. Humiliated by the initial success of the Chechen defense of Grozny, the Russian Army and Internal Forces fought a month-long, bloody battle to take the city, and began the pacification of the countryside.[16]

Pacification and Its Failure

The Chechens conducted a successful withdrawal from the city and then mounted protracted partisan warfare in the countryside. General Anatoliy Kulikov, the commander in chief of internal troops, was given the task of pacification. Russian soldiers occupied more villages but could not uproot the insurrection. Failing to impose their will or find a viable Chechen faction that would serve as Moscow's agent, the Russians began negotiations to end the conflict. Meanwhile, morale and discipline among the Russian forces in Chechnya, which had been low to begin with, declined further.[17] Thanks to bad field sanitation, an outbreak of viral hepatitis, much like those suffered by Soviet troops in Afghanistan, decimated the Russian forces in Chechnya.[18] On the one hand, low morale and lack of discipline led to widespread excesses against the civilian population, turning every village into a source of Chechen intelligence. At the same time, it facilitated transfers of arms for cash between Russian troops and the Chechen rebels. On the other hand, relations between regular army units and units of internal troops deteriorated rapidly. Russian media provided in-depth and largely accurate accounts of the fighting. When Shamil Basaev's band raided the village of Budennovsk in Stavropol' Krai ninety miles inside Russia and took hostages at the local hospital in June 1995, it was the Russian media that depicted the government's incompetent response, turning Basaev into an international figure, and further discrediting the Russian government's cause. As a final straw, the government failed to free hostages held by Basaev, and was forced to negotiate their release while permitting the escape of the Chechen detachment.[19] A major shake-up in the Russian power ministries followed this disaster. Prime Minister Viktor Chernomyrdin initiated negotiations to end the fighting.

Chechen forces continued to conduct raids and terrorist attacks against Russian troops and mounted assassination attempts against Russian officials in Chechnya. In October 1995, the Chechens carried out a bombing attack against General-Lieutenant A. Romanov, seriously wounding the MVD commander and chief Russian negotiator. While the Russian authorities concentrated on trying to create an alternative Chechen government and to carry out the normalization of life in Chechnya—symbolized by Chechnya's participation in the federation's parliamentary elections in December 1995, the Chechens regrouped their forces and mounted daily attacks against Russian posts and convoys. They carried out daring raids into Grozny itself. In January 1996, Salman Rudaev mounted a major raid against Russian forces at Kizliar in Dagestan. Rudaev's band broke off their attack upon the Russian units there and fell back upon the village, where they took civilian hostages. Following negotiations with Dagestani authorities and the release of some of their hostages, Rudaev's fighters were given buses and safe passage to the Dagestani frontier with their remaining hostages. After failing in their initial attempt to capture Rudaev's contingent, Russian special forces found themselves locked into a battle for the village of Pervomaisk. In the course of several days, part of Rudaev's band escaped the encirclement. At the end of a year's fighting Russian forces were no closer to ending Chechen resistance.

Presidential Elections and the End Game

The Yeltsin government swung back and forth between repression and accommodation as the 1996 presidential elections approached. At the beginning of the electoral campaign, Boris Yeltsin's popularity had sunk to rock bottom. Some of his advisors favored postponing the presidential elections and outlawing the Communist Party, the chief opposition force led by Gennadiy Zyuganov. Those supporting the holding of elections mobilized their forces around the theme of preventing the restoration of communism and understood that the war in Chechnya was a chief source of discontent with the government. To win re-election Yeltsin needed both evidence of progress on the ground and an opportunity to begin negotiations with the Chechens. On April 21, 1996, Yeltsin got his evidence of progress when Russian intelligence was able to lock on to Dzhokar Dudaev's cell phone and provide strike coordinates for an Su-25 ground-attack aircraft to launch two laser-guided missiles that killed the Chechen president. With the death of Dudaev, the Yeltsin government proposed a cease-fire as a first step toward a negotiated settlement.

In the following months, the Yeltsin team used the cease-fire to defuse the war issue in the presidential elections, and finished first in the initial round of voting. They then ensured Yeltsin's re-election by forging an alliance with General Aleksandr Lebed, who had finished third in the voting behind Yeltsin and Zyuganov. Yeltsin treated Lebed as his anointed successor and appointed him secretary of the Security Council. Rumors of coups brought major shakeups in the administration, including the removal of General Grachev and the appointment of General Igor Rodionov, a Lebed supporter, as minister of defense. Lebed had been an outspoken critic of the war in Chechnya.

In July, the Yeltsin administration began preparations for renewed fighting, but the Chechens preempted the Russian blow by striking at Grozny. Confronted by the Chechen reconquest of Grozny and serious divisions within the government over the further prosecution of the war, the Yeltsin government was forced to accept a cease-fire negotiated by General Lebed. The immediate axis of this dispute was between General Kulikov of the Ministry of Internal Affairs, who saw Russian control of Chechnya as vital to the territorial integrity of the Russian Federation and its survival, and General Lebed, who saw in Chechnya the collapse of the unreformed army. For Lebed, a cease-fire and settlement of Chechnya were the only way to save the armed forces from disintegration. The peacemakers won, the Russian Army withdrew, and Lebed and Maskhadov signed the Khasavyurt Accords on August 31, 1996. The cease-fire ended the fighting but left the ultimate status of Chechnya unresolved.

BETWEEN WARS, 1996–99

With Yeltsin now seriously ill, a struggle for leadership within the Kremlin became intense. Lebed, who was both popular and strong willed, seemed an immediate threat to the Yeltsin loyalists. They mounted a successful campaign, led by Minister of Internal Affairs Anatoliy Kulikov, to discredit him as a coup plotter and bring about his removal. Management of the Chechen question was left in the hands of the Security Council, with the oligarch Boris Berezovsky appointed deputy secretary for Chechnya. General Rodionov, a champion of military reform, found no support within the government and was removed in May 1997, replaced by General (and then Marshal) Igor Sergeev, the former commander of the Strategic Rocket Forces. Sergeev focused the reform efforts of the Ministry of Defense upon Russia's strategic nuclear forces. Preparation of Russian Army and Internal Forces for possible employment in response to further destabilization of Chechnya or the extension of unrest beyond its borders fell to the General Staff, the Ministry of Internal Affairs, and the North Caucasian Military District.

General Anatolii Kvashnin was appointed chief of the General Staff in June 1997. Former commander of the North Caucasian Military District during the First Chechen War, Kvashnin favored the reform of the Russian Armed Forces along lines that would enhance conventional military power and modernize the force to fight local wars.

Chechen military and political success strengthened the political hand of Colonel Aslan Maskhadov, who served as Dudaev's chief of staff and engineered the victory in Grozny. Maskhadov was elected president of Chechnya in early 1997, but his power base was quite limited. Personal and ideological/religious conflicts projected an image that no one was in charge of a bandit republic. Law and order collapsed and kidnapping and extortion became widespread. Islam defined the splits among the Chechen leadership. Basaev, the most charismatic leader, was a throwback to Shamil's Sufism. Khattab, an Arab who had fought in Afghanistan and Tajikistan, brought foreign Mujahadeen, money, and Wahhabi fundamentalism to the struggle. Both leaders challenged Maskhadov's authority and promoted a renewed and expanded war.

For its part, the Russian government proved utterly incapable of developing a coherent political strategy to deal with Chechnya. Some Russians wanted revenge or had personal reasons to stoke the fires of ethnic hatred using a well-financed media campaign. Even Russian moderates came to view Chechnya as a criminal land and a source of chaos, where kidnapping had become a recognized business. By 1998, both sides were preparing for a confrontation.

THE SECOND CHECHEN WAR, 1999–

The five-year interlude provided by the Russian–Chechen agreement was supposed to provide sufficient time for a political resolution of the core issues: Chechen sovereignty and the territorial integrity of the Russian Federation. An interlude of peace ensued; however, it was marked by increasing violence, banditry, and kidnapping within Chechnya, and by growing Russian concern that the crisis in Chechnya would take a form requiring military action. In 1997–98 it appeared that Russian political and military leaders had agreed upon a limited response to such a crisis. Military command-post exercises, restructuring of command arrangements, and actions in theater all suggested a crisis response that would involve the military isolation of Chechnya from Russia, including an advance to the Terek River but no further.

Several events in the spring and summer of 1999 encouraged the resumption of hostilities. Many Russians viewed NATO's intervention in Kosovo as a precursor to intervention in support of Muslims in the Caucasus. Radical Islamic elements in Chechnya viewed the success of the Kosovo Liberation Army as a model for their armed struggle. The Russian leadership was aware of the possibility of renewed fighting and a raid into Dagestan but were divided over the response. Some saw the optimal response as a Russian attempt to support Maskhadov's authority in Chechnya. Others rejected this path as the surest way to legitimizing Chechen independence in 2001 at the end of the five years of the interim agreement between Lebed and Maskhadov. All sides recognized that Russia was not well prepared to deal with a renewed war. Stepashin's government accepted the military planners' recommendation for an advance to the Terek River in case of renewed hostilities.[20]

In August 1999, Khattab and Basaev led their military formations into Dagestan to ignite an Islamic insurgency. It is still unclear whether President Maskhadov endorsed or supported this move. Russian officials and press accounts stressed the chaos and disorder within Chechnya as a primary source of the external adventure. In his memoirs, General Gennadiy Troshev described Chechnya on the eve of the second war as "an international bandit enclave."[21] Foreign observers mentioned oil and geopolitics but also noted the risk of chaos spreading throughout the region.[22] Anatol Lieven, a leading expert on the First Chechen War, described the second as a struggle against the same extremism that threatened chaos for the entire Middle East.[23]

In response to the Chechen armed incursions into Dagestan, Moscow renewed hostilities and seemed initially to follow a limited course of action designed to drive the insurgents back in to Chechnya and contain them. Tactically, Russian MVD commanders sought to inflict serious damage upon the enemy with indirect fire but to reduce the risks of close battle and Russian casualties. Chechnya was a security problem but not a crusade. This changed in September 1999 under a new prime minister as Yeltsin fired his latest, Sergei Stepashin, and replaced him with the head of the Security Council, Vladimir Putin. A series of bomb blasts in Russian apartment buildings brought the war home to the Russian people. Unlike the First Chechen War, public opinion immediately rallied to the government's cause and has remained supportive. Putin took the war deep into Chechnya, sought to overthrow the Maskhadov government, and vowed to eliminate the bandits/terrorists wherever they were found. "Even if we find them in a toilet, we shall kill them in the outhouse."[24] Unlike the First Chechen War, Russian mass media has followed the government's line on the nature of the conflict and the threat. The advance to the Terek became the preparation for a general assault on Grozny.

Responsibility for the conduct of the campaign in Chechnya belonged to General-Lieutenant Gennadiy Troshev, commander of the North Caucasian Military District. This time the Russian government committed significant forces to the initial campaign. Coordination between army and MVD units had been greatly improved thanks to the efforts of Colonel-General Leontiy Shevtsov, who had served as Chief of the Operations Directorate of the General Staff during the planning of the first Chechen campaign. Shevtsov had gone on to be the Russian representative to NATO's SACEUR under IFOR/SFOR and on his return had been selected by General Kulikov to command Russia's internal troops. When Stepashin became minister of Internal Affairs, Shevtsov took over the task of coordinating internal troop and army operational exercises.

After a deliberate advance to the Terek, MVD units, including Chechens loyal to Moscow, encircled the city of Grozny. A well-prepared Russian assault began on December 24, 1999, and after two months of fighting took Grozny, but only after flattening much of the city with air, artillery, and rocket strikes. The advancing Russian troops were ready for urban combat, using small-unit tactics to find and pin Chechen forces where they could be struck by indirect fire, including TOS-1 fuel-air explosives.[25] The Russian advance over the next two months was slow and methodical and cut the cities into isolated sectors. The Chechen resistance was broken and forced from the city. Russian units trapped the withdrawing Chechens in minefields and delivered devastating fire, inflicting heavy casualties. Shamil Basaev was seriously wounded in a Russian minefield.[26]

The war reverted to insurgency. Withdrawing into the mountains south of the Terek, the Chechen fighters returned to guerilla warfare and began to make greater use of territory outside of Russia for the resuscitation of their units. For example, Russian commanders complained of Chechen sanctuaries within Georgia. Colonel-General Valery Manilov, first deputy chief of the General Staff, charged in May 2000 that no fewer than 1,500 "mercenary gunmen" are based in Pankisi Gorge in eastern Georgia, poised to reenter Chechnya and mount renewed terrorist attacks.[27]

Putin staked his own rise to power on military success in Chechen and achieved it with the capture and destruction of the Chechen capital, Grozny, in March 2000. The uneven struggle, however, continues, pitting regular Russian troops and paramilitary formations against Chechen fighters. Its roots are to be found in the history of the interactions between Russians and Chechens. Moscow has not found credible Chechen leaders to rule through and has not been able to suppress the armed insurrection. Atrocities mount, matched by terrorist incidents. In the spring of 2001, Putin announced the turnover of pacification to the Federal Security Service (FSB) and reductions in troop levels in Chechnya. These have proven premature. After only 5,000 of the 80,000 troops in Chechnya were withdrawn, the government had to curtail the program in the face of mounting Chechen raids. Colonel-General Gennadiy Troshev, who had declared the war in Chechnya over in the fall of 2000, announced only six months later that Russian authorities should resort to the public execution of captured Chechen rebels.[28]

The longer and more bitter the war in Chechnya, the greater the risk of the territorial expansion of the conflict, and of external intervention. The war proved a profound tragedy for Russian democracy and for Chechen national-ism, as violence has driven out any grounds for dialogue and compromise and has made a compelling case for enhanced state power to fight the war successfully. The second war has proven even more destructive than the first. The assault on Grozny effectively leveled the city, leaving its population with-out basic services, and the counterinsurgency operations brought intense physical destruction to outlying settlements, the concentration of refugees into "filtration" camps, and increased brutality—a war without limits against enemy combatants and civilians.[29]

Before the second war began, the Russian military claimed that its actions would be selective, so as to keep damages and casualties among the peaceful civilian population at a minimum. However, the first massive rocket attack upon Grozny, during which hundreds of noncombatants died and Maternity Hospital No. 1 was partially destroyed, serves as definitive proof to the con-trary. The "antiterrorist" operations in the Chechen Republic have, in fact, turned out to be large-scale warfare that inflicted serious casualties upon the Chechen civilian population.[30] With neither side giving or asking for quarter, the war became a protracted, low-intensity conflict. The actual number and size of the armed formations opposing the Russian forces is relatively small, estimated at 100 bands composed of between 1500–2000 fighters at any given time, but the counterterror operations have not brought about a significant reduction in the opposing force.[31] As in the First Chechen War, Russian forces have had successes in strikes against leading enemy commanders, including the capture of Rudaev and the killing of Khattab. Although the Putin government was able to incorporate pro-Russian Chechen units into the MVD forces that assaulted Grozny, it has been less successful in turning the pro-Russian Chechen officials into a legitimate government that enjoys the support of the Chechen population. Akhmed Kadyrov, a former mufti who fought against Russia in the First Chechen War and is now Moscow's man in Chechnya, has proven incapable of bringing stability and legitimacy to the Russian civil administration. While dissatisfaction has mounted with the Kadyrov administration, no loyal alternative has emerged.[32] Kadyrov has expressed his displeasure with the efforts of the military and special services to find the terrorist leadership, even as his own government has been subject to increasing terrorist actions.[33] Even within the Russian government there is open conflict over the efficacy of "cleansing operations" against villages that supposedly harbor terrorist elements. The dispute pitted FSB operatives against military intelligence.[34]

In Chechnya, outsiders should be advised against picking sides and painting one as virtuous and the other evil. The level of chaos and disorder simply overwhelms these categories. General Lebed, a veteran of Afghanistan, once remarked: "I have had occasion to see a lot of combat, and I affirm this fact: There are enough scoundrels in war on both sides—rape and sadism—all of this is present on both sides."[35] Vengeance is an invitation to a perpetual blood feud. But the popular roots of revenge in an armed conflict lie in the pursuit to seek justice against those guilty of injustice. When visited upon a people, and not the culpably guilty, it becomes a source of injustice itself. Such has been the sad particular truth of Chechnya. By the summer of 2001 it appeared that no one involved in the Second Chechen War had found a way to end the bloodshed.[36]

PUTIN'S GAMBIT: THE ANTITERRORIST ALLIANCE AND ENDGAME IN CHECHNYA

The events of September 11 transformed the international security environment and gave President Putin an opportunity to transform the external contexts of the Chechen War. As we have noted earlier, Putin has taken full advantage of these circumstances, emphasizing the linkage between Islamic terrorists in Chechnya and those in Afghanistan, seeking to divide the Chechen nationalist insurgents from the Islamic extremists, and beginning a process of negotiations with the moderates via Victor Kazantsev, his envoy plenipotentiary to the federal district South. In the region, Putin has made clear the paramount importance of a Russian presence for stability. Russia's cause is just and its methods, in the face of this threat, are justified. Russia will negotiate with the Chechens, if they are willing to recognize the error of resisting Russian authority and break with the extremists. For this strategy to work, Putin required that the West stop its criticism of Russian tactics in Chechnya. In exchange, Putin shifted to a policy of finding Chechen partners for political negotiations. Boris Nemtsov, a leading Russian liberal and supporter of Putin, had been keen on such negotiations and declared that Putin's support for the United States and his policy of seeking a negotiated settlement in Chechnya made sense. The underlying premise for success in both ventures was to fight terrorism, but not to make war on the Chechen people.[37]

This emphasis on a political solution comes after two years of fighting in which the Russian armed forces proved effective in conventional war but unable to put down a dogged Chechen resistance. A bloody protracted conflict with its camps and atrocities brought condemnations of Russia's conduct. Western criticism of the Russian military's methods, calls for the creation of an international criminal tribunal to try Russian commanders and officials for war crimes in Chechnya, and unofficial contacts with the Chechen opposition brought sharp objections from Moscow. But this critique of Russian conduct was kept within discrete limits. As Secretary of State Madeleine Albright declared to the Senate Foreign Relations Committee, Chechnya was not Kosovo.[38] In January 2001, Putin placed the counterterrorist operations in Chechnya in the hands of the FSB. Putin stated that FSB leadership would bring "the use of different means and forces and with a different emphasis."[39] The different emphasis did not bring about an end to Chechen resistance, however. At the same time, Putin forcefully argued for linkages between Chechen rebels and international terrorist organizations, especially the Albanian resistance that took up arms in Macedonia in the spring of 2001. Both, he claimed, were terrorist organizations that posed a serious threat to European peace and stability.[40] Frustration with the inability to bring an end to armed resistance in Chechen and the impact of conducting an antipartisan war brought calls for some sort of endgame for Chechnya—a negotiated settlement—but it was unclear through the spring and summer of 2001, with whom Moscow could conduct talks. Both sides still seemed to be looking for a military victory that neither could achieve.[41]

A gradual shift in U.S. policy toward Russia and the war in Chechnya became evident during the Ljubljana summit between Bush and Putin in June 2001. In addition to positive assessments of their trust in each other, the two had a frank exchange on Chechnya, each stating their positions. Bush mentioned freedom of the press and Chechnya, while Putin stressed Russia's security problems in the south. Bush then raised the problem of relations between Georgia and Russia. Russia claimed that Chechen forces enjoyed sanctuary in Georgia's Pankisi Gorge as part of an anti-Russian policy in the region. Russia and Georgia are divided over the solution to the Abkhazian question, where Russian peacekeepers effectively contribute to the continued inability of Georgian refugees to return to Abkhazia. Rebel forces in Abkhazia had driven out the Georgian population and Tibilisi saw the return of the refugees as a vital part of the solution to the conflict in Abkhazia. These exchanges took place in the context of intense discussions of national missile defense and the abandonment of the ABM Treaty.[42] After their second summit in the summer of 2001, Putin and Bush announced that they were seeking a new strategic framework that would address the issue of national missile defense. No solution had been found, but both parties accepted the idea of continuing dialogue.[43]

At the same time, the Bush administration was also reviewing its strategy on terrorism and preparing to mobilize a broader coalition for a determined fight. The focus of the struggle was to be Afghanistan and Pakistan. As Ahmed Rashid reported, one official defined the antiterrorism strategy as one of building a broad coalition. "We are building a global alliance to counter the terrorist threat from Afghanistan and force Pakistan to stop military supplies to the Taliban. . . . The alliance starts from Afghanistan's neighbors and extends to the G-8, NATO, the European Union (EU), East Asia, and the Middle East."[44] In short, before the events of September 11, Russia and the United States had acknowledged the linkage between the global terrorist threat to U.S. interests and the specific challenges in the North Caucasus and Central Asia. Thus, the Russian response to the events of September 11 should not be seen outside this larger context of changed priorities and perspectives.

Since September 11, Putin has moved Russian policy toward supporting the common struggle in Central Asia and seeking to resolve the conflict in Chechnya by negotiations and political means. In what could have been a major step toward a widened war in the Caucasus, Putin acted to defuse the results of the intervention of Chechen fighters in Abkhazia. The Russian press saw this intervention as part of Georgian policy to get the Chechen fighters out of Georgia at a time when their presence had become an embarrassment. Having denied the presence of such fighters on Georgian territory for over a year, President Shevardnadze had to act quickly or face serious complications that could threaten Georgia's stability,[45] as well as relations with Russia and the United States. As the fighting in Abkhazia escalated, Putin asserted Russia's preeminent role as a stabilizing power in the entire region and forced Shevardnadze to acknowledge their importance by threatening to remove Russian peacekeepers.[46] One Russian commentator, Alap Kasayev, spoke of the fighting in Georgia as "the Abkhazian front of the Afghan War," and suggested that Shevardnadze had sought to use Western support and military adventure to undermine Russian interests in the Caucasus.[47] But the outcome of the Abkhazian crisis strengthened Russia's position and Putin's authority as a regional leader.[48]

In Chechnya, Putin's seventy-two-hour deadline brought a positive response by President Maskhadov's government.[49] After six months the two sides are still seeking to find a common agenda for the talks.[50] The Russian strategy here seeks to divide the Chechen opposition between those seeking a political status and those set upon an Islamic revolution. Recent press reports have noted the close ties between Chechen Islamic extremists and the Wahhabis in promoting terrorist actions in Dagestan and Chechnya.[51] Russian special forces successfully eliminated Khattab, the charismatic Wahhabist leader this spring. Western attitudes toward Russian policy have also undergone a sharp change. In a radio interview in Moscow, Alvaro Gil-Robles, the human rights commissioner of the Council of Europe, declared that Chechnya was in transition to normality. He cited both the building of a civil society there and the desire of both Chechen and Russian peoples for peace.[52] While U.S. policy remains concerned about human rights violations in Chechnya and has begun broadcasts by Radio Liberty in Chechen, there is a recognition of the terrorist component to the Chechen conflict. In short, both the domestic and international ramification of the war in Chechnya have been affected by the events of September 11. As one Russian commentator suggested, the geostrategic context of power and interests changed in September. The vital interests of the United States are to be found in the Middle East and Central Asia. Energy may still define the long-term picture, but the immediate threat is the terrorism of Islamic extremism, and in that regard, Putin's Russia and Bush's America share a common if nebulous enemy, a chameleon that changes more than its color and manifests itself quite differently from state to state.[53]

CONCLUSION

In a series of steps, the Putin and Bush administrations have signaled their mutual interests in cooperation during the antiterrorism campaign against Afghanistan. Both have sought to place U.S.–Russian relations on a new foundation of cooperation. On October 17 at a meeting of the Security Council, Putin announced Russia's intention to close its intelligence facility at Lourdes, Cuba, and its naval base at Cam Ranh Bay, Vietnam.[54] While the rationale for the closing of the base was couched in monetary terms, the primary motive seems to have been to solidify the U.S.–Russian alliance against terrorism by a high-visibility step that marked a sharp break with Cold War logic.[55] The Bush–Putin sidebar conversations at the Asia-Pacific Economic Cooperation forum strengthened their mutual commitment to the war against terrorism.[56] National Security Advisor Condoleezza Rice reviewed the

Bush–Putin interactions at Shanghai in positive terms and spoke of an emerging security arrangement that went beyond Cold War remnants to embrace new challenges arising from the war against terrorism, and speculated about the possibility of deeper cooperation. "I do not rule out the possibility, however, that as the war on international terrorism broadens, some new spheres may appear where our countries will find cooperation mutually beneficial."[57] Thomas Friedman, writing a month into the conflict, proclaimed that in the war on terrorism, "We are all alone."[58] He was lamenting the fact that our allies in the fight against terrorism came with their own agendas and commitments. He made no mention of Russia as an ally. Only two days before, Gleb Pavlovsky had written that Moscow had to accept the idea that it would either join the antiterrorist coalition or face similar attacks on its own.[59] Putin has taken a significant domestic risk in supporting the antiterrorist coalition, leading to serious criticism from many former allies within the political elite. But he seems committed to the common struggle against terrorism.[60] Other former allies of the president have been quick to accuse him of selling out Russian interests to the United States. These critics portray the events of September 11 as serving America's efforts to gain global hegemony.[61] Putin has shown a willingness to embrace an American military presence in Georgia, if that military assistance will lead to the termination of a Chechen sanctuary in Pankisi Gorge. U.S. special forces have begun to train Georgian units to combat the terrorist threat in this area.

In this alliance, the perception of a common enemy has been one of the key sources of cooperation. For the Putin administration, it matters that the United States recognizes the centrality of the struggle with Islamic terrorism in Chechnya, even as it fosters a dialogue between the Russian government and the Chechen national resistance. Putin himself has said that the losses inflicted on terrorists and mercenaries in Chechnya contributed to the common struggle.[62] At the same time, this cooperation also demonstrates a desire of both parties to find a new strategic framework that reflects current security concerns and transcends those of the Cold War.

NOTES

1. Tom Heneghan, "Russian Memo Lists Bin Laden Camps in Afghanistan," *Reuters*, September 26, 2001.

2. "Putin Determines Russian Stance on Antiterror Cause," *RIA NOVOSTI*, September 24, 2001.

3. "Putin Determines Russian Stance on Antiterror Cause."

4. "Putin Determines Russian Stance on Antiterror Cause."

5. "Putin Determines Russian Stance on Antiterror Cause."

6. Anatol Lieven, *Chechnya: Tombstone of Russian Power* (New Haven, Conn.: Yale University Press, 1998), 142–43.

7. Samuel P. Huntington, *The Clash of Civilizations and the Remaking of World Order* (New York: Touchstone Books, 1998).

8. Much of this discussion is drawn from Jacob W. Kipp and Lester Grau, "Chechen Nationalism and the Struggle for Independence," *National Strategy Forum* 10, no. 1 (Autumn 2000): 7–12.

9. ANS radio (Baku, in Azeri 1330 gmt 08 May 00) from *BBC Monitoring*.

10. Kerim Fenari, "The *Jihad* of Imam Shamyl," at www.amarelief.org/caucasus/news/Imam_Shamil.htm.

11. Robert F. Baumann, *Russian-Soviet Unconventional Wars in the Caucasus, Central Asia, and Afghanistan* (Ft. Leavenworth, Kans.: Combat Studies Institute, U.S. Army Command and General Staff College, 1993).

12. Moshe Gammer, *Muslim Resistance to the Tsar: Shamil and the Conquest of Chechnya and Dagestan* (London: Frank Cass, 1994).

13. N. I. Pokrovskiy, *Kavkazkie voyny i Imamat Shamilya* (Moscow: ROSSPEN, 2000).

14. Steven Blank, "The Formation of the Soviet North Caucasus 1918–24," *Central Asian Survey* 12 (1993): 13–32.

15. Carlotta Gall and Thomas de Waal, *Chechnya: Calamity of the Caucasus* (New York: New York University Press, 1998), 56–75.

16. Lester Grau, "Changing Russian Urban Tactics: The Aftermath of the Battle of Grozny," Foreign Military Studies Office, at www.call.army.mil/fmso/fmsopubs/issues/grozny.htm.

17. Anatoliy Kulikov and Sergey Lembik, *Chechenskiy uzel: Khronika vooruzhennogo konflikta, 1994–1996 gg.* (Moscow: Dom Pedagogiki, 2000).

18. Lester Grau and William Jorgensen, "Viral Hepatitis and the Russian War in Chechnya," Foreign Military Studies Office, at www.call.army.mil/fmso/fmsopubs/issues/hepatiti/hepatiti.htm.

19. Raymond C. Finch, III, "A Face of Future Battle: Chechen Fighter Shamil Basayev," Foreign Military Studies Office, at www.call.army.mil/fmso/fmsopubs/issues/shamil/shamil.htm.

20. David Hoffman, "Miscalculations Paved Path to Chechen War," *Washington Post*, March 20 2000.

21. Gennadiy Troshev, *Moya voyna: Chechenskiy dnevnik okopnogo generala* (Moscow: Vagrius, 2001), 353.

22. Robyn Dixon, "In Dagestan, Rebel Leader Revives Russian Nightmare," *Los Angeles Times*, August 21, 1999, 1.

23. Anatol Lieven, "Let's Help Russia Against the Chechens," *Los Angeles Times*, September 21, 1999.

24. Moscow, *ITAR-TASS*, September 27, 1999.

25. Les Grau and Timothy Smith, "A 'Crushing' Victory: Fuel-Air Explosives and Grozny, 2000," Foreign Military Studies Office, at www.call.army.mil/fmso/fmsopubs/issues/fuelair/fuelair.htm.

26. Timothy L. Thomas, "Grozny 2000: Urban Combat Lessons Learned," Foreign Military Studies Office, at www.call.army.mil/fmso/fmsopubs/issues/grozny2000/grozny2000.htm.

27. "Russia and Georgia at Odds," *Monitor*, May 18, 2000.

28. David Filipov, "Putin Now Mired in Chechnya: Hopes Evaporate for Closure to War," *Boston Globe*, June 21, 2001; *Johnson's Russia List*, #5314, June 21, 2001.

29. Maura Reynolds, "War Has No Rules for Russian Forces Fighting in Chechnya," *Los Angeles Times*, September 17, 2000.

30. "Devastated by War, Chechnya's Civilian Population Faces Approaching Winter," *Dispatches from Chechnya*, no. 1 (September 18, 2000).

31. "100 Rebel Groups Numbering up to 2,000 Members Operating in Chechnya," *Agentstvo Voyennykh Novostey*, November 1, 2001.

32. Mikhail Ivanov, "Moscow's Muddled Thinking in Chechnya," *IWPR's Caucasus Reporting*, September 22, 2000.

33. Yevgenia Borisova, "Kadyrov's Nephew Fought for Rebels," *Moscow Times*, August 31, 2001, 3; and Marcus Warren, "Rebels Bomb Grozny Leaders," *London Daily Telegraph*, September 3, 2001.

34. Roustam Kaliyev, "Chechen Reality: GRU vs. FSB," *Perspective* II, no. 1 (September/October 2001).

35. *Ogenok*, no. 11 (March 1996): 11.

36. On the problem of ending conflicts see Charles W. Kegley, Jr., and Gregory A. Raymond, *How Nations Make Peace* (New York: St. Martin's/Worth, 1999), 235–36.

37. Yuriy Stroganov, "Boris Nemtsov on Putin's Economic Policies, Afghan Situation," *Trud*, October 16, 2001; *Johnson's Russia List*, #5498, October 19, 2001.

38. Miriam Lansky, "Caucasus: Chechnya, Echoes of Kosovo," *The NIS Observed: An Analytical* Review, Pt. 1, 5, no. 7 (April 25, 2000).

39. Sarah Karush, "Putin Hands Chechnya War to FSB," *Moscow Times*, January 23, 2001, 1.

40. Sarah K. Miller, "US–Russian Relations: Cool Winds Are Blowing," *The NIS Observed: An Analytical Review*, Pt. 1, 6, no. 6 (April 4, 2001).

41. Pavel Felgenhauer, "Chechnya Awaits Endgame," *Moscow Times*, June 28, 2001, 9.

42. "Transcript of June 16 White House Press Briefing by Secretary of State Powell and National Security Advisor [sic] Rice," and "Press Conference by President Bush and Russian Federation President Putin"; *Johnson's Russia List*, #4305, June 16, 2001.

43. David S. Broder, "Bush's Bet on Russia," *Washington Post*, August 1, 2001, 17.

44. Ahmed Rashid, "US Reviews Its Policy on the Taliban and International Terrorism," *World*, July 31, 2001.

45. Timofey Borisov: " 'Fox' Blesses 'Wolf'; Before Attacking Abkhazia Gelayev Met with Shevardnadze" *Rossiyskaya gazeta*, October 21, 2001, 3. Some commentators in Moscow viewed the fighting at Kodori Gorge in Abkhazia as a "provocation" designed to set off a Georgian–Abkhazian war at an advantageous moment. The plan, according to these commentators, failed. See Dmitriy Nikolayev, "Failure of 'Kodori Action,' " *Nezavisimaya gazeta*, October 17, 2001, 1, 5.

46. "Putin Says Abkhazia Georgia's Internal Political Problem," Moscow, TV RTR, 1600 GMT, October 12, 2001.

47. Alap Kasayev, "Abkhazskiy Front Afganskoy voyny," *Nezavisimaya gazeta*, October 9, 2001.

48. Leonid Radzikhovsky, "Policing Asia," *Vremya MN*, October 16, 2001.

49. "Chechen Rebels Make Contact," Moscow: *UPI*, September 27, 2001.

50. Ron Popeski, "Chechens Seek Peace Talks, but Agenda Differs," Moscow: *Reuters*, October 24, 2001.

51. Robert Bruce Ware, "On the Roots of Extremism," *Moscow Times*, November 1, 2001.

52. "European Human Rights Commissioner Says Chechnya Is in Transition to Normality," *Echo Moskvy*, 0910 GMT, October 30, 2001.

53. Leonid Radzikhovsky, "Policing Asia," *Vremya MN*, October 16, 2001.

54. "Putin Announces Russia to Withdraw from Radio-Electronic Center in Cuba," Moscow: *Interfax*, 12005 GMT, October 17, 2001; and Richard Balmforth, "Russia Ends Cold War Chapter by Quitting Cuban Spy Base," Moscow: *Reuters*, October 18, 2001.

55. Alexander Golts, "Putin Finds Way to Deal with Russia's Generals," *The Russian Journal* (October 26–November 1, 2001): 21.

56. Patrick Lannin, "Putin Backs Terror Fight, Says Russia Reforms Work," Shanghai: *Reuters*, October 19, 2001.

57. Yegenyy Bai, "The Threat of Terrorism Brings US Together," *Izvestiya*, October 15, 2001.

58. Thomas L. Friedman, "We Are All Alone," *New York Times*, October 26, 2001.

59. Gleb Pavlovsky: "Are We Prepared to Wait Until the Enemy Hits Us as It Hit America?" *strana.ru*, October 24, 2001, at www.strana.ru.

60. Otto Latsis, "No More Confrontation but Putin's U.S. Stance Faces Opposition," *The Russian Journal* (October 26–November 1 2001); *Johnson's Russia List*, #5511, October 28, 2001.

61. Aleksandr Dugin, "Terakty 11 sentryabrya (sic): Ekonomicheskiy smysl," at www.arctogaia.com/public/teract.html.

62. "Vladimir Putin Talks with American Journalists," *Kommersant*, no. 206 (November 12, 2001); *Johnson's Russia List*, #5541.

Part Five

REGIONAL AND FOREIGN POLICY

Chapter Ten

Putin and the Regions

Nikolai Petrov and Darrell Slider

One of the first and most vital areas that Vladimir Putin identified for a major shift in policy was the relationship between Russia's regions and the federal (national) government. The Yeltsin period had seen a loosening of control by "the center" (the Moscow-based national political and administrative institutions) over Russia's eighty-nine regions. Struggles between Yeltsin and the Duma in the early 1990s ended with the shelling of the parliament building in October 1993, but the new parliament elected two months later was equally contentious. These difficulties forced Yeltsin to make concessions to regional leaders in order to gain their support at critical junctures, including during his campaign for a second presidential term in 1996. The administration was further weakened by the meltdown of the economy and the government's inability to raise taxes needed to finance its policies. This led regional leaders increasingly to take on responsibilities that would normally be carried out by federal agencies. Regional leaders used these opportunities to entrench themselves in power while often willfully flouting federal laws and presidential decrees.

Putin had witnessed the extent of the problem when he supervised Russia's regions for Yeltsin from March 1997 to July 1998. Putin was head of the department within Yeltsin's presidential administration (called the Main Oversight Department, or *glavnoe kontrol'noe upravleniie*) that gathered evidence on violations of federal laws and policies in the regions. Interestingly enough, Putin's predecessor as head of the department was Aleksei Kudrin, who was elevated to minister of finance and deputy prime minister, and his successor was Nikolai Patrushev, who became head of the FSB (the Federal Security Service, successor to the KGB). Both men are key figures in implementing elements of Putin's policy toward the regions. All three, not coincidentally, are from Russia's second city, St. Petersburg.

This chapter will examine the approach Putin has taken to deal with regional leaders through the creation of a new level of administration between the center and the regions in the form of seven federal administrative districts (*federal'nye okruga*) headed by specially appointed presidential representatives. Announced in May 2000, this initiative was one of Putin's first steps as president, and it has the potential to reshape in a fundamental way the nature of the Russian political system. As 2002 began, however, many features of the emerging relationship between center and regions were still open to interpretation.

One possible direction these changes could take would be to solidify Russia's federal system. Federalism requires a fairly explicit distribution of power between national and regional governments, and the new federal districts could be used to implement and refine the Yeltsin constitution of 1993. Article seventy-one of the constitution defines the areas of federal jurisdiction, article seventy-two defines joint jurisdiction, and article seventy-three grants all other functions to the regions. The administrative changes adopted by Putin could be used to reclaim federal powers that were grabbed by the regions and to flesh out the provisions of the constitution with the purpose of creating a functional federal system.

Another interpretation, which we believe fits better with the evidence, is that Putin is aggressively pursuing an anti-federal policy designed to take away or circumscribe most powers exercised by regional leaders. His goal appears to be to establish a unitary state under the guise of "restoring effective vertical power in the country," to use Putin's own description of his intentions. In keeping with Putin's background in the KGB, the main emphasis is on discipline and order. Overall, his approach represents a rejection of federalism—which is still very much a work in progress in Russia—and an attempt at recentralization. At the same time, it is by no means clear that the institutional and personnel choices that Putin has made will have the desired result; nor is it evident that recentralization will be an effective administrative strategy in post-Soviet Russia.

ORIGINS OF THE PROBLEM

Even after the fourteen other former Soviet republics became independent, Russia remained the world's largest country; thus, it is perhaps inevitable that there would be serious problems in administering its far-flung territories. This was true both before and after the Soviet state was established. The usual set of solutions involved efforts to tighten control from the center. Despite some outward trappings of federalism (the Russian republic, for example, was called the RSFSR—Russian Soviet Federative Socialist Republic), the Soviet Union was in essence a unitary state supplemented by a parallel hierarchy— the Communist Party of the Soviet Union (CPSU). Even under Stalin, however, "family circles" or cliques based on personal relations and patronage ties arose in the regions, insulating local politics from Moscow and allowing regional elites a free hand in many matters.[1]

In many of the former communist states of Eastern Europe—particularly those whose leaders set a reformist agenda—a comprehensive redrawing of subnational administrative boundaries took place. In Poland, the Czech Republic, the former German Democratic Republic, Hungary, and Croatia, communist-era regional entities were eliminated or replaced with new ones. In part this was done to meet European Union (EU) entry requirements, but often another important motivation was to break up political and economic power at the regional level that had emerged under communist rule.[2] No such redrawing of the political boundaries took place in Russia, with the consequence that political-economic elites of the communist era emerged largely intact at the regional level. Thus, Russia's current administrative structure closely mirrors that of the Russian republic under communism. Of the eighty-nine administrative entities, or "subjects of the federation," the most numerous are oblasts (forty-nine), followed by republics (twenty-one), six *krais* (which tend to be large territories or border regions), ten autonomous *okrugs* (located within the territory of other entities), one autonomous oblast (the Jewish AO in the Far East), and the cities of Moscow and St. Petersburg.

Russia's republics were, by and large, designated "autonomous republics" in the Soviet period. They received this special status because they were home to a non-Russian ethnic group (most often, though, Russians were the largest ethnic group even in republics; the eight exceptions were Dagestan, Chuvashia, Chechen-Ingushetia, Tuva, Kabardino-Balkaria, North Ossetia, Tatarstan, and Kalmykia). Unlike the "union republics" that became independent with the collapse of the USSR, autonomous republics were typically not in border regions.

Russian and Soviet history had never seen an attempt to apply a federal model as the basis for organizing the relationship between national and regional authorities. In this regard, Yeltsin's policies represented a revolutionary break from past methods of rule. However, because Yeltsin did not take the matter seriously, the result was an improvised series of steps that resulted in a redistribution of power between the center and the regions. As a consequence, Yeltsin's "federalism" was a product of a series of crises and struggles that characterized his nearly ten years in power.

First, there was the battle that took place in 1990–91 over the fate of the Soviet Union. Both Gorbachev and Yeltsin sought the support of regional elites, particularly those in the ethnically based autonomous republics within the fifteen union republics that became independent in late 1991. It was in the context of the struggle with Gorbachev for the loyalty of republic leaders that Yeltsin in 1990 encouraged them to "take as much sovereignty as you can swallow." In most of the republics, local leaders followed Yeltsin's example and created the popularly elected post of president, thus giving them a status and legitimacy lacked by heads of Russia's other regions at that time.

Almost immediately after the collapse of the Soviet Union, Yeltsin faced a new and lengthy conflict—this time with the Russian legislature. Their disputes covered a wide range of issues but centered on the relative powers of the parliament versus the president and on the strategy of economic reform that the country should pursue. In this struggle, Yeltsin sought the support of regional executives—the governors whom he had the right to appoint and dismiss—and the republic presidents. Ruslan Khasbulatov, the speaker of the Russian parliament who became Yeltsin's nemesis, appealed to the regional legislatures in an effort to build an alternative national power base. Since republic leaders had more independence than governors, Yeltsin tended to favor the republics with larger budget subsidies[3] and greater relative autonomy. These concessions were often codified in the form of bilateral agreements between the president and individual leaders. The most generous terms were granted to Tatarstan, Bashkortostan, and Yakutia, the republics with the most potential leverage because of their economic assets.

This battle culminated in the events of September–October 1993, when Yeltsin issued a decree dissolving the parliament. When Khasbulatov and Alexander Rutskoi, Yeltsin's own vice president, resisted and attempted to seize power by force, Yeltsin responded by having tanks shell the building. The new political context led to fundamental changes in regional politics.

First was the drafting of the Yeltsin constitution mentioned earlier, with its enshrined concepts of federalism, including the establishment of a new federal legislature, with an upper house—the Federation Council—comprising two representatives from each region. For the first time, this gave the regions a veto over laws passed by the lower house (the State Duma). Many governors successfully won election to this body and thus achieved additional independence and legitimacy. Yeltsin could not remove members of the Federation Council without its agreement, and council members also received immunity from criminal charges. Second was the dissolution of regional legislatures that had been elected in 1990 (though not in the republics) and the decision of a number of republics to adopt a presidential system to avoid ceding control to the center. Third, as was true at the national level, political power in the regions shifted dramatically toward the executive branch of government. Executive power in the regions was further strengthened in the mid-1990s when Yeltsin gave in to the demand by regional executives for popular elections. Yeltsin's last set of appointments to the post of governor took place in late 1995–early 1996, when he appointed thirteen.[4] After that, all governors were elected to office. This gave governors added legitimacy and made their removal by Yeltsin almost impossible.

In 1994–95, new regional legislatures were elected. The new assemblies were smaller in size than the soviets of 1990, and their powers were substantially reduced. With just a few exceptions, the new deputies tended to be made up of local officials, employees from sectors funded by the government (education and health care), or the regional economic elite—all groups that were dependent on the executive. Only a small proportion of deputies were full-time legislators, and in their legislative role they were both unwilling and unable to challenge the region's governor or president. Very few legislatures had more than token representation by national political parties.[5]

A year after the October 1993 attack on parliament, Yeltsin once again attempted to use force to solve a political problem—this time in Chechnya. Unlike republics such as Tatarstan and Bashkortostan, Chechnya refused to enter into a dialogue with the Kremlin and instead pressed for full independence. Under the leadership of General (and President) Dzhokhar Dudayev, Chechnya created its own military forces and expelled representatives of virtually all central Russian ministries, including the FSB and the Ministry of Finance. It should be said, however, that the Russian leadership did not make a serious attempt to achieve a negotiated solution to Chechnya's complaints, which contributed to the Chechens' resolve to secede. In December 1994, Yeltsin ended several years of neglect of the Chechen problem and ordered Russian Army and Interior Ministry troops into Chechnya in hopes of a quick military victory. The result was a disaster: the army was ill-prepared for a guerrilla war and suffered many casualties while directing much of its military might against the civilian population.

The war in Chechnya and ineffective policies in a number of other areas threatened defeat for Yeltsin in the 1996 presidential elections, and he again turned to regional leaders (as well as the country's business elite) for help. It was at this time that over twenty new bilateral treaties with oblasts and *krais* were signed. Yeltsin further strengthened the status of regional leaders by initiating a change in how the Federation Council was formed. Starting in 1996, sitting governors and chairmen of regional legislatures would automatically have seats in the Federation Council. With the help of regional "administrative resources" such as control over the local press, government workers, and simple vote fraud in some cases, Yeltsin came from behind to win re-election.

These serial political crises took place against a background of persistent economic emergencies that were stabilized in the mid-1990s only by resorting to "virtual" economics and financial trickery. These schemes eventually collapsed in the August 1998 devaluation and default. One common mechanism to formally balance tax receipts and expenses that was used both by central agencies and regional governments was sequestering funds—in other words, reducing expenditures by not paying salaries and not meeting its obligations to suppliers of goods and services. In this way, the federal government effectively lost control of many of its agencies in the regions. Shortfalls in tax collection and nonpayment meant that regional leaders were almost forced to step in to provide funds or in-kind payments (office space, transportation, heat, hot water, electricity, and even food) in order to support the continued operation of federal institutions such as the criminal police, tax police, prosecutors, courts, and even Yeltsin's presidential representatives (created in 1991 to serve as his "eyes and ears" in the regions). Inevitably, federal entities in the regions shifted their loyalty from the center to the regions. Even the Russian military became increasingly dependent on regional leaders for logistical support. The result was "a sustained trend towards increasing compartmentalization and regionalization of military structures, driven primarily by the shortage of resources and underfinancing."[6] It should be emphasized that this was not a power play by regional leaders. In the face of the failure by the Kremlin to carry out its responsibilities, the regions were simply trying to cope.

Another feature of Yeltsin's policies toward the regions was the personalized and bilateral nature of many of the center-region relationships. This was in many ways a continuation of the informal operation of regional lobbying of the central institutions during the Soviet era; both Yeltsin and most regional leaders had practical experience dating back to the Brezhnev era. Some of this bilateralism was formally institutionalized in treaties negotiated between the Yeltsin administration and regional leaders. The first of these agreements was with republics, which provided a set of exceptions and exemptions that went far beyond what other regions were allowed under the 1992 Federation Treaty and the 1993 constitution. These agreements had the effect of making Russian federalism extremely asymmetrical, but in a way that was unsystematic and nontransparent.[7] Much of the enabling documentation at the ministerial level was kept secret. Later, most oblasts and *krais* also negotiated bilateral treaties with the center, though under less-favorable terms. The personalization of politics meant that Yeltsin often turned a blind eye to violations in a region (there were many in Kalmykia, for example) as long as its leader demonstrated loyalty to him in federal elections.

Overall, the institutional framework and dynamics of "federalism, Russian-style" had a number of dysfunctional elements and allowed regions control over other areas of federal responsibility that were atypical of a normal federal system.[8] The nature of federal relations also undermined efforts to democratize the political system as well as efforts to marketize the Russian economy. Governors and republic presidents obstructed the development of a national party system and used their powers to harass political opponents and independent news media. In an effort to protect local industries and markets, regional leaders created barriers to free trade between regions. They also preserved an economic climate that was hostile to outside investment and the rise of small business.[9]

PUTIN'S POLICY AND PERSONNEL CHOICES

Putin's initiatives toward the regions include the following:

1. the establishment of the seven federal districts ("super-regions") headed by presidential envoys, of whom five are generals;
2. increasing central control over federal agencies in the regions, including the courts, police, and television;
3. reforming the Federation Council by replacing sitting governors and chairmen of regional legislatures with full-time representatives who would be appointed by governors and legislatures (in the process regional executives and the heads of regional legislatures lost parliamentary immunity);
4. the adoption of laws that allow the president, under certain conditions, to remove governors and dismiss regional parliaments;
5. the creation of a new body for governors, the Presidential State Council, as a consolation for losing their seats in the Federation Council. The main advantage is that it allows governors to meet with the president four times a year. All regional leaders are members, but its working organ is a presidium (whose membership changes every six months) made up of one governor/president from each of the seven federal districts. The presidium is supplemented by working groups under the leadership of one regional leader (usually drawn from the most influential—such as Moscow mayor Luzhkov). The working groups prepare reports/proposals on important issues, but their role is strictly advisory. As of early 2002, none of their reports was used by Putin or the government; in effect, the purpose seems to be to diffuse opposition by governors by allowing them to let off steam;
6. changes in interbudgetary relations through a new tax code, which increases the center's share and gives the federal government greater control over tax receipts and expenditures.

The first and most important of Putin's innovations, issued in the form of a presidential decree in May 2000, divided Russia into seven administrative districts. The ultimate goal of this new structure was not to replace existing regions, but rather to increase the effectiveness of the center by creating a new administrative structure to coordinate the operation of federal agencies in the regions. The top official in each of these new federal districts was called the "plenipotentiary presidential representative" (*pol'nomochnyi predstavitel' prezidenta* or *polpred* for short). As was mentioned above, this term had been used by Yeltsin to designate his representative in each region. Putin abolished this post in the regions; henceforth virtually every region would have a "chief federal inspector" who would be directly subordinate to (and appointed by) the presidential representative for the corresponding administrative district.

The decree creating presidential representatives provided for their direct accountability to the president. Yeltsin had initially given the same degree of access to his representatives, but later they were subordinated to a department within the administration.[10] In practice, though, while Putin appointed each of his representatives, they did not report solely to the president. The *polpreds* were still part of the presidential administration, which meant that they were supervised by Alexander Voloshin, the head of Putin's staff and a holdover from the Yeltsin era. This was a source of some consternation among the presidential representatives, since they wanted to be closer to the ultimate source of authority at the top of the administrative ladder. A symbolic indicator of the status of the seven representatives was Putin's decision to give each a seat on his Security Council, a body that has been important in establishing strategic priorities in government policy, both foreign and domestic.

The federal districts were not drawn anew based on any particular political or administrative purpose; they corresponded completely to the regional command structure of the Soviet/Russian Interior Ministry troops.[11] The "capital" or administrative center of each district in every case corresponded to the location of the headquarters of the corresponding Interior Ministry district. The following section describes the seven federal regions and Putin's appointees to the post of presidential representative:

1. The Central district is the largest in terms of the number of regions with eighteen. Naturally, Moscow is the center for the district; the capital and surrounding oblast dominate the district in both population and political importance. General Georgii Poltavchenko, named as Putin's representative in this district, was drawn from the upper ranks of the FSB. In the 1980s he served in the KGB in Leningrad oblast, where he first came in contact with Vladimir Putin, and for most of the 1990s he worked as head of the tax police in St. Petersburg. For a brief period before his appointment, Poltavchenko served as presidential representative in Leningrad oblast.

2. The Northwestern district is made up of eleven regions, the most important of which is Russia's "second capital," St. Petersburg. The large number of Petersburg natives in Putin's administration has added to the political significance of the region. One of the most controversial appointments was Putin's choice of General Viktor Cherkesov, first deputy director of the FSB, to serve as his representative in this district. Cherkesov had been a longtime KGB officer in Leningrad/St. Petersburg and was known for his role in the suppression of "anti-Soviet" dissent. His ties to Putin are the closest of any of the representatives, and they reportedly knew one another even before their KGB days.

3. The Southern district comprises the seven non-Russian republics of the unstable North Caucasus region, including Chechnya, as well as five frontline Russian regions. Particularly important regions from the economic standpoint are Krasnodar *krai* and Rostov oblast. The city of Rostov-on-the-Don is the administrative center. As his representative Putin chose General Viktor Kazantsev, at the time serving as commander of the military forces in the North Caucasus military district. As such he was a leading figure in planning the war in Chechnya.

4. The Volga district consists of seven republics, one autonomous *okrug*, and eight oblasts. Among the leaders of these regions are a disproportionate number of nationally known politicians: Presidents Mintimer Shaimiyev of Tatarstan and Murtaza Rakhimov of Bashkortostan, both among the most assertive of all the republics. Also in the district is the republic of Chuvashia, headed by President Nikolai Fedorov, one of the few regional leaders willing to speak out for the record against Putin's policies, and Samara governor Konstantin Titov. Nizhniy Novgorod, the third largest city in Russia after Moscow and St. Petersburg, is the administrative center. Perhaps because of the number of political "heavyweights" in the region, Putin chose a former prime minister, Sergei Kiriyenko, to be his representative there. Kiriyenko, prior to his brief stint as premier (he was dismissed in the wake of the August 1998 financial crisis), had been a Komsomol functionary in Nizhniy Novgorod, a banker, and briefly the federal energy minister. Kiriyenko is also the only presidential representative with a reputation as a liberal reformer; he was one of the founding members of the political movement Union of Right Forces (SPS). Kiriyenko became one of the most visible of the presidential representatives, in part because of effective self-promotion. For example, Kiriyenko launched a nationwide, internet-based search for staff for his office.

5. The Urals district has the fewest regions—only six. The dominant region is Sverdlovsk, along with its capital, Yekaterinburg. Putin named General Petr Latyshev as his representative to the district. Latyshev was at the time of appointment deputy minister of internal affairs and had spent virtually his entire career in the ranks of the MVD. In this capacity he had been active in investigating a number of cases of high-level corruption in regions including St. Petersburg, the most recent case.

6. The Siberian district is, like the Volga district, extremely diverse, made up of three republics, four autonomous *okrugs*, and nine oblasts/*krais*. Novosibirsk, the traditional capital of Western Siberia, was designated as the administrative center of the district, though a number of other regions are of equal or greater importance, including Krasnoyarsk, Tomsk, Kemerovo, and Irkutsk. Despite the size and diversity of the region, it has perhaps the most developed sense of regional identity.

Putin's appointee was Leonid Drachevsky. Once a professional athlete, Drachevsky worked for most of the 1990s in the Ministry of Foreign Affairs, where he served as ambassador to Poland and was deputy foreign minister under Yevgeny Primakov. In 1999 he was the Russian minister for the Commonwealth of Independent States (CIS). Drachevsky is considered the *polpred* with the weakest links to Putin's team.[12]

7. The Far Eastern district makes up the distant edge of the country, separated from Moscow by the Urals and Siberia. It comprises nine regions, including the largest single territorial entity—the republic of Sakha (Yakutia), five oblasts/*krais*, two autonomous *okrugs*, and the only autonomous oblast. Khabarovsk was chosen as the administrative center, though the most important regions are Yakutia and Primor'e (Vladivostok is the capital). The region as a whole is sparsely populated and has long felt isolated from events in Moscow. Konstantin Pulikovskii, a career general in the Russian army with experience in the first Chechen campaign, was named presidential representative for the district. His connection with Putin came when, after being dismissed from the military for his outspokenness, he served as Putin's campaign manager in Krasnodar *krai*.

Thus Putin's "magnificent seven," as they were referred to with some irony in the media,[13] were largely drawn from what are known as the "power ministries"—the FSB, military, and police. The contrast with the early Yeltsin period could not be more vivid. In 1991, Yeltsin created a new institution of "presidential representatives." The largest number of this first set of *polpreds* was drawn from the ranks of radical democrats who had worked with Yeltsin in the Soviet and Russian parliaments. In effect, the early Yeltsin appointees to this post were the type of people that several of the Putin appointees had worked to put in prison camps or psychiatric wards! (Later though, Yeltsin replaced his initial appointees with career bureaucrats, including several FSB officials. An even more major shift took place when Putin became acting president in January 2000. At that time about twenty new presidential representatives were appointed, most with FSB backgrounds.)

The first task awaiting the new plenipotentiaries was to set up their offices and assemble a staff. This process provided additional evidence on the institutional goals and capabilities of the new federal districts. Each was allowed to hire up to eight aides, who was given the title of deputy presidential representative. Each deputy in turn was assigned a specific functional area of responsibility, with two usually designated as the "first deputies." Evidence of the centralizing intent behind the districts is the fact that the vast majority of deputy representatives were not from the district in which they served. One of the first deputies typically came from the subdivision of the presidential administration's Main Oversight Department, which oversaw the region under the old system. Four of the presidential representatives (Kiriyenko, Drachevsky, Kazantsev, and Cherkesov) brought with them their own team of former advisors and close subordinates. Kiriyenko and Drachevsky brought the largest number of Muscovites (more even than Poltavchenko in the Moscow-based district). Kazantsev, since he simply moved from one office in Rostov to another, brought in mostly military aides. Cherkesov, though he had spent about a year in the central apparatus of the FSB in Moscow, continued to have a number of contacts from his Leningrad KGB days whom he tapped as top aides. (In January 2002, Putin named as Cherkesov's first deputy Admiral Mikhail Motsak, who recently had been dismissed in connection with the *Kursk* submarine disaster.) The other three presidential representatives were more dependent on appointees from the presidential administration. Poltavchenko assigned as his first deputy Anton Fedorov, the long-term coordinator of Yeltsin's system of presidential representatives. Pulikovskii brought some of his subordinates from Krasnodar, and was assigned one of Fedorov's deputies from the presidential administration. Latyshev's team was made up mostly of high-level administrators from other regions, including several from outside his district. All of the top aides to the presidential representative were based in the administrative center of the district.

In each of the component regions within the district, chief federal inspectors were appointed, though in a few cases one inspector was assigned two or more regions. Many of these inspectors, while appointed centrally, had roots in the regions to which they were assigned. In especially troublesome regions, however, outsiders—usually from Moscow—were named to the post. Unlike the practice that had emerged in the Yeltsin period, governors and republic leaders were not, as a rule, consulted. However, the ethnic factor was carefully taken into account in appointments to many of the more assertive ethnic republics (Tatarstan, Bashkortostan, and Chechnya, for example). The backgrounds of chief federal inspectors are also revealing. There is a heavy predominance of inspectors who came from the "power ministries"; of those for whom biographical data are available, approximately three of every four came from the military, FSB, or MVD. The majority of federal inspectors are in their mid-forties, all are men, and virtually none of them had a background in any elective office.

Personnel policy consists not just of appointments but dismissals. In this regard, Putin adopted a "hands off" approach toward his presidential representatives in the districts. All seven of the initial group remained in their posts in mid-2002. Yet there were cases where presidential representatives seemed to be inappropriate choices. Pulikovskii, in the Far Eastern district, would undoubtedly be the consensus choice as "worst presidential representative."

He was constantly at the center of controversies in his district, and more often than not his efforts to intervene in regional politics failed miserably.

FUNCTIONS OF THE
PRESIDENTIAL REPRESENTATIVES

Much of the work performed by presidential representatives is secret; as a result their actual role remains hidden. Putin meets regularly—once every three months—with his seven representatives in order to discuss future priorities. Since the system has been in existence, Putin has publicly emphasized three basic tasks:

1. To restore the preeminence of federal law. Much of the first year's work of the presidential representatives was spent overseeing the process of bringing regional legislation (including republic constitutions and regional charters) into conformity with federal law and the Russian constitution.

By the end of the first year's work, it was reported that thousands of regional laws had been "corrected." The effectiveness of this effort is questionable, however, since bringing regional laws into conformity with federal laws was approached as a technical exercise. Given the problems Russia has yet to address in establishing the rule of law, a massive effort to improve the content of laws appears to be premature. Russia, and this is even more true of the regions, is a country where the letter of the law often counts for little in the face of arbitrariness, incompetence, politicization, and corruption in the judicial system and in the bureaucracy.

2. To define the division of powers between the center, regions, and local government. Starting in the latter part of 2001, a major effort was undertaken to formalize relationships between center and regions. Part of this initiative has been to clarify the nature of bilateral treaties that were signed between over half the regions and Yeltsin's government. A commission headed by the deputy head of Putin's staff, Dmitry Kozak, has taken the lead in attempting to formulate the proper relationship between regions and the center, and has worked with the presidential representatives in this area. The general perspective of the Putin team is that the bilateral agreements signed during the Yeltsin period have very limited legal standing; in effect, almost any other form of law or presidential decree takes precedence over them. The presidential representatives have created analogous commissions to inventory how powers are in fact distributed between particular regions and the center and to collect proposals on changes in federal laws defining the competencies of the respective levels.

Part of the division of powers consists of defining the role that would be played by subregional government. Under Yeltsin, the term "local self-management" meant that the regions enjoyed considerable autonomy. This was true both in the 1993 constitution and in the 1995 law on local government. However, resistance from governors turned these provisions into empty promises. Local budgets are completely inadequate to take on the obligations assigned to them, which puts local officials in the role of supplicants to regional leaders. So far Putin's policy toward local government has been ambiguous: in some statements he appears to favor the extension of "vertical authority" down to the lowest level, with mayors and other local officials subordinate to governors. In other statements, he appears to favor some independent role for local officials, including finances independent of the regional government.

3. To coordinate and optimize federal agencies' activity in regions, including a role in appointing and monitoring personnel in federal agencies in the regions. This actually is an extension of actions taken in 1997–98, when collegia of federal agencies under the chairmanship of the presidential representative were created in most regions. These never worked well. Given the nature of the coordinating function, it is logical to expect appointments of FSB officers to play the coordinating role. (FSB appointments as Yeltsin's presidential representatives also became more common starting in 1997–98.) No one else, after all, would have the authority to coordinate such powerful agencies as the FSB, FAPSI (the agency that controls communications security), the Ministry of Internal Affairs, the tax police, and federal prosecutors.

Perhaps more important than the stated functions of Putin's presidential representatives are the undeclared ones. It is here that the need for FSB functionaries becomes even clearer. These more or less covert assignments include:

1. Bringing military, police, and security organs out from under governors and back under the control of the center. This had been largely accomplished by 2002. Presidential representatives created security collegia in their districts, replacing informal structures of this type that had arisen outside the control of the center. Presidential representatives also helped the center establish control over the MVD (see following). In this they were aided by a change in the law in June 2001, which eliminated the governors' effective veto on appointments of regional MVD chiefs.

2. Overseeing and controlling the process of gathering compromising material (*kompromat*) on regional leaders. Officials from the Kremlin's Main Oversight Department have a substantial presence on the *polpred's* staff. Further capabilities that would allow the *polpred* to gather information on corruption or misdeeds in the regions are planned. Most importantly, the Audit Chamber is setting up offices in the districts and regions. This agency, formally under the control of the Russian parliament, in effect has become Put-

in's financial secret police, and it has already been used actively against oligarchs, ministers, and others. The creation of Audit Chamber branches will form a new "financial vertical of power," in the words of its director, General Sergei Stepashin (Putin's predecessor in the posts of prime minister and FSB director).

3. Influencing political developments in the regions. Presidential representatives are clearly involved in efforts to remove from power those regional leaders who are considered obstacles by the Kremlin. In the first two years of Putin's presidency there was a fundamental change in the rules of the game in regional politics. In a number of regions—Kaluga, Kursk, Krasnodar, Primor'e, Yakutia, North Ossetia, and Ingushetia, for example—political figures not to the liking of the Kremlin were removed from the political stage. Elections are a particularly propitious time for action, since it is when governors are at their most vulnerable (much like a crab that has molted and not yet grown a new shell). Under Putin, the Kremlin has not tried to influence elections through the electoral process whereby Putin could use his popularity to help a favored candidate. Instead, secretive, behind-the-scenes maneuvering is common. Methods include exerting influence over the election commission or the local judiciary to remove a candidate from the ballot. In some cases it is clear that the *kompromat* gathered on regional leaders can be mobilized to pressure them not to seek another term in office (the use of blackmail, in other words). In other cases, various incentives are provided for leaders to step down, such as appointment to a new federal post (Primor'e Governor Yevgenii Nazdratenko became head of the agency that awards lucrative fishing quotas) or a seat in the Federation Council. The role that the president's representatives and their staff has played in these developments has not been publicized, but it is fairly obvious.

From the beginning, presidential envoys were denied many of the instruments of real power to control developments in the regions—the right to direct financial flows from the center, for example, or the power to appoint federal officials in the regions. They have, however, found other ways to attain leverage. It is apparent that *polpreds* have worked to expand their links with important regional actors, such as the business community. Behind-the-scenes alliances with prominent industrialists and other local oligarchs can provide presidential envoys the leverage they need to reduce the governors' room for maneuver. The fact that businesses often need to operate on a regional, national, and even international level gives Putin's representatives additional tools of persuasion. *Polpreds* also have power because they control access to the president. The presidential representatives prepare the agenda for meetings between the president and individual governors from their district, thus limiting direct communication with the president. As a result, governors are put in the position of having to work through the *polpred's* staff in order to get to the president. Finally, even though they lack direct appointment powers, *polpreds* can influence personnel decisions by federal agencies and the president in their district through their recommendations for promotions. In effect, over time they can create a kind of web of cadres in the district that could reduce governors' room for maneuver.

PARALLEL STRUCTURES IN THE FEDERAL DISTRICTS

The scheme that Putin established for improving the coordination of federal policy was replicated by many other agencies at the direction of the president. The strategy is to strengthen the vertical chain of command from the ministry in Moscow, to the federal district agencies, and from there to ministry officials in the region. The presence of these new district offices allows presidential representatives to play the coordinating role discussed earlier.

New territorial structures were established in the seven federal districts by the most important federal agencies and ministries—in all, about twenty federal agencies. To illustrate, within a year of Putin's reform there were nineteen federal agencies represented in the Volga district. These included the prosecutor's office, the Ministry of Justice, the Tax Police, the Federal Tax Service, FAPSI (the Federal Agency on Governmental Communication), the Ministry of the Interior for Internal Troops, the Federal Criminal Police, the Federal Service on Financial Restructuring and Bankruptcy, the State Courier Service, the Committee on State Reserves, the Federal Securities Commission, the Property Ministry, the Federal Property Fund, the Ministry on Publishing and TV and Radio-Broadcasting, the Ministry of Natural Resources, the Pension Fund, the Ministry of Transportation, and Health Ministry, the State Committee on Statistics, and the Ministry of Anti-Monopoly Policy (the latter two had other regional branches within which they established federal district departments).[14] A new set of judicial organs—administrative courts—were set up in twenty-one districts, though they fit within the seven federal districts.

Some of the most important changes in administrative subordination took place in the Ministry of Internal Affairs. When Putin came to power, there was a symbiosis between police generals at the center and regional leaders that seemed to be unbreakable. Putin employed chesslike maneuvers to reassert dominance over this key lever of control. Instead of immediately appointing his own man as minister, he began by establishing a new intermediate level that separated the regional bottom from the central top. Seven MVD district directorates were created, headed by high-ranking police officials who are directly subordinate to the minister of internal affairs and appointed by decrees issued by Putin himself.[15] It took almost a year of personnel changes at the regional level to break up existing networks of relationships. Only then, in June 2001, did Putin replace then-minister Rushailo with his ally, Boris Gryzlov, and more far-reaching reforms of the MVD began in earnest. The MVD department that had responsibility for combating organized crime was completely reorganized to bring it under federal control. In this case, the *polpreds* provided a useful mechanism for restoring control by the central ministry over regional police chiefs. This was a source of some dissatisfaction later, when *polpreds* came into conflict with newly centralized police operations. The system of informal governors' control over prosecutors was broken as well, with seven prosecutors' general deputies appointed to head new district offices.

It should be emphasized, however, that none of the heads of the new district agencies is subordinate to the presidential representative in the district. While such a change would make sense from the standpoint of a clear and single vertical chain of command, it would represent a major assault on the prerogatives of the Moscow-based ministries. Ever since Khrushchev's attempt to undermine the ministries and transfer their powers to regional economic councils (the *sovnarkhozy*) the ministries have effectively fought reorganizations that would decentralize power to the district or regional level. The presidential representative cannot order the federal agencies in his district to do anything, though he can complain to Putin if there is resistance to his efforts.

One of the few federal ministries that did not create a new territorial structure based on the federal districts was the FSB. This suggests that the administrative district scheme was conceived by and is, in some respects, itself an extension of the FSB. Otherwise, the FSB would naturally seek to have a voice of its own at the federal district level.

RESTORING ST. PETERSBURG'S CAPITAL ROLE

Putin is the first of the country's Soviet and post-Soviet leaders who was born and raised in St. Petersburg, Russia's imperial capital, rather than coming from a far-flung province. (Interestingly, none has come from Moscow.) Moreover, unlike his predecessors, Putin did not spend a lengthy period of time in Moscow prior to becoming leader. This has had two major consequences. First, there has been a significant flow of elites from "Piter" (as St. Petersburg is known colloquially) to Moscow. The old eastern capital (Moscow) is now besieged by young, Westernizing newcomers. It is reported that on Monday mornings there is a traffic jam of limousines waiting outside the Leningrad railway station in Moscow to pick up officials returning from a weekend with their families in Piter. Second, some capital city functions have shifted from Moscow to Piter. President Putin himself visits the city often and the Constantine palace is being restored as an official presidential residence. There have been serious discussions about moving the capital or at least part of the functions of the capital to St. Petersburg.

St. Petersburg's growing clout can be considered, at least partly, to be the consequence of Putin's reliance on his former colleagues from the Leningrad-St. Petersburg FSB.[16] However, the picture is more complicated than this, even in terms of personnel policy. There are at least three other sources of Petersburg elite recruitment in addition to the FSB: lawyers and former colleagues from Mayor Anatolii Sobchak's administration,[17] liberal economists,[18] and so-called "unallied individuals."[19] In addition to top presidential aides and government officials, the speakers of both the State Duma and Federation Council are from St. Petersburg.

One explanation for the dominance of the "Leningrad group" is Putin's need to fill key posts with people he trusts and who have demonstrated their loyalty to him. Another factor, though, is a desire to systematically dismantle the old Moscow-based bureaucratic machine. Officials from Piter, following long-standing practice, tend to bring with them their own subordinates, so that there has been an exponential explosion in the number of mid-level officials from Petersburg as well. While bureaucrats flow from Petersburg to Moscow, the Kremlin is sending money the opposite direction—in particular, $1.5 billion in federal investment has been allocated for the celebration of the city's three hundredth anniversary in 2003. There is increasing coverage of St. Petersburg life in the national media, and numerous projects have been proposed that would restore some capital city functions to St. Petersburg. Even if the construction of a new parliamentary center in Petersburg is unlikely in the short term, visiting foreign dignitaries are often taken to the "northern capital" as part of their official itinerary.

CONCLUSION

It is clear that the state of center-region affairs under Yeltsin was not sustainable—the regions had become too strong at the expense of the center. But it would appear Putin has swung the pendulum in the opposite direction. The policies he has undertaken threaten both federalism and democratic development in Russia.

There is a Soviet-era joke about a machinist from a defense plant who made Kalashnikovs (machine guns). When he retired from the factory, he decided to make toys for the children in his neighborhood. But whatever he made, whether it was a rocking horse, a doll, or a model ship, it always came out looking like a Kalashnikov! The Putin approach to the regions seems to suffer from a set of limitations that reflects his life experiences and background. Putin's choice of instruments and personnel make it evident that his policies for dealing with the regions will end up "looking like a Kalashnikov"—a recentralized, unitary system. This is in spite of the fact that the goal of his policies is often presented as one of "improving" or "correcting" Russia's federal system.

The methods used by Putin and his team are in large part derived from the standard operating procedures of the KGB and its successor organization, the FSB. These include gathering compromising materials against "targets," using this information to blackmail the target in order to gain its cooperation, planning and carrying out extralegal operations with a maximum degree of secrecy, and the use of diversions and feints to direct attention away from the real purpose of an operation. In the case of the shift of powers to the federal districts, a part of Putin's strategy seems to be to create new institutions that at first seem merely to duplicate functions of existing institutions, but that may later take their place. The emphasis on discipline, carrying out orders without question, and strict hierarchical relations also reflects the internal ethos of the KGB. Democracy and an effectively operating federal system, on the other hand, call for other modes of operation: politics as the sphere for resolving disputes; an emphasis on transparent, lawful action within existing political institutions; and the use of methods such as negotiation, persuasion and compromise.

If one sets aside the obvious exception of Chechnya, the Yeltsin presidency relied heavily on compromise and negotiation to achieve settlements with the regions. What prevented Yeltsin from building a more balanced system of federalism was the center's political and economic weakness. This weakness was exploited by republic presidents and governors to carve out substantial autonomy. Putin, with much higher levels of public support, an effective working majority in the Duma, and a much more favorable economic-budgetary situation, has a much stronger basis to exert leverage. The improvement of the Russian economy after the August 1998 crisis and as a result of higher oil prices cannot be overestimated in this regard. This led to enhanced tax collection and greater budgetary resources that could be used to pay off past debts and to finance federal institutions. The impression one gets from his regional policy is that Putin prefers to use his strength to force the changes he wants largely without bargaining and without employing constitutional mechanisms.

Will recentralization and the attempt to recreate a unitary system be effective in today's Russia? The first two years of experience with the system of federal districts provides contradictory evidence. On the one hand, the new policies do seem to be removing gubernatorial control over the military, police, and federal agencies that rightfully belong under federal jurisdiction. On the other hand, there is little recognition among Putin's advisors that this strategy could go too far, or that excessive centralization was one of the weaknesses of the Soviet system. It is clear from Putin's statements on "restoring" vertical power that his main reference point is the USSR. To someone who is a product of the Soviet system, the elimination of checks and balances appears to increase the manageability and effectiveness of the political system. This may be true in the short run, but there is a huge risk entailed. A highly centralized system runs the risk of collapsing in the face of changing conditions or circumstances.

Putin's top aides and his presidential representatives have only a hazy notion of what constitutes federalism. To an extent this parallels Soviet-era misunderstandings about the nature of a market economy. The absence of a planned or command system for allocating resources was equated with chaos and anarchy. Similarly, the absence of a clear chain of command in the political-administrative sphere is viewed as disorder or a situation that is "out of control" (*bezobrazie*). The idea that certain important decisions would actually be made in Russian regions without a directive from the center is alien to this mindset. The same striving for clarity and order will likely encompass the subregional level—Russia's cities and towns—as well. Yeltsin's declared policy of creating autonomous institutions of local government was an important affirmation of federalist principles. Putin's plans are not likely to increase the effective powers exercised at the local level, and may result in the direct subordination of mayors to governors.

Putin's policies not only threaten the development of a federal system, but democratization as well. The creation of new levels of administrative authority in the form of presidential representatives and new district offices of government agencies does nothing to facilitate Russia's political maturation. Ultimately, the political center of gravity should be in the regions. In the 1990s, normal political institutions, the organizations that constitute civil society, and independent media have been victimized by the disproportionate power wielded by Russia's governors and republic presidents. If the center were to use its power to guarantee political freedoms and rights in the regions it would encourage participation and democratization. Instead, Putin's policies are designed to create a new level of decisionmaking above the regions. This will have the effect of making policy less dependent on governors. But it also puts important policy decisions out of the reach of citizens and their nascent organizations. Needless to say, virtually none of the latter are organized at the federal district level. The few regions that have shown some progress in democratization could very easily see these gains disappear as the locus of policy moves upward.

Illustrative of this point is Putin's policy toward political parties and elections in the regions. Rather than encourage pluralism and allow the "bottom-up" development of grassroots parties, Putin has pushed for the creation of a national superparty through the merger of three of seven parties represented in the Duma: Unity, Fatherland, and All Russia. This new party, "United Russia," is highly centralized under the control of Putin loyalists. As a result of the 2001 law on political parties, regionally based parties will not be allowed to register and compete in national elections. At the same time, Putin's supporters in the Duma launched an effort to change the rules on electing regional legislatures to require a mixed single-member and proportional representation system (by party list). This appears designed to allow United Russia to establish a foothold in regional legislatures and deprive governors of control over them. In addition, the presidential representatives have been mobilized to assist in party formation in federal districts, obviously to benefit United Russia. Finally, plans have been announced to establish an administrative vertical chain of command for election commissions, thus giving the center greater control over the conduct of regional and local elections. This is akin to a restoration of a Soviet-style system using a single party to provide a parallel integration of vertical authority that reaches from the top leadership to the lowest level of society.

Thus, Putin's vision for Russia appears to be one of creating multiple instruments of strong vertical control: administrative (based on federal districts and presidential representatives), police (headed by one of Putin's closest allies, Boris Gryzlov), financial (headed by Sergei Stepashin), political party, electoral commission, and others. If implemented fully, the result will be a vertically integrated and horizontally fractured state.

When looking for parallels from Russian and Soviet history to understand Putin and his policies, the figure who most readily comes to mind is Yuri Andropov. As a long-term head of the KGB in the Brezhnev era, Andropov took part in a struggle between the KGB and party bureaucrats. When he became general secretary after Brezhnev's death, Andropov was considered a modernizer and Westernizer by some observers. He started by emphasizing discipline and order, but was prevented from doing much more due to ill health. Among his unrealized plans, by the way, was a reconfiguring (enlarging) of Russia's regions. Stalin, who like Putin, came to power through intricate bureaucratic maneuvers, also enlarged regions to be led by "loyal followers" and created a complicated system of power verticals that strengthened control over the regions. The leader considered the greatest reformer in Russian history, Peter the Great, introduced a new system of big *gubernias*, hated the city of Moscow and liked Germans, and then paved the road to Europe on the bones of his subjects. More and more frequently Putin is compared to Peter. Yet another historical figure might be a better fit, however— Paul I, Catherine the Great's unloved son. Paul liked Prussia and military parades; he disliked his mother and her reforms, and began his rule with the question of administrative-territorial restructuring. He could well have become the greatest counterreformer in Russian history if he hadn't been removed in a coup d'etat.

NOTES

1. See Graeme Gill, *The Origins of the Stalinist Political System* (Cambridge: Cambridge University Press, 1996) and Gerald Easter, *Reconstructing the State: Per-*

sonal Networks and Elite Identity in Soviet Russia (Cambridge: Cambridge University Press, 1996).

2. Peter Jordan, "Regional Identities and Regionalization in East-Central Europe," *Post-Soviet Geography and Economics* 42, no. 4 (2001): 235–65.

3. Daniel Triesman, "The Politics of Intergovernmental Transfers in Post-Soviet Russia," *British Journal of Political Science* 26 (July 1996): 299–335; and Daniel Triesman, "Fiscal Redistribution in a Fragile Federation: Moscow and the Regions in 1994," *British Journal of Political Science* 28 (January 1998).

4. Michael McFaul and Nikolai Petrov, *Politicheskii Al'manak Rossii 1997*, vol. 1 (Moscow: Carnegie Center, 1998), 149.

5. Darrell Slider, "Elections to Russia's Regional Assemblies," *Post-Soviet Affairs* 12, no. 3 (July/September 1996): 243–64.

6. Pavel K. Baev, "The Russian Armed Forces: Failed Reform Attempts and Creeping Regionalization," *The Journal of Communist Studies and Transition Politics* 17, no. 1 (March 2001): 34.

7. Steven Solnick, "Is the Center Too Weak or Too Strong in the Russian Federation," in *Building the Russian State*, ed. Valerie Sperling (Boulder, Colo.: Westview Press, 2000).

8. Alfred Stepan, "Russian Federalism in Comparative Perspective," *Post-Soviet Affairs* 16, no. 2 (2000): 133–76.

9. Darrell Slider, "Russia's Market-Distorting Federalism," *Post-Soviet Geography and Economics* 38, no. 8 (October 1997): 445–60.

10. Mathew Hyde, "Putin's Federal Reforms and Their Implications for Presidential Power in Russia," *Europe–Asia Studies* 53, no. 5 (2001): 719–43.

11. Nikolai Petrov, "Seven Faces of Putin's Russia: Failed Districts as the New Level of State Territorial Composition," *Security Dialogue* 33, no. 1 (March 2002): 219–37.

12. Ol'ga Blinova, "Polnomochnye predstaveiteli prezidenta Rossii: novaya vlastnaya vertikal" Tsentr politicheskoi informatsii (Moscow: 2000).

13. The reference is to the Western with this title, which was one of the first American films to be widely shown in the Soviet Union during the Cold War. The film was extremely popular in the 1960s when Vladimir Putin was growing up.

14. An additional eighteen federal agencies had regional offices in another location, while forty-three had no intermediate structures between their central headquarters and regional branches. "Federal Agencies on the Territory of Nizhniy Novgorod Oblast," 2001, scheme by the Volga federal district administration.

15. The number of staff (150) assigned to the federal district MVD offices was greater than that assigned to the staff of the presidential representatives.

16. Nikolai Patrushev (FSB Director), Sergei Ivanov (Defense Minister), Victor Ivanov (Deputy Head of Presidential Administration in charge of personnel), Victor Cherkesov (Polpred), Georgy Poltavchenko (Polpred), Viktor Zubkov (Chairman of Ministry of Finance Financial Monitoring Committee).

17. Dmitri Kozak (Deputy Head of Presidential Administration), Vladimir Kozhin (Head of Presidential Administration Property Department), Dmitri Medvedev (Deputy Head of Presidential Administration and Chairman of Board of Gazprom), Igor Sechin (Deputy Head of Presidential Administration), Aleksei Miller (Chief of Gazprom).

18. Anatoly Chubais (Head of United Electrical Systems), German Gref (Minister

for Economic Development and Trade), Aleksei Kudrin (Deputy Prime Minister and Finance Minister), Andrei Illarionov (Chief Economic Advisor to the President), Alfred Kokh (Director of Gazprom-Media), Mikhail Dmitriyev (First Deputy Minister for Economic Development and Trade), Dmitri Vasilyev (Federal Securities Commission Chairman).

19. Valentina Matviyenko (Deputy Prime Minister), Ilya Klebanov (Minister of Industry, Science and Technology and former Deputy Prime Minister), Leonid Reiman (Minister of Communications), Sergei Stepashin (Head of the Audit Chamber), Yuri Shevchenko (Health Minister), Ilya Yuzhanov (Minister for Anti-Monopoly Policy and Entrepreneurship), Sergei Mironov (Federation Council).

Chapter Eleven

Putin and Russian Foreign Policy

Dale R. Herspring and Peter Rutland

In the foreign policy arena, Vladimir Putin marks a dramatic change from his predecessor. In the twilight of the Yeltsin era, it was increasingly common to hear Western commentators refer dismissively to Russia as a country of no consequence, a has-been with an economy the size of Portugal or Holland. While Yeltsin's primary concern was fending off domestic challenges to his authority, Putin has the opportunity and inclination to make the restoration of Russia as a great power a top priority. Putin realizes that the Soviet Union is no more, but he still sees the Russian state as an important player on the world scene.

If there is an "ism" that drives Putin, it is nationalism—nationalism built not on ethnic, cultural, or spiritual values, but on the centrality of state power, which in Putin's case embraces a deep-seated desire to restore Russia's former greatness. In his view, "Patriotism is a source of the courage, staunchness, and strength of our people. If we lose patriotism and national pride and dignity, which are connected with it, we will lose ourselves as a nation capable of great achievements."[1]

Putin is also an advocate of realpolitik. He understands better than most that Russia is playing with a very weak hand. The country's economy faces major problems, the political system is still unformed, and Russia as a whole is riven by social divisions and a profound crisis of identity. The military is in shambles despite Defense Minister Sergei Ivanov's reform efforts. Russia's neighbors view it with suspicion or hostility: its list of trusted allies does not extend much beyond the erstwhile Belarus.[2] Indeed, in the eyes of many, the only reason the country has been a significant actor in the foreign policy field was because it possessed nuclear weapons. But these have been deteriorating to the point that many have become both useless and dangerous to maintain.[3] In short, Putin faces a considerable challenge in trying to forge a coherent and effective foreign policy for Russia.

Putin has shown that he is prepared to tackle foreign policy problems head-on—to be an effective force for Russian interests in spite of the country's weaknesses. He has broken with the mind-set of the Soviet era and is seeking to defend and promote Russia's interests in the world as it is, and not as it used to be. Equally important, he expects other powers to base their policies on a realistic assessment of national interests. Putin is not the kind of individual who neither gives something for nothing; nor does he expect such behavior from an adversary. In a sense, it was easier for the United States to deal with Russian and Soviet leaders like Mikhail Gorbachev and Boris Yeltsin, who saw the world in more ideological terms, than with Putin, who is a calculating pragmatist.

Before discussing the Putin administration's actions in some detail, let us turn to the Yeltsin regime, which is a critical backdrop for understanding the foreign policy world that Putin inherited.

THE PRE-PUTIN PERIOD

The Policy Framework

When he assumed control of a sovereign Russia at the end of 1991, Boris Yeltsin faced a foreign policy disaster. The USSR had collapsed, splintering into fifteen independent states. The Russian Federation took over as its legal successor and inherited what was left of the centralized institutions of the Soviet state, including its massive nuclear arsenal. Russia confronted an unprecedented task: to carve out a foreign policy for itself in the wake of a collapsed superpower.[4]

The effort to create a Commonwealth of Independent States (CIS) that could unify the newly independent states and project Russian power over the post-Soviet space was a failure virtually from the outset.[5] Too many of the former Soviet republics—and especially Ukraine—distrusted the Russians. Memories of the use of Soviet troops in the Baltics, Georgia, Azerbaijan, and other regions in an effort to hold the country together were fresh in their minds. Equally important, leaders such as Islam Karimov and Nursultan Nazarbaev enjoyed their new status as presidents of sovereign states and were understandably reluctant to give up the power that had serendipitously fallen upon them. Many feared that the Kremlin would again use the military to get its way if and when the former republics acted too independently. In the end, the CIS became little more than a fig leaf. Moscow could claim that it had good, close relations with the former Soviet republics, but the fact was that it was not a serious alliance. Russia was alone.

Yeltsin had to go back to the drawing board. He could hardly expect Russia to be the superpower the USSR had been, in spite of the country's nuclear weapons. Furthermore, confrontation with the West would do him little or no good. The country was in chaos. The political system was being reinvented and a new economy was being introduced as the state-owned system was rapidly privatized.

Yeltsin's primary concern was to create a benign external environment in order to free the Kremlin to deal with the critical tasks of domestic political and economic transition. Yeltsin had little alternative but to try to invent a new type of relationship with the West. Given that the United States was the world's only remaining superpower and, in Yeltsin's mind, the primary potential source of economic largesse, his strategy placed primary emphasis on U.S.–Russian relations.

It is important to keep in mind that the Cold War had left a residue of suspicion and even hatred on both sides. Overcoming this legacy would not be easy—and there was a significant part of the Russian populace that opposed Yeltsin's effort to improve relations with Washington; sometimes openly, at other times behind the scenes. Conservatives, and especially some military officers, were entrenched in Cold War habits. Taught for years to fear the West, including the United States, they now were being told that this "enemy" had become a friend.

Unfortunately, while there were certain elements of rationality in Yeltsin's policy, in time, it would become inconsistent, not only because of Russia's weakness and instability but also because Yeltsin himself was erratic, prone to headstrong and at times downright embarrassing behavior. For example, in the summer of 1993, during a trip to Poland, he said that Russia supported Poland's application to join NATO. He quickly reversed himself, but the image of a bumbling leader, who was not in full control of his faculties, was evident to all concerned. Then there was Yeltsin's visit to Ireland, when he was too drunk to leave his plane. He suffered a heart attack during his June 1996 re-election campaign, which left him incapacitated and physically absent from the Kremlin for eight of the following twelve months—a situation that was largely hidden from public knowledge. Because of his erratic behavior, it became increasingly difficult to know what his policy was—other than broadly intending to draw Russia closer to Washington and the West and end the vestiges of the Cold War.

In addition to inconsistency, Yeltsin's reign was also marked by a lack of "geopolitical perspective or political planning, as well as general inertia," a point made by Oleg Levitin in his analysis of the Yeltsin's Kosovo policy.[6] There was a tendency on Yeltsin's part to put off making hard decisions. So Moscow was prone to ignore problems like Yugoslavia, trying to postpone a decision on how to respond to Slobodan Milosevic and his barbaric actions in Kosovo. As a result, the foreign policy establishment hesitated to push him to make important policy decisions.

These problems of erratic leadership were compounded by the administrative chaos in the foreign policy process. In the Soviet era, decisionmaking had been tightly centralized by the politburo, and its implementation overseen by the departments of the central committee. With the Communist Party's collapse, authority shifted from the politburo to the presidential administration, but the newly created security council failed to develop as an effective coordination institution. The huge bureaucracies of the ministries of foreign affairs and defense drifted out of control, often pursuing their own policy goals independent of other government agencies. New, influential players entered the foreign policy arena, such as oil companies, regional governors, and even regional military commanders, adding to the chaos of conflicting policy initiatives.

Yeltsin and the United States

The first official meeting between Boris Yeltsin and President Bill Clinton occurred in April 1993. Both sides declared their interest in and readiness to create a "dynamic and effective Russo–American partnership."[7] Clinton promised financial aid in the amount of $1.6 billion (half credits, half aid). Many believed it would be the beginning of a "special relationship" between Moscow and Washington.

While some may argue that critics such as Stephen Cohen exaggerate the impact the Clinton administration had on Yeltsin's Russia, there is no question that Clinton and his entourage believed that they could remake Russia in America's image. As Cohen put it, "In effect, the United States was to teach ex-Communist Russia how to become a capitalist and democratic country and oversee the process of conversion known as a 'transition.'"[8] Russia found itself swamped by Americans of all backgrounds and specialties, who were convinced that if only the Russians would listen to the West and especially the Americans, they would quickly rebound from the adversity of the transition process. In time, however, it became clear that the recovery process would be much more protracted and complex. Indeed, one could argue that in many ways, the Clinton administration's approach did Russia more harm than good.

In any case, despite growing doubts the Clinton administration continued to forge ties with the Kremlin. Clinton visited Russia in January 1994, and both sides agreed that their relations were closer than ever. A year later another summit took place in Moscow. By September 1998 the two men had met fourteen times—an unprecedented event in U.S.–Soviet/Russian relations. The "Bill–Boris" relationship was in full bloom.

The problem for U.S.–Russian relations—and indeed for Russian internal politics—was that a combination of a U.S. failure to deliver the kind of aid that Russians believed was offered, together with an increasingly corrupt and inept Yeltsin regime, led to gradual disillusionment with the United States.

Many Russians came to see the economic and social chaos of the early 1990s not as the product of a collapsed communist economic system, but as a result of the capitalist regime that was being forced on Russia at Western insistence. Many began to believe that U.S. aid was all part of a "plot" to both embarrass Russia and to enrich the United States at its expense. Not surprisingly, this did not go down well with nationalistic Russians. Accepting help and assistance from the outside world was bad enough; permitting the United States to take advantage of a prostrate country was unacceptable.

In the wake of the strong Communist showing in the December 1995 State Duma elections, Yeltsin appointed former spy chief Yevgeny Primakov as foreign minister. Under Primakov, Moscow adopted a more assertive foreign policy. The overt bias toward the West was replaced by a more even-handed approach, placing more emphasis on good relations with China and the Arab world. But rhetoric aside, Primakov effected only minor course corrections in the Moscow–Washington relationship. He even folded in the face of U.S. determination to enlarge NATO to include Poland, Hungary, and the Czech Republic.

The most serious test of the relationship was the Kosovo crisis in the spring of 1999. In the wake of the August 1998 financial crisis, Primakov was elevated to the post of prime minister, and he soon faced a deterioration in the security situation in the Yugoslav province of Kosovo. Moscow saw itself as having close historical ties with the Serbs (although in reality the relationship had been dormant since World War I). How could it now desert them in the face of American and NATO pressure—notwithstanding the atrocities committed by the Milosevic forces? In the beginning, Russian diplomats went along with actions such as sanctions against the Belgrade government and denying Yugoslavia the country's seat in the UN. But NATO, without consulting Moscow, commenced its bombing campaign on March 24, 1999, just as Primakov was en route to the United States for an official visit. Primakov's decision to turn his plane around above the mid-Atlantic was immediately seen as symbolic of a new chill in U.S.–Russian relations. Russia promptly withdrew from involvement in the permanent joint council that NATO had created in 1997 to give Moscow a voice inside the alliance.

During the crisis, Moscow's policy vacillated from one of limited support for the NATO pressure on Milosevic to vocal opposition. Russia came to realize that the allies were determined to press ahead with their military campaign, since NATO credibility was at stake, and when the opportunity arose to play the peacemaker in June 1999 Moscow seized the chance. Ex-prime minister Viktor Chernomyrdin was sent to Belgrade to deliver the bad news: Russian patience was exhausted; Milosevic could expect no more Russian support. Milosevic quickly decided that he had no alternative but to evacuate his troops from Kosovo, thus ensuring Russian participation in the military occupation of Kosovo and preserving Yugoslavia's formal sovereignty over the province.

As this sorry catalog illustrates, Putin inherited a foreign policy that was neither consistent nor effective. The world knew Russia was weak and not a serious player on the international scene. But recognizing the obvious did not prevent Russians from being deeply resentful of the position in which they found themselves, and of the role the Clinton administration was playing in Russia. Not only did the United States seem to be trying to turn Russians into Americans, in the eyes of many it was gloating over the country's weak position. U.S. involvement in Russia may have been intended to help over-come its problems—but in practice it merely served to draw attention to the unpleasant new reality and to implicate the United States in Russia's weak-ened condition.

As a result, the situation facing Putin when he took over as acting president at the beginning of 2000 was less than ideal. The country was in shambles, its relationship with the United States was troubled, the West seemed to be ignoring Russia, and even the Kremlin's few remaining allies (such as India) had lost faith. It was beginning to look like Moscow was irrelevant in the international arena. Yes, Moscow could be a spoiler by threatening to sell nuclear material or weapons to Iran, or by siding with Iraq in the intermina-ble arguments in the UN Security Council over the sanctions regime, or by selling weapons to China. And it could exploit the presence of Russian "peacekeepers" in Kosovo, Moldova, Abkhazia, and Tajikistan to project Russian influence into those troubled countries. But such actions imposed costs on Russia itself that were equal to or greater than those inflicted on U.S. interests. And when the Russian Bear growled, who paid any attention? The answer was almost nobody.

PUTIN TAKES CONTROL OF FOREIGN POLICY

Putin's first priority was to attempt to rationalize foreign policy. He recog-nized better than Yeltsin not only how weak Russia was, but how important it would be for Moscow to project an activist, participatory image on the international stage. In redesigning Russian foreign policy, Putin had two objectives. First, he believed that Moscow had to be seen as an active global presence. Playing the isolationist game would get the Kremlin nowhere, and in fact would only reinforce the prevailing image of Russian weakness. Sec-ond, he decided that U.S.–Russian relations had to improve. Like it or not, the United States was the world's only superpower.

In carrying out these objectives, Putin's foreign policy has been character-ized by a number of factors. First, he believes in a balance-of-power approach to foreign policy, as opposed to the Soviet-era concept of foreign policy as a clash between rival ideologies. As he stated in his millennium speech shortly after he took over from Yeltsin, "I am against the restoration of an official state ideology in Russia in any form."[9] For Putin, problem solving takes precedence over ideology, whether of the left or the right. U.S. preeminence obliges Russia to "bandwagon" with the U.S.-led coalition of leading powers. Putin understands that there will be times—most of the time, in fact—when he will hold a weak hand. Yet Putin is smart enough to know that the weak partner can deal from a position of strength on occasion.

To make this balance-of-power policy work, Putin adopted a calculated, practical approach to dealing with foreign (as well as internal) problems. Yeltsin himself described Putin as a "somewhat cold pragmatist."[10] According to an article in *Ponedelnik*, "He is in no hurry to make a choice with regard to the reforms and the methods of their implementation. He takes his time, waiting for his team to be formed to the end."[11]

Putin made Russia's position very clear to Russians and the rest of the world shortly after assuming power. On June 28, 2000, he issued a new set of policy guidelines or "foreign policy concept." This replaced a 1993 document, and followed a new "national security concept" published in January and a "military doctrine" released in April. The concept stated that "Today our foreign policy resources are relatively limited. . . . And they will be concentrated in fields that are vital for Russia." Foreign Minister Igor Ivanov described the new approach as a pragmatic effort to help the country to solve its domestic problems.[12] The document itself offered a restrained but critical view of NATO and the West and highlighted the importance of Russia's ties to the Group of Eight (G8) and the European Union. At the same time it took a swipe at Washington by calling for a "multipolar world" in contrast to the "unipolar structures of the world with the economic and power domination of the United States," and reiterated Moscow's opposition to a limited national missile defense plan.[13] In tune with his more realist approach to foreign policy, Putin told an interviewer that Russia "must get rid of imperial ambitions on the one hand, and on the other clearly understand where our national interests are and fight for them."[14]

Putin has outstanding diplomatic skills. He appears to have produced a favorable impression on all of his interlocutors, from Tony Blair to Madeleine Albright to Jiang Zemin. At times he has gone overboard to make a good impression, displaying a Zelig-like enthusiasm for adapting to his current environment. In Japan he took part in a judo contest (allowing himself to be thrown by his fifteen-year-old adversary), in Canada he averred his enthusiasm for ice hockey, in Spain he praised the art of Velázquez, and in Rome he said he came because "we love Italy."

Relations with the United States in Putin's First Year

During Yeltsin's latter years in office, U.S.–Russian relations deteriorated to the point where one source noted that "Washington (was) all but estranged from Moscow for most of the past year over the U.S.-led air war in Yugoslavia and Russia's prosecution of the war in Chechnya. . . ."[15] These same observers argued that Washington hoped to return to a position of influence over the Kremlin, while the latter wanted U.S. assistance to restart its economy.

Putin immediately showed his interest in improved relations by persuading the State Duma to ratify Start 2, a feat that had eluded Yeltsin in the preceding five years. This treaty eliminated multiple warheads on land-based missiles and limited Russia and the United States to 3,000–3,500 strategic warheads each. Putin also announced that he wanted to see even deeper cuts—down to 1,500. While this proposal seemed to carry little weight when it was first announced, Putin would later be able to use it to advantage by suggesting to Washington's allies that his approach offered an appropriate compromise.

Arms control was very much at the fore when President Clinton paid his farewell visit to Moscow in June 2000. The United States again pushed for modifications in the 1972 Anti-Ballistic Missile Treaty so it could begin testing a national missile defense system (NMD). Moscow (and not only Moscow) found the U.S. determination to press ahead with NMD puzzling. Was it really based on the stated objective—fear of a possible nuclear strike on the U.S. mainland (or against U.S. forces?) from a rogue state like Iraq or North Korea? Perhaps its real intention was to intimidate China. Or was it simply a boondoggle for U.S. defense contractors?

Whatever the true motivation behind Washington's enthusiasm, Moscow feared NMD for three reasons. First, no one could predict what kind of "spin-offs" in advanced weaponry the search for NMD might produce. Second, it would leave the United States in a position of unquestioned global strategic dominance with a potent combination of offensive and defensive forces. Third, in addition to lacking meaningful strategic defensive forces, the Kremlin knew that the number of nuclear weapons available to Russia's military leaders would steadily diminish due to lack of funds for maintenance and modernization. In future years Russia's offensive forces could conceivably shrink to the point at which they would be unable to guarantee second-strike retaliation against an overwhelming U.S. first strike.

Despite grave Russian objections, the U.S. Senate had approved in principle the development of theater missile defense in March 1999. In a bid to head off NMD, Putin persuaded the State Duma to ratify Start 2, signed in 1993, which they dutifully did on April 14, 2000. During President Clinton's June 2000 visit there was speculation that Putin was looking for a "grand bargain": Russian agreement to waive the ABM Treaty in return for deep mutual cuts in strategic missiles. However, Senate Republican Jesse Helms made it clear that he would block approval of any such treaty, distrustful of concessions made during the waning months of the Clinton administration. As a consequence, Clinton had to be satisfied with the dubious privilege of being the first U.S. president to address the Duma. He also signed two minor agreements: one to reduce each country's weapons-grade plutonium reserves by thirty-four tons over twenty years, and the other to create a joint early warning center in Moscow by the fall of 2001 in an effort to reduce the risks of an accidental nuclear launch. Meanwhile, on the eve of the summit, Putin mystified observers by suggesting that he was prepared to consider a joint U.S.–Russian NMD to prevent attacks by so-called "rogue states." While he did not describe what he had in mind, "it would be on a smaller scale than the concept being considered by Clinton."[16] Clinton quickly brushed this idea aside.

All in all, Clinton's visit to Moscow was anything but a success. "The Russians signaled their displeasure with the U.S. president by failing to broadcast his speech to the Russian legislature on TV. . . . There was an obvious chill in the air between Clinton and Putin at their final media conference—Clinton looked frustrated, exhausted and exasperated and there was no warmth from Putin. The days of the cheery Boris-and-Bill show are clearly over."[17] Strobe Talbott, at the time assistant secretary of state, has suggested that Putin erred in rejecting Clinton's proposal to loosen the ABM Treaty, since the following year he would be forced to swallow the "shredding" of the ABM Treaty by President Bush in the wake of September 11.[18] The result was that U.S.–Russian relations went into a "stall" for the duration of 2000, while the Russians waited to see who would replace Clinton. As far as they were concerned, there was no sense trying to do business with a lame-duck president. In the meantime, Putin busied himself establishing warm ties with European leaders.

During the American election campaign, Russians were hesitant to come out strongly in favor of one candidate or the other. Senior Russian officials were fully aware that in contrast to the days of the Soviet Union, Russia was not a major issue. There were some grounds for expecting Moscow to prefer a Democratic victory, given that Vice President Al Gore knew the ropes and had put considerable effort into building up the Gore–Chernomyrdin commission, which brokered bilateral relations in trade and technology issues. Others hinted that Moscow favored a Bush victory, since this would represent a clean break with the Yeltsin–Clinton era. Regardless of who won, Russian observers were well aware that Moscow was in a weak position and would have to deal with the United States when it came to regional problems, arms control, and especially economic issues.

Putin continued to take the offensive in arms control, suggesting on the eve of the American elections that Russia was ready for even more radical cuts in both the U.S. and Russian nuclear arsenals. Putin made use of the hiatus in American politics leading up to the election by coming up with a "barrage of policy initiatives,"[19] almost all of which were aimed at challenging Washington's position as the world's only superpower.

Relations with the Bush Administration

U.S.–Russian relations got off to a poor start under the Bush administration. In fact, until the summit in Slovenia in June 2001, it appeared that Washington was simply not taking Moscow seriously as an international player. The new administration seemed to look upon Russia as an economic, political, and social basket case. For example, during his election campaign, Bush denounced Russia's actions in Chechnya and its pervasive corruption—in one presidential debate going so far as to charge former Prime Minister Viktor Chernomyrdin with pocketing Western loan money. Bush seemed to believe that since the Russians had gotten themselves into their present morass, it was up to them to straighten themselves out. Whether or not they had a democracy was a problem for them—not the United States. This was in sharp contrast to the Clinton approach, which was based on the theory of the "democratic peace"—the notion that democracies did not go to war with each other, thus giving the United States a strong stake in Russia's democratization. Some actions by Putin seemed to confirm suspicions about Russian motives held by the conservatives in the Bush administration. In July 2000 on his way to the G8 summit in Okinawa, Putin stopped off in Pyongyang and tried to pull off a diplomatic coup by securing a pledge from North Korea to discontinue its missile program—a "pledge" it later denied. Then in December 2000 Putin made a trip to Cuba, the first by a Russian president since the collapse of the Soviet Union. Putin was well aware that this visit would irritate the United States, and particularly the conservative Bush. He presumably wanted Bush to understand that in contrast to his predecessor he would not kowtow to the United States. To quote an article in the *Guardian*:

> Since succeeding Boris Yeltsin last March, he has been busily challenging America's global hegemony, as seen from Moscow, at every opportunity. He has intervened directly in the US-led Middle East peace process, given succor to Iraq, and resumed arms sales to Iran and Libya. He visited North Korea, that most roguish of US-designated 'rogue states,' and cheekily claimed to have curbed its menacing missiles. He went to India, bidding to revive Soviet-era ties in direct competition with Bill Clinton's efforts to woo Delhi last spring; and has increased military and political cooperation with China.[20]

It was also clear that problems remained between the two sides on issues such as Bush's favorite strategic initiative—a missile defense program. And it was clear from voices within the Russian leadership that Putin would face serious opposition if he tried to change Moscow's position. For example, in December 2000, Defense Minister Igor Sergeev stated that Russia would not agree to any compromise with the United States that modified the 1972 Anti-Ballistic Missile Treaty.

Despite the friction, the two sides shared at least some common interests.

Both were concerned about international terrorism. Both worried about Afghanistan, Pakistan, and Islamic fundamentalism. Putin's pardoning of Edward Pope, a retired U.S. Navy captain and alleged spy, in December 2000 was an obvious effort to improve U.S.–Russian relations. And American policymakers had to realize that there were risks involved in ignoring the Kremlin. In spite of the horrible condition of its economy, society, and political system, Russia would remain vital to U.S. security for years to come. Indeed, after September 11, 2001, Washington would learn just how critical Moscow's role would be.

As the new Bush administration was sworn in, Putin was cagey as ever. When asked about the future of U.S.–Russian relations, he stated that "a lot would depend here on the policy of the new U.S. administration."[21] The Bush administration's policy was equally vague. When the issue of U.S.–Russian relations came up, Secretary of State Colin Powell argued that "Moscow was neither an enemy, nor a potential opponent of the United States." However, Powell pointed out that Washington could not consider Russia a strategic partner. According to commentator Valentin Kunin, this meant that if "the foreign policy of the Bush [administration] becomes the basis of Powell's guidelines, Russia USA relations are unlikely to improve."[22] Condoleezza Rice, Bush's national security advisor, openly called for a decisive break with the "failed" policy of the Clinton administration. She reiterated what Bush had stated previously, that "Russia's economic future is now in the hands of the Russians." Leaving aside any pretense of diplomacy, she argued, "It would be foolish in the extreme to share defenses with Moscow as it either leaks or deliberately transfers weapons technologies to the very states against which America is defending."[23] As a result, the outlook for U.S.–Russian relations was anything but positive as Bush was sworn in.

In spite of this concern over the future of U.S. policy toward Russia, Moscow made it clear from the beginning that it was prepared to talk. On December 30, 2000, Foreign Minister Igor Ivanov said that Moscow wanted a "serious dialogue" with the Bush administration. He went on to note that he "did not believe that differences between the two countries on national missile defense are insuperable." If nothing else, his statement suggested that there were differences of opinion within the Putin regime on this highly sensitive topic."[24] Putin followed up immediately after Bush was sworn in by sending a letter in which he congratulated the new president on his position while at the same time called for improved U.S.–Russian relations. Russia and the United States needed "to find joint answers to the serious challenges which confront us and the entire international community, in the 21st century."[25] Putin was clearly holding out an olive branch.

Lest anyone think that Putin was about to cave in to Bush, however, he made it clear in his dealings with the United States' West European allies that he was prepared to take the fight over NMD into America's own backyard.

He went to Canada where he succeeded in persuading Prime Minister Jean Chrétien to say that "the stability which exists now" should not be "undermined by the plan put forth by the Americans" for missile defenses against rogue nations.[26]

Another key issue was the safeguarding of Russian nuclear materials. The country was clearly unable to spend the kind of money necessary to manage its stockpiles. As a result, the United States had poured $5 billion into an effort to safeguard this material, help destroy it, and pay Russian nuclear scientists enough to keep them from selling their expertise abroad. It was clear that more money would be needed to do the job, but the Bush administration, worried about waste and duplication in the thirty-plus programs being run as part of the weapons dismantling mission, launched an investigative study immediately after taking office. It also was concerned that Moscow was either encouraging or at a minimum permitting sensitive nuclear material to leak to Iran.

To make matters even worse, president-elect Bush gave an interview on January 14, 2001, in which he warned Moscow not to expect economic aid in the future except for nonproliferation projects unless Putin cleaned up the country's economic mess. "He has pledged to root out corruption. I think that's going to be a very important part, but it's his choice to make. That's the point I'm trying to make. It's hard for America to fashion Russia."[27]

The Russian response was mixed. Some, such as State Duma speaker and longtime Communist Party member Gennadii Seleznev, as well as Vladimir Lukin, the former Russian ambassador to Washington and a liberal, agreed with the U.S. president's comments. Others argued that Bush's statement "not only ends any hope of restructuring Russia's debt, but is likely to generate anti-reform reaction in Russia itself."[28]

Meanwhile, those who opposed any improvement in U.S.–Russian relations began repeating the oft-heard refrain that Washington was trying to force its will on others. As one Russian commentary put it, "Washington is trying to subordinate all independent countries to US dictate, to grab key industries and financial systems of the concerned countries and to control their policies. This amounts to Americanization and the assertion of US domination. However, the United States camouflages this process by the 'globalization' concept."[29]

In spite of the harsh polemics, Putin reiterated the Russian position on February 8, 2001, when he stated that he hoped to find common language with U.S. President Bush, especially with the ABM issue. Putin went on to note that he had recently spoken on the phone with Bush and observed that "I give a very positive evaluation to our conversation and its results. I feel that Bush and myself will find a common language."[30] Despite Putin's apparent optimism, Dr. Rice continued the Bush administration's hard line in an interview in *Le Figaro* on February 10, when she commented that "I believe Russia is a threat to the West in general and to our European allies in particular."[31] As if that were not enough, Secretary of Defense Donald Rumsfeld accused Russia of violating the nuclear nonproliferation regime.[32] That was followed by a huge scandal following the February 18 arrest of FBI agent Robert Hanssen, who had spied for the Russians for fifteen years. In response, the United States ejected fifty Russian diplomats: the largest number of expulsions since 1986. Not surprisingly, the Russians reacted by expelling an equal number of American officials. From all appearances, U.S.–Russian relations were headed even farther downhill.

Meanwhile, U.S. and Russian diplomats continued to meet. For example, Secretary of State Colin Powell held what was officially described as a "constructive dialogue" when he met Russian Foreign Minister Igor Ivanov in Cairo in February 2001 to discuss the apparent impasse in U.S.–Russian relations: diplomatic shorthand indicating that the two sides were at least still talking.[33] The two had another positive meeting in April. According to Powell, both countries wanted to put their past difficulties behind them and "move on."[34]

There were a number of indications that U.S.–Russian relations might improve as preparations advanced for the first meeting between the two presidents, scheduled for Slovenia in June. On May 1, Bush gave a speech in which he reversed his administration's confrontational stance toward Russia by calling for a new relationship based on "openness, mutual confidence and real opportunities for cooperation, including in the area of missile defense."[35] For his part, Putin sent a letter to Bush in which he stated that the upcoming summit will "give an additional impetus to Russian–U.S. dialogue and interaction."[36] There were hints that Putin was willing to countenance a deal over NMD that would allow some weakening of the ABM Treaty in return for further mutual cuts in offensive weapons.

The Ljubljana summit had a major, positive impact on U.S.–Russian relations, thanks largely to the personal chemistry between the two leaders.[37] Mr. Bush famously commented after his first meeting with Putin, "I was able to get a sense of his soul."[38] Despite substantive differences, it was clear that the atmosphere between the two countries had improved considerably. It helped that Putin, who had been intensively studying English since becoming president, was able to make some conversation with Bush in English. As Putin stated, "We found a good basis to start building on cooperation, counting on a pragmatic relationship between Russia and the United States." Bush, for his part, said, "I am convinced that he and I can build a relationship of mutual respect and candor."[39] Bush announced that he would support Russia's entry into the World Trade Organization (one of Putin's most important foreign policy goals), and Putin agreed to continue a discussion on a new strategic defense framework—a concession that seemed almost impossible only weeks previously. Both leaders agreed to exchange visits to their respective countries. Putin gave a newspaper interview in which he said he and Bush had forged a "very high level of trust," and referred to the American president as a "partner" and "a nice person to talk to."[40] Putin made no secret that there were significant differences on topics such as Chechnya, NMD, or the Kremlin's relations with Iran, but overall, he painted an upbeat picture. Bush reciprocated in mid-July by telling a *Novosti* correspondent that it was now important not only for the United States and Russia to agree on NMD, but that both countries needed to turn their attention to such threats as cyberterrorism, and—somewhat prophetically—Islamic fundamentalism.[41] In an interview, Bush spoke candidly of his relationship with Putin:[42] "I found a man who realizes his future lies with the West, not the East, that we share common security concerns, primarily Islamic fundamentalism, that he understands missiles could affect him just as much as us. On the other hand he doesn't want to be diminished by America."

The next meeting between Bush and Putin took place at the G8 meeting in Genoa in July 2001. It too went well, with Bush saying of Putin "This is a man with whom I can have an honest dialogue."[43] The two sides issued a joint statement in which they agreed that the issues of antimissile defenses and strategic arms cuts were related and should be dealt with together. In practice it was assumed that this meant that any modifications in the ABM Treaty would be accompanied by large cuts in offensive nuclear warheads. The former was a long-term American goal, while the latter was being forced on the Russians by their increasingly outdated and inoperable nuclear arsenal. The two sides also agreed to begin "intensive consultations," in an effort to better understand each other's position.[44] The talks (or "discussions" as they were termed) would not be easy, but at least the two sides were beginning to debate the issue.

It soon became clear that however much Putin might want to compromise on the ABM issue, he was not able to deliver the Moscow bureaucracy. The Russian military, one of the most conservative institutions in the country, was still locked into the mentality of the Cold War, deeply suspicious of anything that came from the United States and frozen by inertia into anti-U.S. policies—arms proliferation, nuclear deterrence, provocative military exercises.[45] Because of conflicting views and interests among senior commanders, Putin made virtually no progress with urgently needed military reform. In March 2001 Putin reshuffled his top security ministers. Defense Minister Igor Sergeev was replaced with Sergei Ivanov, a former KGB official and close Putin ally, who became the first civilian to head the Defense Ministry in Russian history. Ivanov was replaced as head of the Security Council by Vladimir Rushailo, formerly interior minister. In July Putin removed General Leonid Ivashov, an outspoken hawk, from his position as head of the Defense Ministry's international department.

Perhaps because of Russia's inability to move ahead with concrete concessions, Rice's visit to Russia shortly after the Genoa summit for consultations made little progress. She concluded by insisting that the United States would scuttle the ABM Treaty altogether rather than negotiate amendments to it. Several weeks later, a high-level Russian delegation traveled to Washington for additional discussions. The head of the military delegation, Colonel General Yuri Baluevskii, stressed that no breakthrough had been reached.[46] Oleg Chernov, the deputy secretary of the Security Council, predicted that it would probably take a year or more to reach a substantive agreement on missile defense.[47] It was looking increasingly likely, therefore, that U.S.–Russian relations would founder on the rocks of the ABM Treaty. But then came September 11.

THE WORLD AFTER SEPTEMBER 11

The attack by terrorists on the World Trade Center towers and the Pentagon had a major impact on U.S.–Russian relations. Putin was the first leader to telephone Bush with condolences and an unequivocal condemnation of the terrorist act.[48] Despite Putin's reputation as a cautious and calculating leader, his swift response to September 11 seemed to be driven by instinct and emotion.[49] In a subsequent telegram to Bush, Putin decried the "barbarous terrorist acts aimed against wholly innocent people," and expressed Russia's "deepest sympathies to the relatives of the victims of this tragedy, and the entire suffering American people," calling for "solidarity" in the face of such actions.[50] Equally important was an offer of assistance by Defense Minister Sergei Ivanov to the U.S. Defense Department. Moscow took the unprecedented step of canceling a military exercise by the Russian air force at the request of the United States.

It was clear that September 11 had the potential to mark a sea change in international relations in general and in the U.S.–Russia relationship in particular. As Strobe Talbott noted, U.S. military action in Afghanistan would be targeting a former Russian enemy (Afghanistan) and current Russian threat (Islamic fundamentalism), in marked contrast to previous U.S. actions against Russian allies Yugoslavia and Iraq.[51]

The key question in Moscow, however, was how big a role should Russia play in assisting the United States in retaliating for these actions—and what should it expect in return? The Russians made it clear that they were more than prepared to share intelligence, a gesture that was welcomed by the United States. But the real issue was access to bases in Central Asia, in countries that formerly were part of the USSR. Moscow was anxious to regain some of its former preeminence in the region and had reacted neuralgically to previous U.S. efforts to project its own influence—such as the U.S. military exercise in Uzbekistan in 1998 under the rubric of NATO's Partnership for Peace program. Russia was uncertain of the direction U.S. military action would take and had no desire to be associated with a policy that could involve large-scale conflict in Afghanistan and beyond. Russia was already engaged in what it considered to be a war against Muslim fundamentalists in Chechnya, where there was some evidence of fighters being supported by the same Osama Bin Ladin who masterminded the attacks on New York and Washington. September 11 gave Russia a chance to legitimize its actions in Chechnya, the subject of intermittently harsh criticism by Europe and to a lesser extent the United States. More broadly, an alliance with the United States in the war on terrorism provided Putin with a golden opportunity to make Russia once again a major actor on the world stage.

Meanwhile, the initial response of those below Putin was far from unanimous. Foreign Minister Igor Ivanov said in Washington that the former Central Asian republics (i.e., Uzbekistan, Kazakhstan, Turkmenistan, Kyrgyzstan, and Tajikistan) would be free to make their own decisions when it came to aiding the United States. But Defense Minister Sergei Ivanov ruled out "even a hypothetical possibility" of a NATO military presence in these former Soviet territories. In addition, the chief of the general staff, General Anatolii Kvashnin, stated that "Russia has not considered and is not planning to consider participation in a military operation against Afghanistan." He also reminded the Central Asian republics of "their relevant bilateral and other obligations" to Russia.[52]

It took several weeks for Putin to enforce unanimity in the ranks of his top officials. By September 24 it was becoming clear that in spite of the opposition from some in the military, Putin had decided to actively aid Washington's campaign against the radical Taliban regime in Afghanistan. He agreed to step up support for opposition forces inside Afghanistan, and he gave "tacit approval for the United States to use former Soviet bases in Central Asia."[53] The same day, Defense Minister Ivanov, in a major reversal of his previous position, said that the United States could use military facilities in Tajikistan to launch strikes on neighboring Afghanistan "if the need arises."[54] Access to these facilities was especially important to Washington because of concern over the volatility of fundamentalist Muslim groups in Pakistan, its other major staging area. In addition, Putin agreed to take part in search-and-rescue operations and vowed to share intelligence about international terrorist groups. Presidents Nursultan Nazarbayev of Kazakhstan and Askar Akaev of Kyrgyzstan said that they were willing to provide the antiterrorist alliance with use of their airspace and military bases. By December 1, 500 U.S. troops were deployed at the Hanabad air base in Uzbekistan and the United States had signed agreements granting landing rights in Tajikistan and Kyrgyzstan.

There were limits to Russian cooperation, however. Moscow reportedly encouraged its longtime allies, the Northern Alliance, to move quickly into

Kabul—before the United States had been able to patch together a coalition government with the southern Pashtuns. On November 26, several hundred paramilitary personnel from the Emergency Situations Ministry flew unannounced into Kabul to establish a Russian presence there, in a move reminiscent of the reckless "dash for Pristina" in June 1999, when Russian peacekeepers drove from Bosnia to seize the Kosovo airport before advancing British troops. However, the United States was able to forge a viable coalition government to their liking in the Bonn conference, without Russian interference. And on December 5, Foreign Minister Ivanov announced that Russia had no intention of sending peacekeepers to Afghanistan, signaling its unwillingness to engage more deeply in a country that had been a quagmire for its military in the 1980s.

The unprecedented introduction of U.S. military units into Uzbekistan, Kyrgyzstan, and Tajikistan, on what increasingly looks like a long-term basis, represented a projection of U.S. military power into Russia's "backyard" that would have been unthinkable prior to the September attack. As Dmitri Trenin has noted, Putin's foreign policy was ambiguously polygamous prior to September 11: he was seeking allies from Pyongyang to Ottawa and all points between.[55] After the World Trade Center attack, Putin was forced to prioritize, forced to choose. His decision to align with the United States caused a radical improvement in the tone of the U.S.–Russian relationship. In the summer of 2001, Putin had been getting increasingly bad press in the West because of Chechnya and the crackdown on the independent television station NTV, so as Yelena Tregubova observed, "the Russian president would hardly have made such a breakthrough on the world stage if not for the tragedy of September 11."[56]

Russian foreign policy elites seized upon September 11 as representing a fundamental shift in the international order. Academic Aleksandr Konovalov argued that the event "shattered the myth of absolute power and invulnerability, of the United States as a guarantor of stability," while leading liberal Duma deputy Aleksei Arbatov said it was "the end of the illusion of a unipolar world."[57] Sensing—incorrectly, as it turned out—that the United States was fundamentally weakened, the foreign policy establishment gleefully prepared wish lists of American concessions they expected Washington to proffer in return for Russia's cooperation. However, Putin's choice was a long-term strategic alignment, not a tactical maneuver. He expected—and received—little in the way of immediate payoffs.

Putin's visit to the presidential ranch in Crawford, Texas, in November 2001 symbolized the return of the feel-good factor in U.S.–Russian relations, but it failed to produce any specific rewards for Moscow. President Bush said "The more I get to know President Putin, the more I get to see his heart and soul, the more I know we can work together in a positive way."[58]

At an October meeting on the fringe of the Asia-Pacific Economic Council in Shanghai, Putin had asked Bush to exempt Russia from the 1974 Jackson-Vanik amendment, which forced Russia to vet its emigration policies if it was to maintain normal trade relations with the United States. The Crawford meeting produced a promise by Bush to ask Congress to lift the amendment—something that he still had not done, six months later, when the two men met again in Moscow in May 2002.

Hopes that the Crawford summit would produce some kind of deal to bridge the gap between the two sides on national missile defense were dashed. There were some signs that Russia was open to a quid pro quo—an agreement to deep cuts in strategic forces in return for Russia acquiescing in a reinterpretation of the 1972 ABM Treaty to allow the American NMD program. However, the U.S. administration was reluctant to tie itself down in a major new arms control treaty. Bush suggested that the whole concept of formal treaties defining strategic arsenals was a redundant relic of the Cold War, and that a "handshake" deal was all that was needed.

On December 10, 2001, Secretary Powell traveled to Moscow to inform the Russians that the United States would be withdrawing from the ABM Treaty in six months' time. Russia's response was surprisingly muted. When the news was made public three days later, Putin made a brief televised announcement in which he assured viewers that Russian security was not threatened by the development. Some leading generals had threatened an aggressive response, such as withdrawal from the Start 2 treaty, which commits Russia to dismantle all its multiple-warhead missiles by 2007. But no such response was forthcoming.

However, by the time the two leaders met again, in Moscow in May 2002, the U.S. position had softened. President Bush agreed to sign off on a treaty under which each side pledged to cut its nuclear forces down to between 1,700–2,200 weapons by the year 2012.[59] However, the treaty, a mere three pages long, was vague on specifics. (In contrast, Start 2 ran to 700 pages.) It included no new agreement for verification procedures (still governed by the 1991 Start 1 treaty), and the United States insisted that the two sides be allowed to store and not destroy excess. The treaty was regarded as a political sop to Putin, which did not substantively impact the military programs of either country. Secretary of State Colin Powell himself told reporters that "I'm more worried about chickens going back and forth than missiles going back and forth."[60] (He was referring to a recent trade dispute involving a Russian ban on chicken imports from the United States on health grounds.)

RUSSIA AND THE REST OF THE WORLD

Washington was far from Putin's only concern. In contrast to Yeltsin, Putin engaged actively with the rest of the world—to the point where one could call him the presidential tourist because he always appears to be traveling to one country or another. Between his election in March and the end of the year 2000 he made no fewer than twenty-four visits abroad and hosted dozens of foreign dignitaries in Moscow. These visits had a number of purposes. First, they were aimed at strengthening his hand vis-à-vis Washington by showing the Bush administration that he had alternatives, and that he could be a nuisance factor if he chose. No longer would Moscow's foreign policy be determined in Washington. The United States was far more powerful than Russia, but Putin would not permit his country to be taken for granted by Bush or anyone else. In addition, Putin believed that only by being active all over the world could the Kremlin restore Russia to its proper place. The latter goal is important not only for psychological reasons, but economic ones as well.

Moscow and Europe

Relations between Moscow and Europe developed smoothly under Putin— surprising given the continuing protests at Russian actions in Chechnya from West Europeans. With his fluency in German and familiarity with the European scene Putin was able to woo European leaders, who were more interested than their American counterparts in maintaining steady access to Russia's energy riches. The European Union is Russia's most important economic partner, accounting for 40 percent of Russia's foreign trade, in contrast to 5 percent to the United States.

In Soviet times, Moscow's overtures toward West Europe were aimed at trying to split the NATO alliance by playing on European doubts about American actions, as in the controversy over the deployment of new theater nuclear weapons in the early 1980s. While some commentators still see an anti-American undercurrent to Putin's courtship of Europe, one can equally argue that there is no contradiction in Putin simultaneously pursuing a pro-American and a pro-European policy. Russia is physically part of Europe, Germany is its main trading partner, and it is only natural that a Western-oriented Russia will develop the closest ties with its European neighbors.

A steady stream of Western visitors trooped through the Kremlin corridors in the early months of 2000, sounding out the new Russian leader. The foreign ministers of Italy and Germany came through Moscow in January 2000 to take the measure of the acting president. The next month they were followed by their equivalents from the United States, Britain, and France. Putin's relationship with Britain's Tony Blair ("my friend Tony") grew particularly close. Blair visited Russia in March 2000, in a visible endorsement of the acting president just two weeks before he faced election. Blair defended himself from human rights critics, saying "Chechnya isn't Kosovo. The Russians have been subjected to really severe terrorist attacks."[61] Putin repaid the favor by choosing London as the destination for his first foreign trip in April (although he stopped off in Minsk en route, a favor to Aleksandr Lukashenko). By the time of Putin's official visit to London in December 2001, the two men had met on nine occasions over the preceding two years. Blair, like Putin, was trying to promote his country's international image beyond the level its actual influence would warrant. Putin continued his trips with an official visit to France in late October. Most noteworthy was the fact that the visit took place at all. Relations between the two countries had been strained by Paris's constant criticism of Russian actions in Chechnya and had led Putin to snub French President Jacques Chirac at the G8 meeting in June.

Of all of Moscow's relations with Western Europe, those with Germany have been the closest. Perhaps this was because of Putin's fluency in German and the number of years he lived in that country. In his June 2000 visit German Chancellor Gerhard Schroeder called for "a truly strategic partnership with Russia," and seconded Putin's concerns over the 1972 ABM Treaty.[62] The high point of German–Russian relations came with Putin's visit to Germany in September 2001. He was given the unusual honor of addressing the German Bundestag—which he did in German. In spite of all of this activity, German–Russian relations have been more rhetoric than substance to date. Germany, the largest holder of Russian scrip in the Paris Club of official lenders, has resisted Russian pleas to write down some of the Soviet Union's debts, which Russia took over in 1991. (By the end of 2001 Soviet-era debt stood at $66 billion, of which $36 billion was owed to the Paris Club.[63]) Since Bismark's time, Germany had occasionally used Russia as a counterweight to rival Western powers. But with Germany finally a fully accepted member of the global community, it no longer needs to play such balance-of-power politics.[64]

As mentioned earlier, Putin did an excellent job of turning a state visit to Canada into an attack on Washington's NMD plans. He was able to get Prime Minister Jean Chrétien to agree to a communiqué stating that "Canada and the Russian Federation agree that the 1972 Antiballistic Missile Treaty is a cornerstone of strategic stability."[65] Putin even went to the point of asking the Canadians to become mediators between Moscow and Washington.

Putin had more trouble patching up Russia's relationship with some of its fellow Slavic countries. At the start of his first year, relations with Poland took a turn for the worse. In January 2000 Warsaw expelled nine Russian diplomats for spying, and on February 23 (Russia's Army Day) demonstrators protesting the war in Chechnya attacked the Russian consulate in Poznan. However, in July 2000 President Aleksander Kwasniewski made an official visit to Moscow and patched up the relationship. In January 2002 Putin reciprocated with a visit to Poland, the first by a Russian president since 1993. Good relations are important not least because NATO-member Poland borders the economically devastated and crime-infested Russian enclave of Kaliningrad, a potential flash point for future problems.

In Yugoslavia, Russia blundered by backing Slobodan Milosevic to the bitter end. At the G8 summit in July 2000, Putin had voiced some concerns over Milosevic's policies, but on August 28, 2000, Russia signed a free trade agreement with Yugoslavia, a propaganda coup for Milosevic in the run-up to the September 24 election. It took Moscow until October 6 to acknowledge that challenger Vojislav Kostunica had won the vote. Kostunica was willing to overlook Moscow's sluggish response in order to gain some diplomatic leverage against the West, so he chose Moscow for his first foreign visit on October 26. Russia consistently defended Yugoslavia's interests in the NATO occupation of Kosovo, criticizing the UN administration for failing to disarm the Kosovo Liberation Army and protect the remaining Serbian population.

NATO Expansion

The very existence of NATO is a problem for Russia, given that the alliance was set up to deter the Soviet military threat to central Europe. However, because it obstinately continues to exist, Russia is tempted to bow to the inevitable and regard it not as a barrier but as a bridge for future cooperation.

Russia broke off ties with NATO once the alliance began bombing Kosovo in the spring of 1999, but relations resumed shortly after Putin became acting president. In February 2000 NATO Secretary General Lord Robertson visited Moscow, and the next month the NATO–Russia Permanent Joint Council resumed its meetings after a break of nearly a year.

Putin surprised observers in a BBC interview on March 5, 2000, by floating the idea of Russia joining NATO, saying "it is hard for me to visualize NATO as an enemy." No one was quite sure how to interpret this strictly hypothetical suggestion, other than as a loose sign of goodwill. During his visit to Helsinki in August 2001, Putin for the first time implied that Russia would not violently object if the Baltic States were admitted to NATO. But Putin kept up the pressure on the Baltics to grant more civic and language rights to their Russian residents. Moscow protested the December 2001 decision of the Organization for Security and Cooperation in Europe to stop monitoring ethnic and language policies in Estonia and Latvia.

The question of Russia's testy relations with NATO acquired some urgency, given expectations that NATO would invite some or all of the Baltic States to join the alliance at its November 2002 summit in Prague. In the wake of September 11, British Prime Minister Tony Blair floated the idea of reviving Russian involvement in NATO by creating a new joint council of the nineteen member states plus Russia ("NATO at 20"). U.S. response to the idea was lukewarm, but it did receive support at the NATO ministers' meeting on December 6, 2001, and was formally endorsed at their gathering in

Reykjavik on May 14, 2002. The new council would give Russia a channel to voice its views on matters such as peacekeeping, arms proliferation, and counterterrorism, but few expected that it would give Russia any real influence inside the organization.

The Commonwealth of Independent States

The CIS that Putin inherited from Yeltsin was a hollow shell, and Putin had no serious initiatives to try to revitalize what was essentially a dead organization. On June 1, 2000, Putin officially launched the so-called Eurasian Economic Community, but actual trade ties between Russia and the member states remain anemic. In July 2001, the "Shanghai Five" (Russia, China, Kazakhstan, Kyrgyzstan, and Tajikistan) metamorphosed into the Shanghai Cooperation Organization with the addition of Uzbekistan. The grouping could have provided an important vehicle for joint Russian and Chinese supervision of the security situation in Central Asia, but its prospects were shattered by the September 11 attacks and the unexpected projection of U.S. military and economic power into the region.

Putin did find one new way to pressure uncooperative CIS members. In September 2000 Russia announced that it was withdrawing from the 1992 Bishkek agreement on visa-free travel for CIS countries, and would henceforth conclude agreements on a bilateral basis. The next month Azerbaijan's Foreign Minister Vilat Gulei traveled to Moscow and secured the continuation of visa-free travel for Azeri citizens: this was presumably a reward from Moscow in return for Azerbaijani concessions over the legal deadlock regarding the status of the Caspian Sea. Putin made an official visit to Baku in January 2001, pointedly visiting the monument to those killed during the Soviet army crackdown in January 1990. On December 5, 2000, Russia imposed a visa regime on Georgia, while exempting the separatist regions of South Ossetia and Abkhazia. This step threatened serious disruption for the estimated 650,000 Georgians living inside Russia, whose remittances were vital to the Georgian economy.

A most dramatic development in the wake of September 11 was Russia's acquiescence in the deployment of U.S. security personnel in Georgia. In February 2002, Georgia requested U.S. help in battling Chechen rebels holed up in the Pankisi Gorge in the north of the country. Russian forces had made occasional raids on Georgian territory in pursuit of Chechen guerrillas—most recently on the Khodori Gorge in the Abkhaz region of Georgia in October 2001. Washington agreed to provide $64 million worth of equipment (such as helicopters) and 150 Special Forces troops as trainers. Speaking on March 1, Putin raised no objection to the deployment, saying that it was "no tragedy," even though just a week before Foreign Minister Ivanov had spoken out against the plan.[66] Putin presumably reasoned that it was a good thing to get the United States directly involved with his campaign against the Chechen rebels. Also, for the first time he won from Washington public acknowledgement of the Russian argument that there were direct ties between the Chechen rebels and elements of Al Qaeda.

Developments in Ukraine seemed to signal a tilt back toward Moscow after several years of vocal enthusiasm for closer ties with NATO and the EU. In September 2000 President Leonid Kuchma fired the pro-NATO Foreign Minister Borys Tarasiuk and replaced him with Anatoly Zlenko, who had served in that post from 1990–94 and is regarded as pro-Russian. Meeting with Putin in Sochi in October 2000, Kuchma agreed to sell Russia an unspecified stake in Ukraine's natural gas transit system to offset the roughly $2 billion which Ukraine owed Moscow for gas deliveries. The huge scandal that erupted toward the end of the year, after the disappearance and murder of crusading journalist Heorhy Gongadze in September, seriously damaged Kuchma's credibility in the West, while Moscow remained loyally supportive.

The Middle East

Putin has also tried to involve Russia more actively in the Middle East. Moscow continued to observe the UN sanctions against Iraq while urging that they be lifted. Moscow also pressed Iraq to allow the return of UN arms inspectors. Moscow has high hopes that once sanctions are lifted lucrative contracts for oil exploration and weapons purchases will head its way—not to mention the $3 billion-plus Iraq owes for prior arms deliveries. In November 2000 Putin sent Foreign Minister Ivanov to Baghdad with a letter to Saddam Hussein "confirming the firm intention of the Russian administration to work to get the Iraq issue resolved as soon as possible and to normalize the situation in the Persian Gulf." From the U.S. and Western standpoint, Moscow took a very hostile position, calling for an end to sanctions and violations of Iraqi airspace and the "bombing of Iraqi territory by U.S. and British warplanes."[67]

By the following April, Russian policy was shifting. Iraqi Vice President Taha Yassin Ramadan's visit to Russia was a very low-key affair. News coverage was modest. Indeed, one source called the visit one of "restraint and caution." And some of the news the Iraqi official received was almost certainly not welcome. For example, Foreign Minister Ivanov told the Duma "in unusually straight terms the need for Baghdad to accept the restoration of UN weapons inspections in order for sanctions to be lifted," a clear change from past rhetoric.[68] In November 2001 Russia suddenly dropped its opposition to a U.S.–British plan to revise UN sanctions against Iraq. With Russian approval, the UN Security Council approved the revised regime of "smart sanctions" allowing more oil sales but with specific bans on military-related purchases, to take effect in May 2002.

Russia also continued to be active in Iran. In October 2000 it was revealed in Washington that Russia had agreed to terminate arms deliveries to Iran by 1999, in a confidential deal struck with Vice President Al Gore back in 1995. One month later, Moscow announced it was going to resume conventional arms sales, and in December 2000 Defense Minister Sergeev paid a visit to Tehran, the first of its kind since 1979, to explore the sale of missiles, patrol boats, diesel submarines, and spare parts. In return, President Muhammad Khatami traveled to Russia in March 2001 to talk directly with Putin about arms sales. Putin also reiterated Russia's intention to help Iran complete a long-stalled nuclear power plant in Bushehr—one that some American experts believe could advance Iran's nuclear weapons program.[69]

Putin tried to justify Russia's increased involvement with Tehran by claiming: "There are changes taking place in Iran. We must take into account our interests, we must help our companies work there."[70] In fact, the economic stakes in this budding relationship were significant. One source estimated that it could earn Moscow up to $7 billion during the next few years.[71]

Russia was offended by not being invited to the Sharm-el-shaik Israeli–Palestinian peace talks in October 2000, despite the fact that it was a sponsor of the 1993 Oslo accords, and despite Foreign Minister Ivanov's feverish shuttle diplomacy in Syria, Lebanon, and Israel over the preceding weeks. In September 2001 Moscow dispatched a special envoy for the Middle East, Andrei Vdovin, to meet with all the sides in the Israeli–Palestinian conflict in an effort to show the world that Moscow had a productive role to play in its resolution. More important from Putin's point of view was that at the same time Israeli Prime Minister Ariel Sharon told Prime Minister Mikhail Kasyanov that Israel was prepared to open more credit lines for Russian firms in order to expand upon the current $6 billion in trade between the two countries.[72]

Latin America

Putin seemed to be going out of his way to express his interest in Latin America with a highly publicized visit to Havana in December 2000. He clearly knew that this visit would irritate the United States, but he wanted to show the world that Russia was again a force to be reckoned with in the region. It was the first by a Russian leader since the collapse of the Soviet Union. The two sides signed agreements to "continue the long standing trading of Russian oil for Cuban sugar and to expand it to other products."[73] In addition, both sides denounced efforts by the United States to dominate the world. All in all, however, the talks were longer on rhetoric than substance. And Fidel Castro was stunned by the abrupt Russian decision announced in October 2001 to close down their 1,500-man electronic listening post in Lourdes, Cuba, complaining that the $200 million annual rent was too high.

Asia

Putin was determined from the outset that Russia would remain an Asian power. He is acutely aware of the economic and geopolitical precariousness of the Russian Far East, whose eight million residents are outnumbered one hundred to one by their Chinese neighbor to the south. Putin has sought to build trust with both China and India—the continent's two giants.

Apart from moral support, the one sphere where Russia could really be of help to China is in supplying military hardware. Russia's motives in these sales are strictly pecuniary: it does not want to strengthen China's military capacity, but it desperately needs China's cash to keep Russian defense plants afloat. Since 1994 China has bought four Kilo-class submarines, and two Sovremenny-class destroyers equipped with Sunburn antiship missiles. China has a license to produce the Zvezda H-31 antiradar missile, which can counter the American Patriot and Aegis systems. China is producing 300 SU 27 aircraft under license, and is buying sixty advanced SU-30 aircraft, four S-300 air defense systems, and the A-50 Sheml airborne early-warning radar aircraft. China needs such technology if it is to seriously threaten an invasion of Taiwan. But Russia is wary of strengthening its huge Eastern neighbor, and it is not clear how a confrontation over Taiwan would serve Moscow's interests.

In July 2001 Chinese President Jiang Zemin traveled to Moscow to sign a twenty-year Treaty on Good Neighborly Friendship and Cooperation, which reflected the two sides' joint opposition to U.S. supremacy along with a desire to settle the border disputes that had been a source of friction for years. However, the treaty lacked substance. There was no reference to military cooperation and if anything, the document appeared aimed at regularizing the existing arms sales relationship.[74] The Russian press optimistically dubbed the meeting the "oil and gas" summit since the leaders revived the idea of an oil pipeline to China. However, September 11 would complicate Russo–Sino relations. Although Beijing welcomed the crackdown on Islamic terrorism, it was decidedly unenthusiastic about a U.S. military presence in Central Asia, which they saw as part of a plot to encircle China.

India is less than happy to see Russia adding to China's military arsenal. After two years of negotiations, and two months after Putin visited the country, Moscow finally signed a major arms agreement with India in December 2000 under which India agreed to purchase 310 Russian T-90 main battle tanks. India also signed a license to manufacture 140 Sukhoi-30MKI fighter aircraft over the next seventeen years—a deal worth around $3 billion.[75]

The frostiest relationship in Asia is that with Japan. The Soviet Union and Japan failed to sign a peace treaty at the end of World War II, and Russia still occupies the southern Kuril Islands, which it seized in August 1945. Russia had agreed in the 1993 Tokyo Declaration that the territorial issue should be solved before a peace treaty could be signed, a step that Japan took as signaling the legitimacy of their claim. In 1997 Yeltsin and Premier Ryutaro Hashimoto set 2000 as a deadline for a peace treaty, a point reaffirmed in the 1998 Moscow Declaration. With the end-of-year deadline looming, Putin traveled to Tokyo in September 2000 and reportedly offered Prime Minister Yoshiro Mori two of the four disputed islands. Mori rejected the offer, and reaffirmed that Japan would not sign a peace treaty without the return of all the islands. A few days later a scandal erupted as a Japanese official was arrested on charges of spying for Russia. Clearly, Tokyo will not normalize relations with the Kremlin until and unless Moscow agrees to return all four islands, a step Putin is not prepared to take.

Putin also spent some time and political capital visiting other Asian countries such as North and South Korea, and Vietnam. Putin's trip to Vietnam and South Korea in February 2001 was aimed at opening up business opportunities for Russian companies. But Russia's commercial presence in East Asia is marginal at present. For example, the United States conducts more than $55 billion in annual trade with Seoul, while Russia's trade reached $2.5 billion in 2000. Russia has almost no trade with its former close ally, Vietnam, while trade between the United States and Hanoi is close to $1 billion.[76] In October 2001 Putin announced that Russia would not renew its lease of the Cam Ranh naval base in Vietnam, due to expire in 2004. In the meantime, Russia agreed to permit North Korea to repair and modernize its Soviet-era tanks, fighter planes, and submarines.

In a bizarre footnote to Putin's Asia gambit, in August 2000 North Korean President Kim Jong-il traveled to Moscow by train (he is said to be afraid of flying). News reports of the Supreme Leader's entourage wending its way across the expanse of Russia seemed like a throwback to the Stalin years. Presumably this was not the sort of signal Putin wanted to send about Russia's outlook as it enters the new millennium.

CONCLUSION

Despite its weakened position, Russia is a far more active and influential player on the international scene that it was when Putin took over as president. He is no longer Washington's vassal, as Yeltsin appeared to be during much of his presidency. Early signals by the incoming Bush administration that Russia would be relegated to the ranks of middle-range countries also seem to have reversed as relations between the two countries have improved significantly. The best example is the positive role Russia (and Putin) played during the American response to the attacks on the World Trade Center and the Pentagon. While it would be wrong to suggest that the United States could not have responded without Russian assistance, it is fair to say that

Moscow's cooperation made the process much easier. Intelligence, access to air facilities, search and rescue assistance, etc., not to mention Putin's public support for the United States, all played important roles in helping the United States carry out its military and diplomatic operations.

Putin's assistance came with a price, of course. The West modified its position on Chechnya, linking the rebels to the terrorist Osama bin Laden and backing off the stringent criticism that had characterized Western policy in the past.

Putin also ensured that Russia would play a more important role in the world as a whole. Cuba, China, Iran: Putin was everywhere during his first two years in office. It could be argued that Russia was never a critical factor in key foreign policy decisions around the world, but what was important was that in contrast to the Yeltsin regime, other countries began to take Russia seriously, even in its weakened position. Putin's foreign policy success is all the more remarkable given the paucity of diplomatic experience in his previous career.

Most important, Putin paid a small price for Russia's higher visibility. In sharp contrast to Yeltsin, he avoided giving the impression that he was selling out Russia to the United States or anyone else. The main cost he incurred for this successful foreign policy was that his efforts and energies were to some degree diverted away from the domestic reform agenda. Although Putin was quite vigorous in pursuing political reform, his economic policy was sluggish and his willingness to grasp the nettle of military reform almost nonexistent. As a result, the gulf widened between Russia's Soviet-legacy military establishment and its twenty-first-century foreign policy rhetoric.

A further item of concern is that Putin's pro-Western stance, especially after September 11, moved him far ahead of the Russian security establishment. Even the most liberal foreign policy commentators were somewhat taken aback by the extent of Putin's cooperation with Washington. Polls indicate that the general public, while suspicious of U.S. motives, were prepared to trust their president to defend Russia's interests. So long as Putin's general approval rating remains strong, he will be able to continue defying the foreign policy establishment. However, should his domestic support falter (because of an economic crisis, for example), his pro-Western foreign policy could be a point of attack for his opponents.

For the future, we expect Putin will continue his efforts to make Russia an increasingly important player on the international stage. He knows that his success will be dependent to a large degree on the domestic scene—how successful Russia will be in getting its economy moving again, and in achieving and maintaining the kind of political stability the country needs for global influence. Regardless of what happens, however, there is no question that Putin has discovered the "bully pulpit," when it comes to foreign affairs—and he will continue to make as much use of it as possible.

NOTES

1. Vladimir Putin, "Russia at the Turn of the Millennium," *Parvitel'stvo Rossiyskoy Federatsii*, January 17, 2000, at www.government.gov.ru/english/stat VP_engl_1.html.

2. National Intelligence Council conference "Russia in the International System," February 2001, at www.odci.gov/nic/pubs/conference_reports/russia_conf.html (last accessed June 1, 2001).

3. See chapter 7.

4. Nikolai Kosolapov, "Stanovlenie sub'ekta rossiiskoi vneshnoi politiki" [Becoming a Subject of Russian Foreign Policy] *Pro et contra*, vol. 6 (Winter 2001) at www.ceip.org.

5. Martha Olcott and Anders Aslund, *Getting It Wrong* (Washington, D.C.: Carnegie Endowment, 2001).

6. Oleg Levitin, "Inside Moscow's Kosovo Muddle," *Survival*, vol. 42, no. 1 (Spring 2000): 130.

7. *Diplomaticheskii vestnik*, no. 7–8 (1998): 18, as cited in Stephen White, *Russia's New Politics* (London: Cambridge University Press, 2000), 224.

8. Stephen Cohen, *Failed Crusade* (New York: Norton, 2000), 7.

9. "Russia at the Turn of the Millennium," Government of the Russian Federation at www.pravitelstvo.gov.ru.

10. Cited in *Russian Journal*, November 2, 2001.

11. "Putin in 2001: Burden of Choice," *Ponedelnik*, February 2001.

12. www.mid.ru/mi/eng/econcept.htm.

13. *Los Angeles Times*, July 11, 2000.

14. Jamestown Foundation *Monitor*, January 4, 2001.

15. Sharon LaFraniere and Steven Mufson, "Putin's Victory Could Bring Thaw in U.S–Russia Ties," *Washington Post*, March 28, 2000.

16. "Arms Control Reverts to a Waiting Game," *Washington Post*, June 6, 2000.

17. "Moscow's Chilly Rebuff Leaves Clinton in a Bind," *Time*, June 5, 2000.

18. Strobe Talbott, "Putin's Path: Russian Foreign Policy after September 11," lecture, Yale University, January 27, 2002.

19. Ron Popeski, "Russia's Putin Fills US Vacuum with Initiatives," *Reuters*, November 27, 2000.

20. "Mr. Putin Gets to Work. George Bush Will Find Him a Handful," *The Guardian* (London), December 15, 2000.

21. Valentin Kunin, "What Moscow Expects from the New US Administration," *RIA-Novosti*, December 19, 2000 in *Johnson's List*, December 21, 2000.

22. Kunin, "What Moscow Expects."

23. Martin Walker, "Commentary: New Hard Line on Russia," *UPI*, January 5, 2001.

24. "Moscow Seeks 'Serious' Dialogue with the New US Bush Team," *RFE/RL Daily Report*, January 3, 2001.

25. "Putin Writes to Bush, Wants Better US-Russia Ties," *Reuters*, January 24, 2001.

26. "Putin Takes up Debt and Defenses with German Chief," *New York Times*, January 7, 2001.

27. "Excerpts from the Interview with President-Elect George W. Bush," *New York Times*, January 14, 2001.

28. "More Russian Reaction to Bush Interview," *RFE/RL Daily Report*, January 17, 2001.

29. "Russian-US Dialogue: Heeding Current Realities," *Krasnaya zvezda*, January 19, 2001.

30. "Russia's Putin Confident of Finding 'Common Language' with US President," *Interfax*, February 8, 2001.

31. "The President's Lookout," *Le Figaro*, February 10, 2001, in *Johnson's List*, February 17, 2001.

32. "Rumsfeld's Accusations May Worsen Russia-US Relations," *ITAR-TASS*, February 15, 2001, in *WNC Military Affairs*, February 16, 2001.

33. "'Excellent' Talks Belie Chill in US-Russia Relationship," *Los Angeles Times*, February 25, 2001.

34. "Russia, US Appear to Mend Fences after Powell-Ivanov Meeting," *AFP*, April 12, 2001, in *CDI Russia Weekly*, April 12, 2001.

35. "Russian-US Ties on the Eve of Washington Talks," Jamestown Foundation *Monitor*, May 17, 2001.

36. "Putin Says Summit to Give Impetus to US-Russia Ties," *RFE/RL Daily Report*, May 21, 2001.

37. Seigel Oznobishchev, "Will the 'New Partnership' Succeed?" Jamestown Foundation *Prism* VII, no. 7 (July 2001); S. Oznobishchev and I. Runov, "Chto delat' s Amerikoi?" [What Is to Be Done with America?] *Dipkurier NG*, supplement to *Nezavisimaya gazeta*, May 24, 2001.

38. *Washington Post*, June 16, 2001.

39. *Los Angeles Times*, June 16, 2001.

40. "Not Quite Buddies, but Maybe Partners," *Washington Post/National Weekly Edition*, June 25–July 1, 2001.

41. "George Bush: USA and Russia Should Not View Each Other with Suspicion," *RIA/Novosti*, July 19, 2001, in *Johnson's List*, July 19, 2001.

42. Peggy Noonan, "A Chat in the Oval Office," *Wall Street Journal*, June 25, 2001.

43. *New York Times*, July 23, 2001.

44. "White House Finding Putin a Friend Indeed," *New York Times*, July 23, 2001.

45. Alexander Golts, "Tough Challenge Ahead as Putin Looks West," *Russia Journal*, October 5, 2001.

46. "Russians: No Breakthrough in Missile Talks," *UPI*, August 9, 2001.

47. "No Deal Soon on Missile Defense Plan, Russia Says," *Washington Post*, September 6, 2001.

48. Although he in fact talked to National Security Advisor Condoleezza Rice, and not President Bush himself. Dan Balz and Bob Woodward, "America's Chaotic Road to War," *Washington Post*, January 27, 2002.

49. Andrei Piontkowsky, "Putin Chooses US over Political Elite," *Russia Journal*, October 5, 2001.

50. "Russia Expresses Solidarity with US in Fight against Terrorism," Jamestown Foundation *Monitor*, September 12, 2001.

51. Strobe Talbott, "Putin's Path: Russian Foreign Policy after September 11," lecture, Yale University, January 27, 2002.

52. "Russia Joins Coalition," *Time.com*, September 23, 2001.

53. "Putin Vows to Aid Taliban Foes, Clarifies Position on Air Bases," *Washington Post*, September 25, 2001.

54. "Russia Says US May Use Facilities in Tajikistan," *Washington Post*, September 26, 2001.

55. Dmitrii Trenin, "Vladimir Putin's Autumn Marathon," Carnegie Endowment Briefing, November 2001 at www.ceip.org.

56. Yelena Tregubova, "The Results of 2001," *Kommersant-Vlast*, December 25, 2001.

57. Remarks at a conference organized by the Marshall Center for European Security and Ebert Foundation, Moscow, October 6, 2001.

58. *New York Times*, November 16, 2001.

59. Peter Slevin and Walter Pincus, "Treaty Means as Much Politically as Militarily," *Washington Post*, May 14, 2002.

60. Todd Purdum, "NATO Strikes Deal to Accept Russia in a Partnership," *New York Times*, May 15, 2002.

61. *The Guardian* (London), March 11, 2000.

62. Jamestown Foundation *Monitor*, June 19, 2000.

63. Vladimir Kucherenko, "Russia's Book of Debt," *Rossiiskaya Gazeta*, January 9, 2001.

64. Point made by Hans Joachim Spanger at a conference organized by the Marshall Center for European Security and the Ebert Foundation, Moscow, October 6, 2001.

65. "Putin Pays a Visit to Canada, Winning Support on Missile Issue," *New York Times*, December 19, 2000.

66. He was speaking at a meeting of CIS heads in Kazakhstan. Sebastian Alison, "Putin Says No 'Tragedy' in U.S. Troops in Georgia," *Reuters*, March 1, 2002.

67. "Further on Putin's Message on Resolving Iraq Issue," *Interfax*, November 15 in *WNC Military Affairs*, November 16, 2000.

68. "Russia: An Honest Broker in the Middle East?" Jamestown Foundation *Monitor*, April 25, 2001.

69. "Putin to Sell Arms and Nuclear Help to Iran," *New York Times*, March 13, 2000.

70. "Putin Sees Positive US Ties but Defends Ties with 'Rogue' States," *AFP*, December 26, 2000.

71. "US Alarm at Russian Arms Sale to Iran," *The Times* (London), December 30, 2000.

72. "Putin Sends Special Envoy to Middle East," *RFE/RL Daily Report*, September 6, 2001.

73. "In Cuba, Putin Signals Russia's Return to Region," *Washington Post*, December 25, 2000.

74. It is worth noting that one of the authors was part of a high-level U.S. military delegation that traveled to Russia to visit the Far Eastern Military District. In private conversations with Russian military officers it became clear that many are suspicious

of the Chinese and some are downright hostile, worrying aloud if these weapons would end up being used against Russia.

75. "India, Russia Sign Another Major Defense Deal," Jamestown Foundation *Monitor*, February 19, 2001.

76. "Putin, Ending Asia Trip, Appears Pleased with Renewed Stature," *New York Times*, March 3, 2001.

Chapter Twelve

Conclusion: Putin and the Future of Russia

Dale R. Herspring

Based on the analyses in this book, there are a number of reasons to believe that some form of democracy will be possible in Russia in coming years. I would emphasize, however, my use of the phrase "some form of democracy," and the word "possible."

As Colton and McFaul demonstrate, there are good reasons to believe that the concept of democracy remains popular among Russian citizens. As they suggest, the last ten years have had a major impact on the psyche of the average Russian. This is important because it suggests two conclusions. First, Putin will continue to face pressure from the populace for the implementation of democratic policies. Second, should Putin decide to rely more on democratic institutions, many if not most Russians will be receptive.

There are indeed some aspects of a democratic polity already functioning in Russia today. This is evident from Putin's involvement in a bargaining process with the Duma—even if he is in the dominant position—and his support for the creation of political parties. The actual establishment of political parties as we in the West understand them is still some time off, but they are developing, albeit rather slowly.

Despite Putin's indecisive approach to economic reform, Russia appears to be moving closer to the European Union. Should this process continue, and should Russia's GDP continue to grow, along with a viable middle class, the kind of economic stability that is a prerequisite for a healthy democracy could become a reality.

Putin's effort to reform the judiciary is also a positive development. Again, we are far from seeing the kind of democratic legal system that exists in the West, but clearly efforts are being made not only to better protect individual rights, but to give business and international trade a legal basis as well.

After a decade of neglect under Yeltsin, Putin has begun to address the military's problems. While it may seem peripheral, military reform is especially critical to the future of democracy in an unstable country like Russia. Nothing could more quickly undermine a fledgling democracy than a military that is demoralized, bitter, and prepared to intervene in the political arena. To date, despite its involvement in the events of 1991 and 1993, and the decision of a number of Russian generals to enter politics, Russia has been spared a politicized, politically active military. By attempting to resolve the military's problems, Putin is taking a very important step toward political stability.

Finally, Putin's ability to use the events of September 11 to move Russia toward the West could have a positive influence on the country in the long run. Fuller interaction between Russia and the West in the economic sphere is bound to have some positive political spillover. If nothing else, Russian students studying at American universities, German businesspeople inspecting their Russian investments, or closer ties between NATO and the Russian military could over the long run not only break down existing negative stereotypes, but could also help Russians better understand how democratic institutions function outside their own country.

Unfortunately, there are also some negative signs on the road to democracy in Russia. There is no doubt that Putin has restricted media freedom—or at least he sat by while Russian bureaucrats restricted it for him. The only promising aspect is that the media, especially the press, is still permitted considerable latitude in criticizing the government.

Like the media, the oligarchs have only been suppressed when they openly opposed Putin—as Gusinsky and Berezovsky did. He seems to treat them like the "robber barons" in the United States during the nineteenth century, who remained behind the scenes with considerable political and economic power.

There is also no doubt that Putin needs to take a fresh look at the issue of corruption. He rails against it and calls for its demise, yet seems not to really understand its underlying causes. And if he does, is he prepared to make the fundamental changes that are needed in the Russian political system to control it? He is overseeing a reform of the country's legal system, yet much, much more needs to be done to rid the country of the corruption that permeates and cripples every aspect of society.

Chechnya, too, seems an intractable problem. As long as Russian troops continue to butcher Chechens (and Chechens return the favor), it will be difficult to take advantage of the spirit of democracy that Colton and McFaul write about. It demonstrates to Russians all too clearly that when faced with a difficult problem, the preferred solution is to use force.

Finally, there is the issue of center-periphery relations and here there is no question that Putin wants to limit local autonomy. If local control is a key indicator of democracy, there is no doubt that Russia is moving in the opposite direction for the immediate future. Putin clearly feels that Moscow has ceded too much authority to local authorities, and if there is any chance for Russia to reform and reconstruct a stable political, economic, and social infrastructure, the Kremlin must exert strong central control.

Now back to the man himself. As I see it, there are five factors that characterize Putin's approach to political and economic problems. The first, which should come as no surprise given his career in the KGB, is his devotion to the state. To Putin, the state is just a larger form of the bureaucracy he once served in. Indeed, this is key to his somewhat ambivalent attitude toward democracy. During his time in the KGB, Putin was part of an organization in which meritocracy, discipline, and order were paramount. If he was given an order, he was expected to carry it out and for many years he did exactly that. He appears to be trying to impose that model on the country he is governing.

While Putin sees the whole Russian system as one big bureaucracy, I would disagree with suggestions that he is trying to reimpose a Soviet- or Stalinist-type regime on Russia. That danger always exists, of course, but to date he has shown no interest in enforcing conformity throughout the system. Rather, as is normal in a bureaucracy, Putin believes the leader on top should be able to set the organization's parameters and that those who work in it should operate within them. This helps explain his approach to the press. Putin's government has set certain parameters for what can be criticized and what cannot, and it is up to the media to abide by those limits. Putin's Russia must avoid the kind of political chaos that an unrestrained press helped create during the Yeltsin years.

Putin's bureaucratic mind-set also helps explain his approach to issues such as legal reform, the military, and even Chechnya. He has developed a structural paradigm that he expects the rest of the system to follow. In his own mind, the answer to many questions he faces comes in the form of bureaucratic modifications. He seems to believe that once the bureaucracy is well ordered the system will work better.

A second and equally important factor is political culture. While he does not use the social science term, Putin is very conscious of it and its implications for Russia. In short, he does *not* believe Russia should import a Western-style democratic system. In his mind, it goes against everything Russian. To paraphrase Stalin on the introduction of communism in Poland, he thinks it would fit the Russian people "like a saddle fits a cow." Indeed, he expressed his doubts about the appropriateness of the Western model in his millennium speech in January 2000.

It will not happen soon, if it ever happens at all, that Russia will become the second edition of, say, the US or Britain in which liberal values have deep historic traditions. Our state and its institutions have always played an exceptionally important role in the life of the country and its people. For Russians a strong state is not an anomaly that should be got rid of. Quite the contrary, they see it as a source and guarantor of order and the initiator and main driving force of any change.[1]

In essence, the above quote describes exactly what Putin has been doing since he took office: strengthening state authority while permitting freedom, but only to the degree that it doesn't get in the way of the effective functioning of the country's bureaucratic structures. Besides, from his perspective, the Russians want it that way.

Third, and even stronger in Putin than his bureaucratic mind-set, is his anti-ideological attitude toward dealing with problems. As he put it in his millennium speech, "I am against the restoration of an official state ideology in Russia in any form."[2] What this means in practice is that with the exception of his proclivity to look to the state to resolve problems, he is open and pragmatic when it comes to solving problems. The key question for Putin is, "Does it work?" If the answer is yes, then let the solution be tried. If the answer is no, then another approach will be sought. This too should come as no surprise given his background. When it came to problem solving, the KGB was one of the least ideological organizations in the Soviet Union. The key task was "to get the job done, to solve the problem at hand." Talking to KGB agents over the years, I have the impression that while they were the "shield and sword" of the state, they were primarily evaluated on their ability to solve the problems given to them by the "center."

This implies that if Putin were convinced that the introduction of greater forms of what we in the West understand as democracy would help him deal with Russia's problems, even if it ran counter to his understanding of the Russian mind-set, he would probably move in that direction. If, on the other hand, he believed that further restrictions were required, he would have no hesitation in reversing course. While this pragmatic approach may be a bit unnerving to those who fear that Russia could revert back to a more authoritarian state if the political and economic situation were to deteriorate, it also leaves open the option for a movement in the opposite direction.

Fourth, Putin is not a forward planner. His focus tends to be on the here and now, just as it was when he was in the KGB. This helps explain why he has yet to come up with a long-range plan for solving the country's economic problems. His focus has been on factors like the price of oil, or getting rid of obnoxious oligarchs, or forcing generals to go along with the American request to station troops in Central Asia. He has had neither the time nor the inclination to look at problems from a conceptual standpoint.

Finally, as many writers have noted, Putin is cautious—a common characteristic among bureaucrats. His decisionmaking approach tends to be incremental. This is most evident in his dealings with the regions or in his attitude toward legal reform or his hesitation to adopt an economic reform plan. Rather than the "harebrained schemes" of a Khrushchev, Putin's attitude is to try one approach after another, even if, as in the case of Chechnya, they do not seem to work very well. It is the approach of the tortoise rather than the hare.

This is not to suggest that Putin cannot react quickly when the opportunity presents itself. This is clearly what he did in the aftermath of the events of September 11. He used this tragic event not only to move Russia closer to the West, but to overcome opposition on the part of the military and other conservatives to his desire for closer ties with Washington, in particular. It is worth noting, however, that he is far from secure. A number of key individuals who opposed this move toward the United States remain bitter—and powerful. However, I would not be surprised if we encounter this willingness to seize on events in the future when Putin sees an opportunity to advance his political agenda.

In conclusion, what should one call Putin's form of governance? No title—especially one taken from another political system—would fit the Russian system exactly. Yet Putin's preference for reliance on the state, his nonideological approach, his pragmatic attitude, his problem-solving attitude, his belief in the importance of culture (a system of governance must fit the political beliefs and attitudes of the populace), as well as his cautious, incremental approach to problem solving suggests that the term "managed democracy" may fit best.

As Putin sees it, he was unexpectedly given the task of trying to lift Russia out of the mess in which it found itself at the beginning of the year 2000. He has accepted that responsibility and is trying to solve its myriad problems as he "manages" the country. He fears that if he does not impose order through the power of the state, Russia will collapse. This is his paramount concern. At the same time, despite the restrictions he has placed on the media, for example, he believes that controls are necessary while he guides Russia toward a more stable, "democratic" political future. Besides, from Putin's point of view, Russians want a strong manager during a "time of troubles."

It is difficult to say how long this period of "managed democracy" will last before the democratic impulses that Colton and McFaul described are allowed to flower. Indeed, I suspect that if asked, Putin himself would not be able to answer that question. Nor would he be able to explain where he believes the country is heading (beyond clichés such as political stability, economic affluence, and yes, democracy). Like most bureaucrats around the world, Putin's primary concern is to put out the many fires he faces on a daily basis. Yesterday it was trying to manage the sinking of the submarine *Kursk*, today it may be getting a recalcitrant governor to behave in the Russian Far East, while tomorrow it may be convincing arms manufacturers to agree to work on the basis of the profit motive. One suspects that he never knows what kind of a disaster he will face when he walks in his office in the morning.

The best that one can hope for Putin and Russia in coming months and years is that the economic situation will improve, that the country will remain stable, and that Putin will become increasingly convinced that movement toward greater democracy (as defined in the West) will be in his and Russia's interest. All that appears clear now, however, is that Putin does not seem to favor a highly repressive regime. If that were the case, he could have created such a system by this time. Given his bureaucratic orientation, he probably realizes that it would be highly dysfunctional.

The French political scientist Bertrand de Jouvenel once answered the question about solutions to political questions by arguing that they are too complex to be "solved." As soon as one is "solved" it gives rise to another. Political problems, he admonished us, can only be "settled" temporarily.[3] I am not sure if Putin has ever heard of de Jouvenel, but I suspect he would agree with his comment concerning the fleeting nature of political "solutions."

NOTES

1. Vladimir Putin, "Russia at the Turn of the Millennium," *Pravitel'stvo rossiyskoy federatsii* at www.government.gov.ru/english/statVP_engl_1.html, 6.

2. Putin, "Russia at the Turn of the Millennium," 5.

3. Bertrand de Jouvenel, *The Pure Theory of Politics* (New Haven, Conn.: Yale University Press, 1963), 207.

Suggested Reading

BOOKS

Arbatov, Alexei, et al., eds. *Eurasia in the 21st Century: The Total Security Environment*. Armonk, N.Y.: M. E. Sharpe, 1999.

Aron, Leon. *Yeltsin: A Revolutionary Life*. New York: St. Martin's Press, 2000.

Ashwin, Sarah, ed. *Gender, State, and Society in Soviet and Post-Soviet Russia*. Manchester, UK: Manchester University Press, 1999.

Barany, Zoltan, and Robert G. Moser. *Russia's Politics: Challenges of Democratization*. Cambridge: Cambridge University Press, 2001.

Breslauer, George W. *Gorbachev and Yeltsin as Leaders*. Cambridge: Cambridge University Press, 2002.

Brown, Archie, and Lilia Shevtsova, eds. *Gorbachev, Yeltsin and Putin: Political Leadership in Russia's Transition*. New York: Carnegie Endowment for International Peace, 2001.

Cohen, Stephen F. *Failed Crusade: America and the Tragedy of Post-Communist Russia*. New York: Norton, 2000.

Colton, Timothy J. *Transitional Citizens: Voters and What Influences Them in the New Russia*. Cambridge, Mass.: Harvard University Press, 2000.

Cox, Michael, ed. *Rethinking the Soviet Collapse: Sovietology, the Death of Communism and the New Russia*. London: Pinter 1999.

Dunlop, John. *The Rise of Russia and the Fall of the Soviet Union*. Princeton, N.J.: Princeton University Press, 1995.

Ellman, Michael, and Vladimir Kontorovich, eds. *The Destruction of the Soviet Economic System*. Armonk, N.Y.: M. E. Sharpe, 1998.

Ellis, Frank. *From Glasnost to the Internet: Russia's New Infosphere*. New York: St. Martin's Press, 1999.

Field, Mark G., and Judyth Twigg, eds. *Russia's Torn Safety Nets: Health and Social Welfare During the Transition*. New York: Palgrave, 2000.

Gall, Carlotta, and Thomas de Waal. *Chechnya: Calamity in the Caucasus*. New York: New York University Press, 2000.

Gustafson, Thane. *Capitalism, Russian-Style*. Cambridge: Cambridge University Press, 1999.

Handelman, Stephen. *Comrade Criminal: The Rise of the Russian Mafiya*. New Haven, Conn.: Yale University Press, 1997.

Hesli, Vicki, and William Reisinger, eds. *Elections, Parties and the Future of Russia: The 1999–2000 Elections*. Cambridge: Cambridge University Press, 2003.

Huskey, Eugene. *Presidential Power in Russia*. Armonk, N.Y.: M. E. Sharpe, 1999.

Klebnikov, Paul. *Godfather of the Kremlin: Boris Berezovsky and the Looting of Russia*. New York: Harcourt, 2000.

Kotz, David, and Fred Weir. *Revolution from Above: The Demise of the Soviet System*. New York: Routledge, 1997.

Ledeneva, Alena. *Russia's Economy of Favors. Blat, Networking and Informal Exchanges*. Cambridge: Cambridge University Press, 1999.

Lieven, Anatole. *Chechnya: Tombstone of Russian Power*. New Haven, Conn.: Yale University Press, 1999.

———. *Ukraine and Russia: A Fraternal Rivalry*. Washington, D.C.: United States Institute of Peace, 1999.

Marsch, Christopher. *Russia at the Polls: Voters, Elections, and Democratization*. Washington, D.C.: Congressional Quarterly Press, 2002.

McFaul, Michael. *Russia's Unfinished Revolution: Political Change from Gorbachev to Putin*. Ithaca, N.Y.: Cornell University Press, 2001.

Mickiewicz, Ellen. *Changing Channels: Television and the Struggle for Power in Russia*. Durham, N.C.: Duke University Press, 1999.

Odom, William. *The Collapse of the Soviet Military*. New Haven, Conn.: Yale University Press, 1999.

Putin, Vladimir. *First Person*. New York: Public Affairs, 2000.

Reddaway, Peter, and Dmitrii Glinsky. *The Tragedy of Russia's Reforms*. Washington, D.C.: United States Institute of Peace, 2001.

Remington, Thomas F. *Politics in Russia*. 2d ed. New York: Longman, 2001.

———. *The Russian Parliament: Institutional Evolution in a Transitional Regime*. New Haven, Conn.: Yale University Press, 2001.

Remington, Thomas F., and Steven Smith. *The Politics of Institutional Choice: Formation of the Russian and State Duma*. Princeton, N.J.: Princeton University Press, 2001.

Sachs, Jeffrey D., and Katharina Pistor, eds. *The Rule of Law and Economic Reform in Russia*. Boulder, Colo.: Westview Press, 1997.

Shevtsova, Lilia. *Yeltsin's Russia: Myths and Reality*. Washington, D.C.: Carnegie Endowment for International Peace, 1999.

Simes, Dmitri K. *After the Collapse. Russia Seeks Its Place As a Great Power*. New York: Simon & Schuster, 1999.

Smith, Gordon B., ed. *State-Building in Russia: The Yeltsin Legacy and the Challenge of the Future*. Armonk, N.Y.: M. E. Sharpe, 1999.

Sperling, Valerie, ed. *Building the Russian State: Institutional Crisis and the Quest for Democratic Governance*. Boulder, Colo.: Westview Press, 2000.

Stoner-Weiss, Kathryn. *Local Heroes: The Political Economy of Russian Regional Governance*. Princeton, N.J.: Princeton University Press, 1997.

Varese, Federico. *The Russian Mafia*. Oxford: Oxford University Press, 2001.

Wedel, Janine. *Collision and Collusion: The Strange Case of Western Aid to East Europe*. New York: St. Martin's Press, 1998.

Weigle, Marcia. *Russia's Liberal Project: State-Society Relations in the Transition from Communism.* University Park: Pennsylvania State University Press, 2000.

Woodruff, David. *Money Unmade: Barter and the Fate of Russian Capitalism.* Ithaca, N.Y.: Cornell University Press, 1999.

Yeltsin, Boris N. *The Struggle for Russia.* New York: Times Books, 1994.

———. *Midnight Diaries.* New York: Public Affairs, 1999.

ARTICLES

Aslund, Anders. "Russia and the International Financial Institutions." February 2000. At www.ceip.org/files/Publications/IFIAC.asp?pr=2&from=pubdate

Gel'man, Vladimir. "Regime Transition, Uncertainty and Prospects for Democratisation: The Politics of Russia's Regions in a Comparative Perspective." *Europe-Asia Studies* 51, no. 6 (September 1999).

Hellman, Joel. "Winners Take All. The Politics of Partial Reform." *World Politics* 50, no. 2 (January 1998).

Herspring, Dale, and Jacob Kipp. "Searching for the Elusive Mr. Putin." *Problems of Post Communism* (September/October 2001).

Hyde, Mathew. "Putin's Federal Reforms and Their Implications for Presidential Power in Russia." *Europe-Asia Studies* 53, no. 5 (2001).

Lynch, Allen. "The Realism of Russia's Foreign Policy." *Europe-Asia Studies* 53, no. 1 (January 2001).

Menon, Rajan, and Graham Fuller. "Russia's Ruinous Chechen War." *Foreign Affairs*, March 2000.

"Russia: Ten Years After." Carnegie Endowment Conference, June 2001. At www.ceip.org/files/programs/russia/tenyears/panel8.htm.

Remington, Thomas. "Putin and the Duma." *Post-Soviet Affairs* 17, no. 4 (November/December 2001).

———. "Russia and the 'Strong State' Ideal." *East European Constitutional Review* 9, no. 2 (Winter/Spring 2000).

Rutland, Peter. "Putin's Path to Power." *Post-Soviet Affairs* 16, no. 4 (December 2000).

Stepan, Alfred. "Russian Federalism in Comparative Perspective." *Post-Soviet Affairs* 16, no. 2 (April/June 2000).

Treisman, Daniel. "Fighting Inflation in a Transitional Regime." *World Politics* 50, no. 2 (January 1998).

Index

About the Contributors

[V]irginie Coulloudon is associate director of communications and director [of re]gional analysis at Radio Free Europe/Radio Liberty, Prague. Coullou[don i]s an associate of the Davis Center for Russian and Eurasian Studies at [Harv]ard University, where she has been directing a research project entitled ["the Elite and Patronage in Russia." Coulloudon received her Ph.D. in his[tory fr]om the École des Hautes Études en Sciences Sociales, Paris, in 1997. [She is] the author of one of the first scholarly studies of Soviet organized [crime,]*La mafia en Union soviétique* (1990).

[Jame]s Collins is a retired foreign service officer with the Department of [Stat]e. Mr. Collins served as U.S. ambassador to Russia from 1997 to 2001.

Timothy J. Colton is Morris and Anna Feldberg Professor of Government and director of the Davis Center for Russian and Eurasian Studies at Harvard University. He is the author of a number of books on Russian politics, most recently *Transitional Citizens: Voters and What Influences Them in the New Russia* (2000).

Dale R. Herspring is professor of political science at Kansas State University, a member of the Council on Foreign Relations, and a retired foreign service officer with the Department of State. He is the author and editor of nine books and more than sixty articles dealing with the former East Germany, Poland, Russia, and the USSR. His most recent book is *Soldiers, Commissars, and Chaplains: Civil-Military Relations since Cromwell* (2001).

Jacob W. Kipp is senior analyst with the Foreign Military Studies Office of the U.S. Army Training and Doctrine Command at Ft. Leavenworth, Kansas. He is the past editor of *European Security* and the author of numerous articles on Russian military matters, including Soviet and Russian concepts of space as a theater of military actions.

Masha Lipman is deputy editor of the Russian news weekly *Ezhenedel'ny Zhurnal*. She regularly writes op-ed articles about Russian politics for the *Washington Post*.

Michael McFaul is associate professor of political science and the Peter an Helen Bing Research Fellow at the Hoover Institution, specializing in er nomic and political reform in post-communist countries. He is also a se associate at the Carnegie Endowment for International Peace. His lates is *Russia's Unfinished Revolution: Political Changes from Gorbachev t* (2001).

James R. Millar is professor of economics and international affairs Washington University, where he previously served as director c tute for European, Russian and Eurasian Studies. He is also the ' journal *Problems of Post-Communism*. He is the author and editor and more than forty articles. Millar served as president of the Ame ciation for the Advancement of Slavic Studies as well as treasurer of ican Council of Learned Societies. He is currently vice presid International Council for Central and Eastern European Studies ar ber of the board of governors of the International Research and E Board. Millar has been a Guggenheim fellow and Woodrow Wilson fellow.

Nikolai Petrov is visiting associate professor at Macalester College an of the Center for Political-Geographic Research. He obtained his Ph.D. Moscow State University in geography and urban studies and he is the at of numerous works dealing with regionalism and internal Russian politi including the three-volume *The Political Almanac of Russia* (1998) with Michael McFaul.

Thomas F. Remington is professor of political science and chair of the political science department and Claus M. Halle Distinguished Professor of Global Learning at Emory University. He is the author of *The Russian Parliament: Institutional Evolution in a Transitional Regime, 1989–1999* (2001) and other books and articles on Russian politics.

Peter Rutland is professor of government at Wesleyan University. From 1995 to 1997 he was assistant director for research at the Open Media Research Institute in Prague, and in 2000 he was a Fulbright visiting professor at the European University in St. Petersburg. His most recent book is the edited collection *Business and the State in Contemporary Russia* (2001).

Darrell Slider is professor of government and international affairs at the University of South Florida. He has been the recipient of numerous awards and is the author of more than thirty-five articles dealing primarily with regional and local politics in the former USSR and Russia.